# TEDDY *and* BOOKER T.

*President Theodore Roosevelt visits his friend Booker T. Washington at the Tuskegee Institute on October 24, 1905.*

# TEDDY *and* BOOKER T.

HOW TWO AMERICAN ICONS BLAZED
A PATH FOR RACIAL EQUALITY

## BRIAN KILMEADE

SENTINEL

SENTINEL
An imprint of Penguin Random House LLC
penguinrandomhouse.com

Most Sentinel books are available at a discount when purchased in quantity for sales promotions or corporate use. Special editions, which include personalized covers, excerpts, and corporate imprints, can be created when purchased in large quantities. For more information, please call (212) 572-2232 or e-mail specialmarkets@penguinrandomhouse.com. Your local bookstore can also assist with discounted bulk purchases using the Penguin Random House corporate Business-to-Business program. For assistance in locating a participating retailer, e-mail B2B@penguinrandomhouse.com.

Image credits may be found on pages 315–318.

Library of Congress Cataloging-in-Publication Data

Names: Kilmeade, Brian, author.
Title: Teddy and Booker T. : how two American icons blazed a
path for racial equality / Brian Kilmeade.
Description: [New York] : Sentinel, [2023] | Includes bibliographical references and index.
Identifiers: LCCN 2023036261 (print) | LCCN 2023036262 (ebook) |
ISBN 9780593543825 (hardcover) | ISBN 9780593543832 (ebook)
Subjects: LCSH: Roosevelt, Theodore, 1858–1919—Influence. |
Washington, Booker T., 1856–1915—Influence. | United States—Race relations—20th century. |
Presidents—United States—Biography. | African American intellectuals—Biography.
Classification: LCC E757 .K56 2023 (print) |
LCC E757 (ebook) | DDC 973.91/1092—dc23/eng/20230811
LC record available at https://lccn.loc.gov/2023036261
LC ebook record available at https://lccn.loc.gov/2023036262

Printed in the United States of America
1 3 5 7 9 10 8 6 4 2

BOOK DESIGN BY MEIGHAN CAVANAUGH

*To Jim Brown,*
*my former radio cohost and UFC broadcast partner,*
*who taught me so much about race in America.*
*I grew up hearing about his legendary exploits at the bar*
*my family owned on Manhasset, Long Island, where Jim*
*also grew up. Getting to work with Jim for over thirty years*
*was a great honor, but the greatest honor of all was getting*
*to call myself his friend. Jim, I know you would have loved*
*this project, and my only regret is that you're not around*
*to read it. Without your influence, I never would*
*have been able to tackle it. Rest in peace.*

It is not hyperbole to say that Booker T. Washington was a great American. For twenty years before his death he had been the most useful, as well as the most distinguished, member of his race in the world, and one of the most useful, as well as one of the most distinguished, of American citizens of any race.

THEODORE ROOSEVELT

One thing that impressed me about Mr. Roosevelt is that I have never known him, having given a promise, to overlook or forget it; in fact, he seems to forget nothing, not even the most trivial incidents. . . . I have no hesitation in saying that I consider him the highest type of all-round man that I have ever met.

BOOKER T. WASHINGTON

# CONTENTS

*Preamble*                                          *xiii*

CHAPTER ONE
## BORN "BOOKER"                                    *1*

CHAPTER TWO
## "TEEDIE" GROWS UP                                *15*

CHAPTER THREE
## FROM STUDENT TO TEACHER                          *26*

CHAPTER FOUR
## THEODORE, HUSBAND AND WRITER                     *39*

CHAPTER FIVE
## "MY LIFE-WORK"                                   *46*

CHAPTER SIX
## LESSONS AND LOSSES                               *63*

CHAPTER SEVEN

"LIKE CLOCK WORK"                      *81*

CHAPTER EIGHT

ROOSEVELT THE REFORMER                 *93*

CHAPTER NINE

THE SPEECH THAT ECHOED                 *103*

CHAPTER TEN

AMERICA THE UNREADY                    *121*

CHAPTER ELEVEN

THE MOSES OF HIS PEOPLE                *134*

CHAPTER TWELVE

A SPLENDID LITTLE WAR                  *144*

CHAPTER THIRTEEN

THE CROWDED HOUR                       *161*

CHAPTER FOURTEEN

MAN IN THE MIDDLE                      *176*

CHAPTER FIFTEEN

THE NEW CENTURY DAWNS                  *192*

CHAPTER SIXTEEN

DEATH OF A PRESIDENT                   *207*

CHAPTER SEVENTEEN

GUESS WHO'S COMING TO DINNER           *217*

CHAPTER EIGHTEEN

## THE MORNING AFTER                                231

CHAPTER NINETEEN

## "THE NEGRO QUESTION"                              241

CHAPTER TWENTY

## SOUTHERN DISCOMFORTS                              254

CHAPTER TWENTY-ONE

## WINDING DOWN                                      272

CHAPTER TWENTY-TWO

## ROAD'S END                                        288

EPILOGUE

## POSTMORTEM                                        298


*Acknowledgments*                                   305

*For Further Reading*                               309

*Image Credits*                                     315

*Notes*                                             319

*Index*                                             335

# PREAMBLE

The adoption of the Fifteenth Amendment to the Constitution completes the greatest civil change and constitutes the most important event that has occurred since the nation came into life.

ULYSSES S. GRANT, MARCH 30, 1870

In April 1865, the Union won the Civil War. For the next dozen years, the country both rebuilt infrastructure that had been destroyed in battle and reformulated American society; historians call that era *Reconstruction*. Though Lincoln was dead, his Republican Party remained in power and worked to integrate four million newly freed Americans into the body politic. The nation ratified the Thirteenth Amendment, which abolished slavery. The Fourteenth granted formerly enslaved people citizenship. By 1870, when the Fifteenth Amendment became law, all male citizens, regardless of race, were granted the right to vote. The federal government stationed troops in the South in an attempt to assure that newly freed men could exercise their right to vote and run for office. The United States of America seemed about to fulfill the Founders' great promise of equality for all men.

Black men were winning national, state, and local elections, many of them in the South—but there was a growing backlash, too, led by the newly founded Ku Klux Klan and Southern Democrats; this rise in white supremacist sentiment would soon reverse the tide that raised Black hopes. White people frustrated by the elevated status of Black Americans began undoing the freedoms so recently granted their fellow citizens.

The watershed moment came when no clear winner could be declared in the presidential election of November 1876. Disputed results in a number of states meant neither Samuel J. Tilden, the Democratic candidate, nor Rutherford B. Hayes, the Republican, gained a majority in the Electoral College. After months of behind-the-scenes wrangling, Hayes emerged as the winner—but only after making a bargain with the devil. In the so-called Compromise of 1877, he got the electoral votes he needed from South Carolina, Louisiana, and Florida by agreeing to return the power to define race relations to the states. The deal brought the Reconstruction Era to an abrupt and painful end as the white supremacists swooped in to fill the political vacuum. In the years that followed, legislatures in the South were free to pass laws requiring separation of the races in public accommodations, schools, theaters, and transportation. In many places, interracial marriage was forbidden. With Black citizens increasingly deprived of voting rights across the South, the number of Black men holding elective office rapidly dwindled.

The Jim Crow era, as it came to be called, named for a black-faced character in minstrel shows, was also a time of intimidation. There were countless episodes of horrific violence, ranging from the lynching of individuals to massacres in various Southern cities in which dozens died; the death toll would rise into the thousands. As the century drew to a close, Black people in the South were virtually powerless to resist region-wide segregation and institutional racism.

In moments of need, American heroes have always arisen. In the mid-nineteenth century, Abraham Lincoln and Frederick Douglass formed a unique friendship to confront slavery; by century's end, Theodore Roosevelt and Booker T. Washington, an equally unlikely pair, emerged as the heirs of the Lincoln-Douglass partnership. Although his background was privileged, Roosevelt lived through a childhood riddled with illness that left him physically weak; at times, his parents worried he might not survive to adulthood. Washington was born into slavery, fatherless, and was forbidden an education in his early years. Despite such challenges, however, the two men became the leaders America needed, and together they confronted the forces that were rapidly rolling back hard-won rights for Black Americans.

Theirs is a story of triumph and tragedy, of cooperation and disagreement, and ultimately of the kind of courage that makes America great. Although their work remains unfinished even today, the progress Booker T. Washington and Theodore Roosevelt made is undeniable. Only by understanding how they worked together, how they decided when to push society and when to pause, and where their drive and determination came from can we carry on the work of these two icons.

—*Brian Kilmeade*

# TEDDY *and* BOOKER T.

# CHAPTER ONE

# BORN "BOOKER"

> There was never a time in my youth, no matter how dark and
> discouraging the days might be, when one resolve did not con-
> tinually remain with me, and that was a determination to se-
> cure an education at any cost.
>
> BOOKER T. WASHINGTON, *Up from Slavery*, 1901

No one could have predicted he would become famous when a brown baby boy with reddish hair was born atop a pile of rags in a slave quarter. On entering the world, that child got one name only. For a decade, he would be called Booker, just Booker.

Nothing about his arrival seemed promising. Booker would never know his date of birth. His slaveholders kept scant records on their western Virginia farm, a few miles from Hale's Ford, a crossroads town that Booker later said was "about as near to Nowhere as any locality gets to be."[1] Family recollections narrowed the season of his birth to spring, and he later guessed the year was 1858 or 1859, though more likely it was 1856.* He never knew his father's identity—"I only know he was a White man," Booker later wrote.[2] His enslaved mother, Jane, would never confirm the rumor that Booker's father lived on a nearby farm.

Home was a log cabin, roughly fourteen feet by sixteen; a one-room structure that doubled as dwelling and cookhouse. Inside, Jane prepared meals for slaveholder James Burroughs and his family on an open fire. Together with his mother and older brother, John, Booker slept on the floor, as did his half sister, Amanda, and Booker's stepfather, Washington ("Wash") Ferguson, an enslaved man from a nearby plantation who came and went depending on the whims of his slaveholder. A crude wooden door hung on unreliable hinges. Two unglazed holes in the sidewalls provided limited natural light and ventilation when the weather was warm but were shuttered when it turned cold. A few boards on the shanty's dirt floor covered a deep hole in which sweet potatoes were stored. The cabin was witheringly hot in summer, cold and drafty in winter, and always cramped and smoky.

The stark difference in his family's status from those they served struck the child at unexpected moments. One day as he held the reins of the horses while the Burroughs ladies mounted for a pleasure ride, "just before the visitors rode away a tempting plate of ginger cakes was bought out and handed around to the visitors. This, I think, was the first time that I had ever seen any ginger cakes, and a very deep impression was made upon my childish mind. I remember I said to myself that if I could ever get to the point where I could eat ginger cakes as I saw those ladies eating them the height of my ambition would be reached."[3]

For the 1860 census, James Burroughs listed ten enslaved people. Booker's sister, Amanda, still a small child, was worth the least at $200.

---

* After Booker's death, his older brother, John, remembered having seen the date April 3, 1856, noted in the slaveholder's Bible. However, as John did not learn to read until long after leaving the Burroughs farm, Booker's date of birth remains uncertain. Louis R. Harlan, *Booker T. Washington* (New York: Oxford University Press, 1972), p. 325, n1.

*The cramped and crude cabin in which Booker and the rest of his enslaved family lived prior to emancipation, in Hale's Ford, Virginia.*

Women of birthing age and sturdy men were valued higher. Jane, entering her forties, was assessed at just $250, and young Booker $400.[4] In the eyes of the United States government, these people were legal property, along with Burroughs's 207 acres, five-room farmhouse, two cabins for the enslaved, and a miscellany of horses, cattle, pigs, and sheep.[5]

Booker's childhood was without comforts. "[We got] our meals very much as dumb animals get theirs," he remembered. "It was a piece of bread here and a scrap of meat there."[6] His family never ate at a table together, and he wore no shoes until he was eight. Brutalizing punishment was a fact of life; Booker once witnessed an uncle, naked and tied to a tree, whipped bloody with a strip of cowhide. The sight, Booker said, "made an impression upon my boyish heart that I shall carry with me to my grave."[7]

One deprivation in particular frustrated the boy as he looked around him. He played with the Burroughs children; they fished and wrestled and enjoyed games together. When it came to education, however, the schoolhouse door was always closed in Booker's face. He asked his mother why.

"Learning from books in a schoolroom," she explained, "[is] forbidden to a Negro child." He was told reading was "dangerous," but that only upped his curiosity. "From that moment I resolved that I should never be satisfied until I learned what this dangerous practice was like."[8] His lust for learning and, subsequently, his passion for teaching, would come to mean almost everything to the man who became Booker T. Washington.

# FREE AT LAST

Despite an ignorance of reading, writing, and arithmetic, the Black inhabitants of the Burroughs farm knew more of the world beyond its boundaries than their overseers realized. For years the "grape-vine telegraph" had brought the enslaved in the South stories about abolitionists in the North who were agitating to free those in bondage. By the time Booker heard whispered nighttime conversations about Abraham Lincoln and the secession of many states from the Union, freedom had begun to seem possible.

With the fall of Fort Sumter in the spring of 1861, the war became a family matter to the Burroughs. One after another, the sons volunteered to fight for the Confederacy, joining the ranks of the Virginia Cavalry to serve under J. E. B. Stuart, who would soon gain fame as one of Robert E. Lee's most effective fighters. The well-liked William died in battle, in 1863, and "Marse Billy" was much mourned not only by his family but by Black residents on the Burroughs farm, some of whom had nursed him or been his playmates in childhood. Two of his brothers returned wounded, one shot at the Battle of Gettysburg in Pickett's Charge. Another Burroughs son died in a Union prison.

The Black man charged with walking the three miles to the village to collect the mail—often, he was Booker's brother John—did double duty. His official task was to return with letters for the worried Burroughs women, but on behalf of his brothers and sisters, he would linger in Hale's Ford. He could not read the newspapers, but he listened, distilling the conversations around him. The enslaved on adjacent farms gathered bits of information, too, and because of the grapevine, "often the slaves got knowledge of the results of great battles before the white people received it."[9]

By April 1865, Union soldiers were rumored to be in the neighborhood. As brother John escorted the Burroughs women to the nearby Baptist church one Sunday, he saw a company of Yankee soldiers approaching. That night, the voices raised in song in "the quarter," where those enslaved lived, grew louder and bolder, unafraid to sing out the word *freedom*. The arrival of the Yankee army could mean only the approach of "the day of jubilo," the long-awaited emancipation.[10]

In the morning everyone on the farm assembled at the Big House. The Burroughs men and women, along with their children, stood or sat on the veranda looking down upon the rest of their little community. From the perspective of Booker, who was probably about nine years old, what came next was not entirely clear.

"Some man who seemed to be a stranger," he would write later, "made a little speech and then read a rather long paper." As he listened, Booker studied the faces of the Burroughs family. They looked sad but not bitter, he thought, but he himself didn't quite know what to feel.

He heard the words, and "after the reading we were told we were all free, and could go when and where we pleased." But to a child who had known nothing beyond the rigid structure of his home farm, this required translation. His mother, standing with Booker, John, and Amanda, bent

*This drawing, first published in Booker Washington's autobiographical* The Story of My Life, *pictures the young Washington (center, stick in hand) listening to the joyful but almost incomprehensible news of emancipation.*

to kiss each of them. When she did, Booker could see the tears—they were tears of joy, he realized—running down her cheeks. "She explained to us what it all meant, that this was the day for which she had been so long praying, but fearing she would never live to see."

Young Booker's world had just undergone a radical shift. The document the soldier read was most likely the Emancipation Proclamation. Though issued more than two years before, on January 1, 1863, the order to free the slaves at first meant nothing in jurisdictions where the Confederate government retained control. But with General Robert E. Lee's surrender to General Ulysses S. Grant at Appomattox, on April 9, 1865, just sixty miles east of Hale's Ford, Lincoln's proclamation came into full force and effect. With the Civil War at an end, freedom had finally come for Booker and every other enslaved person in the newly reunited nation.

Yet with freedom came uncertainty. Booker later recalled that at first, "there was great rejoicing, and thanksgiving, and wild scenes of ecstasy." But the simple joy of the moment did not last for the newly freed people.

> I noticed that by the time they returned to their cabins there was a change in their feelings. The great responsibility of being free, of having charge of themselves, of having to think and plan for themselves and their children, seemed to take possession of them. It was very much like suddenly turning a youth of ten or twelve years out into the world to provide for himself.[11]

# ABC BREAKTHROUGH

While many formerly enslaved people had no choice but to remain where they were, becoming sharecroppers on terms dictated by their former slaveholders, Booker's family went west. Jane took the reins of a wagon loaded with what few household goods and clothes they owned. Booker, John, and Amanda followed on foot. They walked some two hundred miles, crossing the Blue Ridge Mountains to reach their destination, a town called Kanawha Salines, West Virginia.* There, Jane was reunited with her husband, Wash Ferguson, who had escaped during the war.

"Uncle Wash," as Booker called him, had found work in an industrial town along the Kanawha River that was one of the country's major sources of salt. Dozens of great furnaces boiled the briny water that bubbled to the surface at a natural salt lick nearby. The evaporation

---

* Later in the century the town came to be known as Malden. It survives today as a suburb of the state capital, Charleston.

process produced salt crystals that were much in demand downstream in Cincinnati's pork-processing plants. Wash was among the unskilled laborers paid a small wage to compress the dried salt into barrels for shipment, and within days of their arrival, Booker and John were awakened before sunrise to trudge off with their stepfather for the 4:00 A.M. shift at the Snow Hill Furnace.

The family settled into a hovel only slightly better than their cabin in the quarter. This one, at least, had windows, but Booker thought little of the neighbors, whom he described as "the poorest and most ignorant and degraded white people." The boy was disgusted by their "drinking, gambling, quarrels, fights, and shockingly immoral practices."[12]

Every cent the boys earned went into Wash's pocket, but Booker found an unexpected dividend in the work of shoveling and pounding salt. At the close of each shift, a supervisor came to inspect their day's work. Booker noticed that he marked the barrels with the same two symbols. He soon learned they were numerals—a *1* and an *8*—and that *18* was the number assigned to Wash Ferguson. "After a while," Booker wrote much later, "[I] got to the point where I could make that figure, though I knew nothing about any other figures or letters."[13]

The urge he had felt at the schoolhouse door in Hale's Ford returned. "If I accomplished nothing else in life," he resolved, "I would in some way get enough education to enable me to read common books and newspapers."[14] After his mother managed to get him a worn copy of Noah Webster's *The American Spelling Book*, he pored over the little blue-bound volume for hours. In a matter of weeks, he mastered much of the alphabet, but he had no one to teach him how to use these new tools to help him decode words. Schools for the formerly enslaved existed in some places, but education was still out of reach for many Black people. Yet the presence of a local school for Black children only added to Booker's frustration because Wash refused to give him time off from the furnaces to attend. Once again, though, Jane found a solution, arranging for a few hours of evening instruction. Finally, she reached an understanding with her husband: If Booker worked two half shifts, one each before and after school, the boy could go to class.

When the roll was called on his first day, he noticed that the rest of children replied with two names. But he had just one. He thought fast, and by the time his turn came, "I calmly told him 'Booker Washington,' as if I had been called by that name all my life." He was on his way to both literacy and becoming a self-made man.*

## THE DEMANDING MRS. RUFFNER

Around the time of his twelfth birthday, Booker left the salt mines for a job working in the household of a former teacher, a Vermonter named Viola Knapp Ruffner. Miss Knapp had arrived in Kanawha Salines as a governess for Lewis Ruffner, a mill owner and one of the town's richest men. Eventually, the widower Ruffner had asked Viola to marry him, and she became the lady of the house, helping manage his sizeable estate.

At first, Washington admitted, the well-to-do and educated White woman intimidated him. "[I] trembled when I went into her presence." He knew that most of the other boys who previously worked for her lasted no more than two or three weeks and had grumbled that she was too strict and impossible to please. But as he struggled in the early days, determined to meet her rigid requirements, he recognized a simple fact: Yes, she had high standards, but that didn't make her mean. As he explained later,

---

* He would add the middle initial *T* later, after his mother told him that she had named him *Booker Taliaferro* (pronounced *Tolliver*) as a baby, borrowing a familiar Virginia surname.

I had not lived with her many weeks . . . before I began to understand her. I soon began to learn that, first of all, she wanted everything kept clean about her, that she wanted things done promptly and systematically, and that at the bottom of everything she wanted absolute honesty and frankness.[15]

Before emancipation, the prevailing approach among slaveholders had been to discourage any sense of autonomy among the enslaved: Ignorance and dependence went hand in hand on the plantation. Teaching them to read and write had been forbidden in most Southern states—Virginia had passed one such law an 1831—and anything short of complete obedience was often met with whippings or other punishment. But when Mrs. Ruffner insisted Booker do things her way, he gradually recognized an open door. She didn't want him merely to obey her orders; she wanted him to share her standards and independence, and Booker, reaching deep within himself, found a new self-discipline. The result was a fresh sense of himself, of what he could do, that she reinforced. She trusted him with added responsibilities—but he knew he had earned them.

Once a Black child to whom most White people paid little regard, Washington felt his view of himself change. If Mrs. Ruffner had opened a door, he chose to walk through it and to begin the process of remaking himself into a newly independent person. He would define himself and not be defined by others.

Booker moved into the Ruffner house. Together, he and Mrs. Ruffner raised vegetables and fruit, which they loaded into a wagon that he drove to and from nearby Charleston, selling the produce along the way. He handed over the money he collected. Since his duties didn't keep him occupied every second, Mrs. Ruffner encouraged him to pursue his studies and allowed him to attend school in the afternoons. She tutored him at home, too. "I would help and correct," she remembered, "and he was more than willing to follow direction. . . . He never needed correction or the word 'Hurry!' or 'Come!' for he was always ready for his book."[16] While at Mrs. Ruffner's, Booker began a lifelong habit of collecting books, storing the first ones in a dry-goods box he turned into bookshelves. Booker called his aging and lovely employer "one of my best friends."[17]

As she helped him with his studies, Mrs. Ruffner saw in him a desire to succeed that perhaps Booker himself was just beginning to grasp. "He seemed peculiarly determined to emerge from his obscurity. He was ever restless, uneasy, as if knowing that contentment would mean inaction. 'Am I getting on?'—that was his principal question."[18]

And he certainly was "getting on." Booker made more of the opportunity of the four formative years in Mrs. Ruffner's employ than she or anyone expected. He adapted to her sense of thrift and her Yankee principles. He lost his plantation dialect, gaining a fluency in speaking and writing that enabled him to communicate effectively with educated people. And as he entered his middle teens, the dream taking shape in his mind grew larger. Might he truly raise himself up well beyond what even his mother might have hoped for her curious and clever middle child?

That idea was fostered by a conversation between two miners. Deep in a coal mine where he briefly worked digging coal to fire the salt furnaces, Booker overheard the men speaking of a new kind of educational institution, "[a] college that was more pretentious than the little coloured school in our town."[19]

Moving with stealth in the dark of the mine, Booker crept quietly in the direction of the talking men. At the school, he learned, the students were also Black. It served not only those with money, but those without, seeking to teach them skills to advance themselves in post–Civil War society. The worthy student might work and study at a place the men called Hampton. To Booker, it sounded like "the greatest place on earth," and he set his sights on enrolling in a school that welcomed Black students as hungry as he was for formal education—and a better life.

# GIDEON'S BAND

The war was nearly five years in the past when Booker, still in the employ of the Ruffners, saw a stark sign that the divide between the races was far from resolved.

Saturday was payday in Kanawha Salines, and on December 4, 1869, a mix of strong drink, angry words, and racial hatred led to a fight between two miners. A Black man and a White man exchanged blows— but Preston, the Black man, "came out first best."[20] To many a White Southerner, that was unacceptable.

When Preston heard that his humiliated White opponent had vowed revenge and was out to kill him, he swore out an arrest warrant. Fearing the law might trump their brand of vigilante justice, a group of the White man's friends, members of an offshoot of the Ku Klux Klan called Gideon's Band, let it be known that the Black man would not be permitted to attend the proceedings to make his case.

When trial day arrived, however, Preston walked into town surrounded by ten Black men armed with revolvers. When the Gideons confronted them, another fight broke out, and one member of Preston's posse went to the ground, struck by a brick. When gunshots were exchanged, Preston and company sought cover nearby at Georges Creek Bridge.

Hearing the report of the guns, General Lewis Ruffner came running, with Booker just behind. Seeing the assembled Black men at the bridge, Ruffner ordered them to put down their guns. When they complied, he then approached the Gideons to broker a peace. He had stature in the town, having been a militia general and the delegate from Kanawha County at the convention to establish West Virginia as a state. But the White mob didn't care, and one among the agitators lobbed another brick. He scored a direct hit, striking Ruffner above the ear. The old man collapsed to the ground, unconscious.

Two White men would sustain minor bullet wounds in the melee that followed, one in the arm, another in his leg. But no one died and, despite a grand jury investigation, no one, Black or White, went to jail. The Klan issued further threats of violence, but the only real casualty of the affair was General Ruffner. After helping carry the unconscious man back to his home, Booker had continued to work in the household, observing the general's struggle to recover. But the seventy-two-year-old's memory and vision were permanently diminished. He would never again be able to walk without crutches.

The traumatic scene at Georges Creek Bridge was seared into Booker's memory: A peaceable man, a pillar of the town who wanted only fairness and justice, Ruffner had been assaulted and nearly murdered by a white supremacist mob. The anger and resentment Booker had seen in the crowd were such that, as a thirteen-year-old, he, despite his own emerging sense he could make something of himself, saw that the prospects for Black people were even bleaker than he had thought.

In Booker's recollections, General Ruffner was an accidental victim. The goal of the Gideons had plainly been to intimidate the recently emancipated; the White men involved wanted "to crush out the political aspirations of the negroes."[21] Their fear of the Black vote was such that, as one newspaper editor observed, the Klan wanted "to make things so *hot* among the darkies that they will have to leave."[22]

Booker found a lesson in witnessing pure racial hatred firsthand. He would face it himself, again and again, in the years to come. He would fight back, whenever and however he could. Unlike the general, however, he recognized the need for less-confrontational strategies. He saw that General Ruffner had both failed in his effort to stand up for justice and been gravely injured trying. If a White man paid such a price, what would the cost be for a Black man? In time, Booker Washington would find ways to exercise a soft power uniquely his own.

# CHAPTER TWO

# "TEEDIE" GROWS UP

I was a sickly, delicate boy, suffered much from asthma, and frequently had to be taken away on trips to find a place where I could breathe.

THEODORE ROOSEVELT, *An Autobiography*, 1913

As a man, Theodore Roosevelt Jr. would change history. As a small boy known to his family as "Teedie," he simply witnessed it.

In April 1865, the nation was in mourning: Just days after Robert E. Lee's surrender at Appomattox Court House, the sixteenth president had been assassinated at Ford's Theatre in Washington, D.C. Abraham Lincoln's shocking murder reverberated across the country, and his remains, returning home by funeral train to Illinois, made stops in many cities along the way. New York was no exception, and on April 24, a long procession accompanying Lincoln's casket marched north on Broadway,

*Looking down from a second-story window of his grandfather's home was Teedie Roosevelt, age six.*

the street lined with thousands of mourners bidding their fallen leader a sad farewell.

Abraham Lincoln would forever hold a place of admiration in the impressionable boy's mind. As an adult, Roosevelt repeatedly called Lincoln "my great hero." On the day of his 1905 inauguration, Roosevelt would wear a ring containing a snip of Lincoln's hair. Behind his desk at the White House, the twenty-sixth president hung a large portrait of Lincoln.

Once, when asked about the picture by a reporter, Roosevelt replied that, upon being faced with a great problem, "I look up to that picture, and I do as I believe Lincoln would have done."[1]

But that was four decades later, long after the boy had become the man. In childhood the biggest influence in Teedie's life would be one of the saddened New Yorkers who marched in that funeral cortege, his father, Theodore Roosevelt Sr.

# "I'LL MAKE MY BODY"

Born October 27, 1858, Theodore had been, in his mother's words, a "most affectionate and endearing little creature."[2] His family was well-to-do, his parents were loving, and Teedie seemed to have every advantage. But colds, stomach upsets, and fevers had become a way of life in early childhood, threatening to prevent the clever boy from living up to his potential.

At age three, he developed asthma; the attacks of breathlessness became so frequent and terrifying that he had a recurring nightmare of a werewolf coming for him from the foot of his bed. He had to sleep propped up. Then he began to experience acute bouts of diarrhea and vomiting, which his doctors called cholera morbus.* His health was so fragile that his parents feared he might not survive and chose to educate him and his siblings at home.

Theodore was fourteen and had suffered years of sickness when his father sat him down for a man-to-man conversation about his health. He was frank: "You have the mind, but you have not the body," Theodore the elder told his namesake son. "Without the help of the body the mind cannot go as far as it should."

As young teenager, the boy, as if channeling the man he would become, seemed ready—even happy—to rise to his father's challenge. Throwing back his head, he smiled and looked his father in the eye. "*I'll make my body*," he promised.[3]

Over a period of months, Teedie set out to do exactly that with a rigorous program of lifting weights, wrestling, and boxing lessons at Wood's Gymnasium, which catered to New York's upper crust. Proprietor John Wood himself supervised the boy until his father, seeing his son's

---

* In today's medical literature, *gastroenteritis* is the preferred term for cholera morbus.

seriousness and progress, equipped the back piazza at the Roosevelt row house with all the needed apparatus. Theodore persisted and, as one of his sisters observed, he "widen[ed] his chest by regular, monotonous motion—drudgery indeed."[4]

He worked his mind, too, reading voraciously, his tastes varying from boys' fiction to travel books and works on zoology and natural history. His effort at remaking himself meant he was ready to make the most of it when his father announced he was taking the family on a grand journey down the river Nile.

The two winter months, beginning in December 1872, would be some the happiest days of Theodore's childhood. A new world opened to the fourteen-year-old. He wore a pair of spectacles, having just learned he was profoundly nearsighted. He walked the banks of the world's longest river carrying his first gun, a double-barreled breechloader. Pursuing a great passion for natural history, he added more than a hundred specimens to his collection of stuffed birds. "This trip," he recalled much later, "formed a really useful part of my education."[5] He even mastered the craft of taxidermy, which, to the disgust of some members of his family, involved arsenic and the evisceration of his many kills.

Better yet, this would be a rare period of good health; with Teedie reveling in his freedom to roam the strange terrain, he built himself up in every way. The steady diet of yogurt and salads agreed with him, as did the dry desert air—not once did it rain during the Roosevelts' Egyptian idyll.

They headed upstream in a chartered boat, the *Aboo Erdan*. It was named for a bird sacred to Egyptians, the ibis, one of which Teedie shot for his collection. He noted in his diary that the vessel was "the nicest, coziest, pleasantest little place you ever saw."[6] The flat-bottomed and barge-like dahabeeyah was a craft like countless others that had cruised the Nile since the days of the pharaohs. Sailing at just two or three miles

*Teedie, age ten. In his autobiography, Roosevelt captioned this photograph* THE PROPRIETOR OF THE "ROOSEVELT MUSEUM OF NATURAL HISTORY."

per hour, it carried the family from Cairo to the desert city of Aswan, a journey of six hundred miles, then back again. Each morning Teedie, brother Elliott or "Ellie," not yet twelve, and the baby of the family, nine-year-old Corinne, known as "Conie," sat for two hours of lessons. Their tutor was the eldest of the four Roosevelt children, "Bamie," born Anna, who would soon turn eighteen. Once freed of his lessons, Teedie promptly went ashore, tracking birds, sometimes riding a donkey, exploring the groves of palms and dates.

Often his father went, too. The elder Theodore Roosevelt was a member of the eighth generation of New York's powerful Roosevelt clan. He was a descendant of Dutchman Claes Van Rosenvelt, who had arrived in New Amsterdam about 1650. Teedie's father had been born to considerable wealth, as many in the clan were principals at Roosevelt and Son, merchants and bankers; on their return to New York, the family would be moving into their fine new mansion, at 6 West Fifty-Seventh Street, one of the city's most prestigious addresses, near both Fifth Avenue and Central Park. There, every Roosevelt need would be tended to by a full downstairs staff of butler, housekeeper, cook, footmen, and ladies' maids.

The elder Theodore was capable enough at business, but his great public passion was his philanthropy—as he himself put it, "something higher for which to live." He had earned the nickname Greatheart after helping establish such charities as the Children's Aid Society, which provided clean beds for homeless boys, most of them newsies, and the New York Orthopedic Dispensary and Hospital, for the treatment of children with spinal deformities. He was a founder of the Metropolitan Museum, too, but in his son's eyes, the most important of his good works was his father's role in establishing the American Museum of Natural History. Its charter had been signed in the parlor at the Roosevelt home, inspiring Teedie in his collecting quest.

Tirelessly cheerful and a man with a warm and affectionate nature, Theodore Sr. always found time for his children. He had often been Teedie's particular caregiver when the boy's asthma attacks left him feeling strangled and breathless. He gave his son black coffee, ipecac, and even cigars, all believed in that era to be treatments for acute asthmatic episodes. But best of all, Theodore had regularly whisked his son off to the fresh air of the countryside, the seashore, or the mountains. For Teedie, the privilege of having his father to himself—whether in the United States or exploring Egypt's ancient temples—was a pure joy.

In Egypt, the son truly began the process of becoming himself, separating from the protective cocoon of his father's household. Though he had barely begun his transformation from a short, skinny boy of fragile health, he possessed extraordinary concentration and nearly infinite curiosity about the world. After his Egyptian days, he exuded a newfound confidence.

# CONFEDERATES IN THE FAMILY

Born shortly before the Civil War, Theodore Roosevelt the younger did not see Bulloch Hall, his mother's Georgia home, until he was a man in his forties. As a boy, however, Teedie had a dreamy familiarity with the antebellum mansion. "My mother told me so much about the place that . . . I felt as if I knew every nook and corner of it, and as if it were haunted by the ghosts of all the men and women who had lived there."[7] Though a Yankee by birth, he was thus a child of the American South, too. This dual inheritance would inform the way Roosevelt looked at regional divisions later in life.

The Bulloch family was old Savannah—one ancestor had been a Georgia delegate to the Continental Congress—but Martha "Mittie" Bulloch, born in 1835, grew up northwest of Atlanta in what had been Cherokee country before the tribe's removal. The town of Roswell had developed around a new cotton mill, and Major James Bulloch, Mittie's father, was part owner. He had also commissioned a Connecticut carpenter to supervise a crew of enslaved workers to build him a fine house for his family, with a generous porch shadowed by gargantuan Doric columns.

Mittie Bulloch's girlhood had been a time of grace and ease. She was tended to by a dozen enslaved house servants, and remembered being surrounded by kith and kin of "the most delightful gifts . . . good looking [people] who all had entrancingly stormy love affairs."[8] When nineteen-year-old Theodore Roosevelt had arrived unannounced, in 1850, he, too, fell under the spell of Roswell and, in particular, of Mittie, then just fifteen. She was blue-eyed, dark-haired, and fine-featured, a beautiful belle with many admirers. But she took an immediate fancy to this stranger—he stayed in Roswell for weeks to woo her—and, on his return three years later, they became Mr. and Mrs. Theodore Roosevelt in the dining room of Bulloch Hall, on December 22, 1853.

Mittie and her new husband left Roswell for married life in his native New York, but she never tired of telling Teedie and her other children "tales of life on the Georgia plantations; of hunting fox, deer, and wildcat; . . . and of the queer goings-on in the Negro quarters."[9] Mittie celebrated "the atmosphere of dignity, ease and courtesy that was the soul of the Old South," as Margaret Mitchell, a reporter for *The Atlanta Journal*, wrote of Roswell in 1923. Not so many years later, Mitchell would write the novel that made her famous, *Gone with the Wind*, a nostalgic drama of the Lost Cause and the culture that Mittie Bulloch had treasured.[10] But Mittie and Mitchell's shared view of the "Old South" differed radically from the experience of the men and women in bondage.

The Civil War had brought Mittie and Theodore, by then the parents of three children, face-to-face with impossible choices. Mittie's primary loyalties lay with her husband, whom she loved deeply. She lived among Unionist in-laws, all solid Lincoln Republicans. Yet back home three of her brothers headed off to war to defend the Confederacy and slavery. One was a Georgia Volunteer, another a midshipman in the Confederate navy. The third, Mittie's half brother James, was a retired veteran of the U.S. Navy and, more recently, the captain of merchant ships. He moved to Great Britain to become an agent for the Confederate government.

In contrast to Teedie's Bulloch uncles, none of his Roosevelt relations would fight for his country. His own father, though just twenty-nine and in robust good health when the war broke out, paid a substitute to avoid military service, as did many others in monied New York society. He did involve himself in a plan to enable Union soldiers to send home their pay but remained out of uniform—and out of the line of fire. That decision, made partly out of respect for his wife and his Bulloch relations, would weigh on him. Over time, he would conclude that avoiding military service had been "a very wrong thing."[11]

Young Teedie was barely of school age when Robert E. Lee surrendered to Ulysses S. Grant at Appomattox, though his allegiance to the North was unquestioning—the boy was overheard asking the Lord in his bedtime prayers "to grind the southern troops to powder."[12] But when Theodore came to know Captain Bulloch after the war, Uncle Jimmie seemed to him "a dear old retired sea-captain, . . . as valiant and simple and upright a soul as ever lived." Both James and Mittie's younger brother Irvine Bulloch lived in exile in England, ineligible for amnesty because of their war work.[13]

As in so many American families, the Civil War left a scar. Although he never said so, young Theodore Roosevelt almost certainly regarded his father's failure to fight as the man's greatest mistake, one which, according to his youngest sibling Corinne, left her brother with a yearning to fight in a war and a compelling need to somehow make up for their father's decision not to.[14] Ironically, the Yankee boy took great pride in the bravery of his uncles in fighting for the short-lived Confederate States of America.

# A FATHER'S FAREWELL

On September 27, 1876, seventeen-year-old Theodore waved goodbye to his father as the lad boarded a train. His destination was Harvard College, but neither Theodore could know that during the younger man's years in Cambridge, Massachusetts, he would experience the shocking departure of a man and the joyful entrance of a woman, both of which would be defining events in his life.

From day one, college life was strange for the first-year student who, in his many letters home, couldn't quite settle on whether to sign himself *Theodore, Teddy, Ted,* or even *Tedo.* Until that autumn, his entire education had been at home and he had never sat in a classroom with other students. For the preceding two years, the last of his private tutors had drilled him in history, geography, science, mathematics, and Latin in preparation for Harvard's entrance examinations. Theodore Roosevelt's wealth also opened doors: In his era, fewer than one in a thousand earned a bachelor's degree, and a tiny minority of those gained entry to hallowed Harvard Yard.

For the first time in his life, he lived alone, in an apartment near campus his older sister Bamie had chosen and decorated for him. He missed his mother, whom he addressed with the endearment "Beloved Motherling" in his correspondence. But he found consolation in his firm sense of belonging to the Roosevelt tribe. "I do not think there is a fellow in college," he wrote his father a month after his arrival, "who has a family that love him as much as you all do me."[15]

# NEW FRIENDS

Despite living in a strange town with no close confidants and few acquaintances, he adjusted. The other boys seemed content to overlook the thick spectacles and prominent front teeth that, later in life, would be repeatedly caricatured. Among so many Bostonians, his squeaky voice and posh New York accent set him apart, but his health was better than it had ever been. By winter, he was attending dances, going to sleighing parties, and spending an occasional weekend at the homes of other boys who lived in the comfortable towns surrounding Boston. He bonded with a classmate who shared his passion for collecting natural history specimens, and the names of "sweet" and "pretty girls"—*Miss Richardson, Miss Andrews, Miss Wheelright*—peppered his letters.

He maintained his regimen of physical exercise, with rowing, swimming, and skating in season, still devoted to building up his body as his father had prescribed. Boxing in particular seemed to suit his highly competitive temperament. By the middle of his sophomore year, however, it would be his father's health, not his own, that worried the younger Theodore.

Late in autumn 1877, the older man experienced intense abdominal pains. Bamie wrote to Theodore in Cambridge, and though the news left him "uneasy," he chose not to imagine the worst. "The trouble is the dear old fellow never does think of himself in anything," he told his sister.[16]

A week before Christmas, the patient's condition worsened. The doctors diagnosed an acute attack of peritonitis, inflammation of the bowel. Theodore hurried to New York. Though he found his father was desperately ill, he confided in his diary a few days later, "Xmas. Father seems much brighter."[17] The apparent remission was such that the son went back to college on January 2.

Not until early February did a second telegram arrive for Theodore in Harvard Square. He raced home, but on arriving early on Sunday, February 10, he learned that his father, just forty-six, had succumbed to an inoperable tumor. He had suffered thirteen and a half hours of agony, broken only by doses of chloroform and brandy, before breathing his last at 11:30 P.M. the evening before.[18]

Theodore Roosevelt turned to his diary, "He has just been buried," he wrote. "I shall never forget these terrible three days; the hideous suspense of the ride [home]; the dull, inert sorrow, during which I felt . . . as if part of my life had been taken away." Suddenly as fatherless as Booker Washington, he resolved that "with the help of my God I will try to lead such a life as he would have wished."[19]

# CHAPTER THREE

# FROM STUDENT TO TEACHER

I was on fire constantly with one ambition, and that was to go
to Hampton. This thought was with me day and night.

BOOKER T. WASHINGTON, *Up from Slavery*, 1901

A few years prior to Theodore's move to Cambridge, Booker
Washington had, in September 1872, said goodbye to his family, to the Ruffners, and to West Virginia. This time, he took
to the road by himself, headed for the Hampton Normal and Agricultural Institute, the institution he had heard the miners discussing years
before. There Washington hoped to fulfill his ambition of continuing
his education: "My whole soul," he later remembered, "was . . . bent
upon reaching Hampton."[1] He had learned much from the Ruffners, but
perhaps the biggest lesson of all was that he still had so very much to
learn.

He departed with twelve dollars.[2] Much of it came from older brother
John, who gave him what he could spare from his miner's wages. Other
former enslaved people chipped in, too. After spending most of their

lives in bondage, they saw in Booker's dream a realization of their own hopes for a better future for their people. But even with their hard-earned nickels and quarters in his pocket, the sixteen-year-old had far from enough funds to cover the cost of a four-hundred-mile journey.[3]

At first he traveled by train, then stage coach. Nearly out of money, he walked and begged rides in wagons going his way. By the time he reached Virginia's capital city of Richmond, he was flat broke, his stomach empty, and still almost a hundred miles from his destination. He was entirely alone, a teenager armed with nothing but his ambition to learn, to make something of himself. Everything around him was strange, the dangers unknown.

He walked the streets of the largest town he had ever seen, knowing no one and tempted at every turn by the delicious smells of fried chicken and apple pies that he had not a penny to purchase. "I was tired, I was hungry," he remembered later, but "I was everything but discouraged."[4] Finally, in the midnight dark, the exhausted Booker crawled beneath a boardwalk near the docks, resting his head on his satchel. He tried to sleep with the footfalls of pedestrians overhead.

He awoke to the sound of men unloading pig iron for Richmond's foundries from a large ship moored nearby. "I went at once to the vessel and asked the captain to permit me to help unload the vessel in order to get money for food." Taking pity on the hungry boy, the captain agreed. "As I remember it now," Booker wrote more than a quarter century later, he soon enjoyed "about the best breakfast that I [had] ever eaten."[5] Impressed by the lad's work, the captain offered him a small daily wage as a stevedore. Washington accepted, and when he left Richmond days later, his earnings in hand, he felt confident he could complete his journey.

On October 5, 1872, he at last arrived at the campus located near the mouth of Chesapeake Bay. He knew almost nothing about Hampton Normal, but he was thrilled at the sight of Academic Hall, a just-completed three-story brick structure that he thought was the handsomest building he had ever seen. "I felt I had reached the promised land, and I resolved to let no obstacle prevent me from putting forth the highest effort to fit myself to accomplish the most good in the world."[6]

*Academic Hall at Hampton Normal and Agricultural Institute was unlike any school building Booker had ever seen. One message it conveyed was the sense that Black students had as much right to learn as White ones did.*

But the name Booker T. Washington meant nothing to anyone at Hampton Normal. He hadn't applied; he had simply arrived. And when he met the head teacher, he wasn't an impressive sight:

> Having been so long without proper food, a bath, and change of clothing, I did not, of course, make a very favourable impression upon her, and I could see at once there were doubts in her mind about the wisdom of admitting me as a student. I felt that I could hardly blame her if she got the idea I was a worthless loafer or tramp.[7]

Hampton was a destination for applicants from all over the region. For several hours, Booker watched as the White woman, Miss Mary F. Mackie, admitted several other students who had arrived better dressed and better prepared than he. When Miss Mackie finally turned to him, she hesitated before asking a series of a searching questions, leaving him with the impression that she doubted he belonged at Hampton. But then she gave him an assignment.

"The adjoining recitation room needs sweeping," she told him. "Take the broom and sweep it."[8]

He seized the moment: *"Here was my chance."*

Mrs. Ruffner's rigorous training served Booker well. He swept and re-swept the room, then dusted every surface, once, twice, thrice. When Miss Mackie inspected his work, she wiped her handkerchief across windowsills and walls, tables and benches. It came away clean.

"I guess you will do to enter this institution," she told the overjoyed young man.

Booker Washington got himself a place at Hampton, despite having exactly fifty cents to pay for his further education.

## THE SEEKERS

The first class at Hampton for Black students had convened in the shade of a tree sixteen years before Booker arrived. So-called "contraband of war"—men, women, and children in bondage who managed to escape their slaveholders—had begun arriving at Union-held Fort Monroe in May 1861, soon after the battle at Fort Sumter. As their numbers rose in the months that followed, so did the desire among the African Americans to learn to read and write. The landmark moment arrived on September 17, 1861, when some twenty students got their first lessons beneath what came to be called Emancipation Oak. Their teacher was a member of the American Missionary Association.

The educational tradition at the contraband encampment in Hampton survived the Civil War, evolving into much more than a place for free Black children to learn the three R's. When it became the Hampton Normal and Agricultural Institute, on April 1, 1868, the larger mission was clearly stated:

> To train selected Negro youth who should go out and teach and lead their people first by example, by getting land and homes; to give them not a dollar that they could earn for themselves; to teach respect for labor, to replace stupid drudgery with skilled hands, and in this way to build up an industrial system for the sake not only of self-support and intelligent labor, but also for the sake of character.[9]

Both women and men wanted to learn, even in the face of stubborn resistance from former slaveholders. The White administrators at Hampton ran the place like a military school, with students rising and retiring to the tolling of the school bells. They marched to classes, with a fixed schedule established for prayer and dining. Everybody worked, too, with men in the fields or as waiters, carpenters, or painters, the women as seamstresses or in the kitchens or laundries. When Booker Washington arrived, he became a janitor, for which he was paid two dollars a week against the cost of ten dollars per month for his board.

In the classroom, Hampton's students learned English language skills, mathematics, history, and biology, but their hunger to improve themselves went beyond the classroom. Washington, for one, found "life at Hampton was a constant revelation," even down to daily living habits. "The matter of . . . eating on a tablecloth, using a napkin, the use of the bath-tub and of the tooth-brush, as well as the use of sheets upon the bed, were all new to me."[10] On the other hand, the study of Latin, Greek, and ancient history, central to Roosevelt's Harvard education, had no place at Hampton, where the virtues of manual and industrial training were treasured above the liberal arts. Upon earning their degrees, Hampton graduates would seek jobs in primary schools in order to share their gains by instructing African American children.

Miss Mackie was "lady principal," but Brigadier General Samuel Chapman Armstrong was the founder of Hampton Normal. The son of a Presbyterian minister, he brought both the missionary zeal of his upbringing in Hawaii and the experience of commanding Black regiments in the Union army during the Civil War. He saw that gaining their freedom was only the first step for enslaved people, who had been brutalized and degraded by generations in bondage, to take control of their lives. His ideas were both advanced for his times and of them; he once wrote, "Especially in the weak tropical races, idleness, like ignorance, breeds vice." But he believed that a "deficiency of character" could be corrected by establishing "a routine of industrious habits, which is to character the foundation is to the pyramid."[11] His life's work became the education and training program he developed at Hampton, a demanding twelve-hour-a-day regimen that would give students at his school the chance to demonstrate that the Black man was "so skilled in hand, so strong in head, so honest in heart, that the Southern white man cannot do without him."*

General Armstrong made a profound impression on Booker Washington, who described him as "a great man—the noblest, rarest human being" that he had ever met. When Booker arrived at Hampton, Armstrong was just thirty-three, handsome and athletic; the first time Booker came into his presence, he was nearly bowled over. "He made the im-

---

* The words are Washington's but he was channeling Armstrong's mantra. "Letter to the Editor," *New York Herald*, October 20, 1895.

*Samuel Chapman Armstrong: Civil War general, founder of Hampton Normal, and the man who more than anyone else inspired Booker Washington's educational aspirations.*

pression upon me of being the perfect man; I was made to feel that there was something about him that was superhuman."[12] Armstrong was someone to be like, a model of commitment and vision. Booker thought of Armstrong as his mentor, himself the disciple, but over time, Washington would elevate himself from to the status of follower to leader in his own right.

Armstrong, General and Mrs. Ruffner, and Miss Mackie all had been struck by the determination and respectful manner of the likable young Booker; each became an ally and even a friend. But one teacher at Hampton would help him develop a particular talent that would be invaluable to his rise to the role of public man and spokesman for his people.

## BOOKER'S GIFT

Booker Washington was working for pay: His teacher, Nathalie Lord, gave him a few dollars he badly needed for his Hampton expenses, and in return, he took care of her little rowboat and was her boatman on days suitable for pleasure rides. But she also became a woman he trusted, in whom he could confide.

"[During] these quiet rows on Hampton Creek," Nathalie Lord would recall, "I learned something of Booker Washington's hopes and aspirations."[13]

Lord recognized that the seventeen-year-old Booker stood out from his fellow students. "His quiet, unassuming manner, his earnestness of purpose and faithfulness greatly impressed me." She recognized he was bent upon "improving himself in every possible way," concluding that someday he would truly be *someone*, someone *important*.

When Miss Lord had arrived, Booker was a "middler," a second-year student in the school's three-year course. She was twenty-five, a slim and pretty young New Englander whose spectacles added to a look of seriousness. She brought solid credentials to her job teaching rhetoric, the art of persuasive writing and speaking. She was the daughter of a Christian magazine editor and had studied at Vassar College.

She began investing extra time and energy in this special student. He came to Hampton to learn the rules of grammar and how to spell, but she encouraged him to read the Bible daily. He would make such study a ritual, spending fifteen minutes a day with the Good Book for the rest of his life. Miss Lord was also among the teachers who exposed him to the writings of Abraham Lincoln and Frederick Douglass.

Even before he could read, Booker had heard Douglass's name; his mother and others had spoken of the great abolitionist. "I had heard so much about Douglass when I was a boy that one of the reasons why I wanted to go to school and learn to read was that I might read for myself what he had written and said."[14] Douglass's historical perspective differed from the standard version of history that saw Western civilization in terms of Anglo-Saxon progress and that held African people and cultures in low regard. For the enslaved, Douglass's notion of equality was a revelation; to a young thinker like Booker, Douglass's ideas became building blocks for his own racial views.

Booker was a hard worker—"I think I may safely say he was never idle"—and during their quiet hours out on the water, Booker unburdened himself. *"To help his people,"* Miss Lord learned, "was foremost in his mind." But she also saw a particular skill in the quiet, self-effacing young man, a particular talent that she could help him develop.

"He had an unusual gift for public speaking even then, and his soul was fired with a longing to use this gift in behalf of his people." As she coached him, he gained a new facility for talking in public. She helped him learn to control his breathing, to shape his articulation, to recognize when to modulate his voice from "powerful and earnest" to "gentle and tender." She encouraged him to participate in the school's debating society.

Miss Lord continued the work Mrs. Ruffner had begun. His exposure to the New England ladies in his life enabled Booker to speak educated English and to shape and convey his thoughts with new clarity. In a world where most White people regarded the Black man as ill-educated, he learned to speak as they did and to persuade and to move an audience.

Much later, as the famous Booker T. Washington, he would choose to be generous in crediting those who aided in his self-making. "Whatever ability I may have as public speaker," he wrote two decades later, "I owe in a measure to Miss Lord."[15]

## BOOKER WASHINGTON, TEACHER

Washington the student flourished at Hampton Normal. He earned his teaching certificate in the allotted three years, and General Armstrong tapped him to be a graduation speaker.

His time at the school had been transformative:

> I was surrounded by an atmosphere of business, and a spirit of
> self-help that seemed to awaken every faculty in me and cause
> me for the first time to realize what it means to be a *man* instead
> of a *piece of property*.[16]

Still, he had more lessons to learn.

He left Hampton owing $23.05 in school fees. A summer job working as a waiter at a Connecticut resort would earn him money to pay what he owed, but he was mortified at his own incompetence and ignorance—he had never eaten in a formal restaurant—when a table of hotel patrons "scolded me in such a severe manner that I became frightened and left their table, leaving them sitting there without food." But the persistent Washington, after being demoted to bus boy, eventually regained his former position waiting tables. The time was not wasted, since during this first visit to the North he observed the manners and attitudes of the sort of "wealthy and aristocratic people" whose respect and support he would later come to rely on.[17]

That autumn he put his teaching skills to work. A job awaited the new graduate teaching Black children in Kanawha Salines. Washington had charge of ninety day students, mostly children, and a similar number of adults attending evening classes. He taught Sunday school, too.

One subject he taught was self-care, which had also been an emphasis at Hampton. To many students raised in dirt-floor shacks with no running water, the rituals of bathing, hair combing, and washing were a challenge. Booker, both as a teacher and later as a public speaker, preached cleanliness. He targeted toothbrushing in particular: "I am convinced," he said, "that there are few single agencies of civilization that are more far-reaching."[18]

He himself became a role model, a man who had risen from the lowest caste; he would inspire a number of his students to follow his path and further their studies at Hampton. But he also had family obligations, among them helping to care for his younger sister, Amanda, then fifteen, and a younger adopted brother, James. Their mother, who had been in ill health for years, had died the previous summer; to Booker, her death had been "the saddest and blankest moment of my life." He regretted not having been with her at the end, but he would honor her memory by helping James attend Hampton.

Simply standing before a class meant that Booker had achieved a great goal. Yet one of his students would remember that their young teacher, just twenty his first year, "always appeared to be looking for something in the distant future."[19] Getting an education for himself had been his first aspiration; having achieved it, he shared the gift of learning with other children who had been born with as little as he had. But he was beginning to realize he possessed even larger ambitions.

He confided in Miss Lord that he felt more Black lawyers were needed and began reading law under the guidance of an attorney in nearby Charleston. Growing bored with his legal studies, he took the chance to polish his oratorical skills during a statewide debate in 1877 about relocating West Virginia's capital. He stumped for Charleston, hoping to attract Black voters to the cause. He spent that summer speaking around the state. Just as important, he also made the case to his Black listeners for the quiet power the ballot gave them in a society where their voices were rarely heard. Little did he know that in years that followed the precious right to vote would be challenged across the South, and, in many states, lost to Black citizens.

In the fall of 1878, he moved on, leaving the Kanawha River Valley to enroll at Wayland Baptist Theological Seminary, in Washington, D.C. His time there would be limited. The sheer size and energy of the large city left him wondering whether the many freedmen and -women who had come to the nation's capital wouldn't be better off working the soil back home. He also felt a little lost in Washington: He had no strong religious vocation to anchor him in his studies at the seminary, and he was shocked at what seemed to him the very indulgent lifestyle in the city's large Black community, where it seemed to him that less money was saved than was wasted on carriage rides and stylish clothes.

Booker found his bearings after receiving a letter from General Armstrong in early 1879. Armstrong asked Washington to deliver the "post-graduate address" at commencement. This time he could afford to ride the rails in comfort the full distance, and he thought about how he had transformed his prospects in the nearly seven years since he slept under a boardwalk on his first journey to Hampton. Reunited with Miss Lord, he asked for her help, and she coached him as he rehearsed his speech—"The Force That Wins"—in the school chapel. In it Washington would lay out goals for the new graduates:

> My humble experience as a teacher in the South for the last four years teaches me that there is a force with which we can labor and succeed and there is a force with which we can labor and fail. It requires not education merely, but also wisdom and common sense, a heart set on the right and a trust in God. . . .
>
> Will we be a success is the question that each one must answer for himself. It must be answered not in planning but in *doing*, not in talking noble deeds, but *doing* noble deeds. It must be answered by a life spent in the cause of truth and virtue, by the number of men made better for our having lived in the world.[20]

Washington impressed his audience. Armstrong, then adding Black teachers to his faculty for the first time, invited his former student to join the staff at Hampton. In return for payment of twenty-five dollars per month, Washington would demonstrate over the next two years that he was more than a teacher. He ran Hampton's night school. He took charge of a dormitory for Native American students, newly arrived from reservations in the West. General Armstrong recognized in his protégé a capacity that perhaps equaled his own, making Washington the inevitable choice when Armstrong was asked to recommend a candidate to run a new independent educational experiment. Booker Washington, faced with the chance of a lifetime, had prepared himself to take on a challenge that all too few White Southerners thought any Black man could possibly meet.

Meanwhile, another young man, a soon-to-be Harvard graduate, was about to make his own life-changing decisions.

# CHAPTER FOUR

# THEODORE, HUSBAND AND WRITER

I grew into manhood thoroughly imbued with the feeling that a man must be respected for what he made of himself.

THEODORE ROOSEVELT, *An Autobiography*, 1913

He mourned his father that spring and summer, but Theodore's return to college, in September 1878, was just the distraction he needed. He had been bookish from childhood: One Harvard classmate remembered the first-year Roosevelt, seated in a noisy room, surrounded by rough-housing friends, his nose in a book, "oblivious to all that was going on around him."[1] Now, as an upperclassman, he was ready to expand his horizons.

The sheltered young man found the right clubs. He was surrounded by people of his own kind, almost entirely members of the Northeast's Protestant and patrician upper class. In October, he wrote to his mother, "Funnily enough, I have enjoyed quite a burst of popularity."[2]

A classmate named Richard Saltonstall had become a particular friend. "Old Dick," as Theodore called him, would also play the role of matchmaker when Teddy met Alice on a weekend visit to his friend's family home, a rambling Victorian house six miles from Cambridge.

Alice Hathaway Lee was Dick's cousin—their mothers were sisters—and the Lee and Saltonstall households had all but melded into one, separated as they were by a short, much-used footpath in rural Chestnut Hill. Between them, the two families had eleven children, and the scenes of intimate family life Roosevelt witnessed felt instantly familiar. The setting was tailor-made for him to fall in love with seventeen-year-old Alice. They met on October 18, 1878, and by Thanksgiving, he made a secret promise to himself that they would marry. Like father, like son: He recognized the woman with whom he wanted to spend his life almost at first sight.

Winning her hand, however, and the approval of her father, would take time. Trips to New York were required. Alice and her parents visited Mittie at 7 West Fifty-Seventh Street. Theodore's sisters traveled to Chestnut Hill. At dances, tennis parties, luncheons, woodland walks, and carriage rides, Alice grew fond of the insistent young man from New York; for him, as he explained to a friend, his was an "eager, restless, passionate pursuit of one all-absorbing object."³ Then, in January 1880, Theodore noted in his dairy, "after much pleading, my own sweet, pretty darling consented to be my wife."⁴ He went to New York to tell his family in early February and buy her a ring. A date for the marriage was set after the couple agreed to live in a third-floor apartment in the Roosevelts' Fifty-Seventh Street mansion, where the young bride could learn about managing a rich man's house under Mitty's guidance. As Theodore told his younger sister, "I don't think Mr. Lee would have consented to our marriage so soon on other terms."⁵

On Wednesday, October 27, 1880, Theodore, by then a Harvard graduate, and his betrothed exchanged vows, at the Unitarian First Parish Church in Brookline, Massachusetts. He felt immensely lucky to have her. She stood a slender and athletic five-foot-eight, an inch shorter than he. With honey-colored hair and gray-blue eyes, Alice was a very pretty girl and, by nature, cheerful and affectionate (her childhood nickname had been "Sunshine").[6] She was nineteen and, on their wedding day, he turned twenty-two.

New responsibilities rested on Theodore's shoulders. As a husband, a child of privilege, and now a man of the world, he took on the obligation he felt to become the man his father would have wanted him to be.

# ROOSEVELT THE WRITER

After his father's death, Roosevelt abandoned his boyhood dream of devoting himself to natural science. Drawn to the life Theodore Sr. lived as a man of good works, the son had recognized that "pretty much the whole duty of man lay in . . . making the best of himself."[7] Happily married and ready to join "the big world," he decided, like Booker Washington, to study law, thinking it might be "preparatory to going into public life."[8] He enrolled that fall at the Columbia Law School in what would be his first step toward a career in politics.

The winter social season in New York kept the newlyweds busy, as Alice got acquainted with many new faces and places. Each morning Theodore left early, walking more than fifty blocks downtown to law school. Some days he read law at an uncle's offices, but the energetic young man—he slept little, always in motion—also found time to pursue a growing fascination with military history.

Many men his age in the North had been raised on Civil War stories told by fathers or older brothers who had fought for the Union in the South. In contrast, Roosevelt's taste for tales of battle had been primed by two Confederate uncles whose experiences had played out far away, in England and on the world's oceans. Though they had become successful cotton merchants after the war and lived in exile in Liverpool, the wartime exploits of James Dunwoody Bulloch and Irvine Bulloch in creating a navy for the Confederacy had fascinated Roosevelt as a boy.

James Bulloch had repeatedly outsmarted both British officials and a network of U.S. intelligence agents. He commissioned the cruiser CSS *Florida*, which would capture or destroy thirty American ships, and the famous CSS *Alabama*. A sloop-of-war armed with a half dozen muzzle-loader guns and a pair of larger pivot cannons, the *Alabama* seized or burned sixty-five union merchant vessels and boarded some two hundred more in a twenty-two-month rampage. When the U.S. Navy finally destroyed her, Irvine Bulloch had been a member of her crew.

His uncles' stories lived in Theodore's imagination: They were men who believed so deeply in their cause that they risked their lives and liberty to fight for it. In the book he decided to write, he would not tell their stories—but they certainly helped inspire him to tell the tales of another war.

# THE NAVAL WAR OF 1812

While still a student at Harvard, Theodore had begun researching the War of 1812. "When the professor thought I ought to be on mathematics and the languages, my mind was running to ships that were fighting each other," he recalled.[9] After his marriage, he revisited what he had written at Harvard, and though he thought the opening pages "so dry that they would have a made a dictionary seem light reading by comparison," he decided to expand them into a book.[10]

Some of the most important battles in what some people called "the second war of independence" were fought at sea. The navies had been far from evenly matched. After defeating Napoleon war's machine, the British Royal Navy was indisputably the most powerful in the world with almost a thousand warships. In contrast, when President James

Madison declared war on America's former masters, in June 1812, the upstart nation had four seaworthy frigates and barely a dozen sloops, brigs, and unrated vessels.

The stories were many. In an epic battle with the HMS *Guerrière*, the USS *Constitution* had gained its name "Old Ironsides" after an eighteen-pound cannon ball struck its live oak bulwarks and fell harmlessly into the sea. Commander Oliver Hazard Perry had memorably reported after the Battle of Lake Erie, "We have met the enemy, and they are ours!" And Captain James Lawrence, though mortally wounded, had ordered the crewmen aboard the USS *Chesapeake*, "Don't give up the ship!" The battle had been lost, but Lawrence's dying words became the motto of the U.S. Navy.

A passionate competitor, Roosevelt was always drawn to the underdog, and he saw that this was a classic David-and-Goliath clash. To his delight, the tiny U.S. Navy had managed to win five of the first six ship-to-ship confrontations, thus both demonstrating the prowess of American sailors and ending the illusion that His Majesty's Navy was invulnerable.

All this would have been thrilling for a wide-eyed boy, but Theodore was no longer a child. Once spellbound by his uncles' stories, he now brought to his own research a more sophisticated understanding of the world. Battles at sea, dramatic as they were, were to war as the tip of an iceberg was to the dangerous nine-tenths of an ice floe beneath the surface. He dug deeply into naval records, logbooks, captain's logs, other documents. He counted ships and casualties. He read the battle narratives to understand the tactics—and more, too. Embedded in the War of 1812 were larger lessons about domestic and international politics and especially economics. Jimmie Bulloch had known he couldn't build a Confederate navy one ship at a time, but he did know his commerce raiding would punish the enemy, panic the coastal population, and upset the maritime industry. Nephew Theodore, too, began to understand that his world would be, to some degree, shaped by powerful armies and, in particular, navies.

Over the course of 1881, Roosevelt put to use every spare minute, mastering the lexicon of naval warfare—*cannon* versus *carronades, frigates* and *brigs* and *ships of the line*—as well as nautical terminology, with ships "hauling off," "wearing round," and "sheeting home." The pages began to add up, together with many of Theodore's sketches of the maneuverings of opposing ships in battle.[11]

When he and Alice took a European vacation that summer, he carried his research with him, writing wherever he could. Their twelve-day stop in Liverpool was the longest of their trip. There he got the good guidance that he would soon acknowledge in the book's preface. Without Uncle Jimmie's "advice and sympathy," he wrote, "this work would probably never have been written or even begun."*

Their author-editor relationship went both ways since Bulloch, no doubt with Theodore's encouragement, was also at work on his own book. He would write about his Civil War exploits, and though the old captain's stories of derring-do on the high seas would find few readers back in the United States, it also contributed to a growing forgetfulness. As he celebrated the bravery of the Confederate navy, the reason for the war—the fight over slavery, which the rebels had lost—was beginning to fade from public consciousness. The result might not have been evident to Roosevelt then, but as Booker Washington could clearly see living in the South, it also meant that the rights granted Black Americans during Reconstruction were beginning to fall away.

By the time he delivered the pages to his publisher, on December 3, 1881, Roosevelt understood why the U.S. Navy had succeeded six

---

* In a notable omission, Roosevelt identifies his uncle simply as "Captain James D. Bulloch, formerly of the United States Navy," skipping over Bulloch's Civil War services to the Confederacy. James Bulloch's two-volume *Secret Service of the Confederate States in Europe* was published a year later.

decades before. Its frigates had been more maneuverable, efficient, and technically advanced than the immense ships of the line that had been the standard for more than a century. He saw a lesson there, too, for his own time. "It is folly," he noted in the book's preface, "to rely for defense upon a navy composed partly of antiquated hulks and partly of new vessels rather more worthless than the old."[12]

When it appeared the following year, *The Naval War of 1812* was widely admired. Roosevelt would publish thirty-eight books in his lifetime, but this first one was perhaps his most enduring, and even today it remains a basic reference for naval historians. At twenty-three, he became an accomplished author. Yet soon he embarked upon another career altogether.

CHAPTER FIVE

# "MY LIFE-WORK"

Booker T. Washington will suit us. Send him at once.

GEORGE W. CAMPBELL TO SAMUEL
ARMSTRONG, JUNE 5, 1881

As for Booker Washington, he was just weeks away from his own life transition, the most important of his life. The instrument of change was a letter, dated May 24, 1881, which landed on General Armstrong's desk.

Three state commissioners from Tuskegee, Alabama, wanted Armstrong's guidance. They explained that a school to train Black teachers was being organized in their state. They hoped he might recommend someone to be its principal and "seemed to take it for granted that no coloured man suitable for the position could be secured."[1]

Armstrong thought otherwise.

He summoned Washington, now in his mid-twenties, to his office. He asked his protégé if he thought he was ready to take on a job as head of school. With his usual humility, Booker replied that he was willing to try, while beneath the surface, a sense of elation blossomed. Here it was, he thought to himself, the opportunity to begin his "life-work."[2]

The general wrote back to the commissioners, his handwriting the business-like scrawl of a military man accustomed to issuing orders:

> The only man I can suggest is one Mr. Booker Washington a graduate of this institution, a very competent mulatto, clear headed, modest, sensible, polite and a thorough teacher and superior man. The best man we ever had here.
>
> I am satisfied he would not disappoint you.[3]

Five days later, Sunday chapel at Hampton was interrupted by the arrival of a messenger with a telegram addressed to the general. When the service ended, Armstrong rose to read its contents aloud to the student body.

Yes, Booker Washington would suit them, the Alabamians said. "Send him at once."[4]

## TUSKEGEE, ALABAMA

Washington packed his bags. He bid a fond farewell to his many admirers at Hampton, in particular a second-year student named Fanny Smith, whom he had been courting. He detoured to West Virginia to visit family before arriving in the county seat of Macon County, Alabama, on June 24, 1881.

He had not known what to expect in Tuskegee, but he found merely hopes and dreams. He again arrived in a strange town, knowing no one. He found that the school existed only on paper, in a document, House Bill No. 165, which allotted two thousand dollars per year for teacher salaries. There were no buildings or students and no site had been designated. Nor was there money to pay for them. Finding the needed funds and assembling all the pieces was Washington's job.

Bill No. 165 had come about thanks to Lewis Adams, a man, like Washington, born into slavery. A skilled tinsmith, he fabricated kitchen utensils and roofed houses; a trained leather worker, too, he made shoes and harnesses, and owned a substantial store on the town square. As a leading Black citizen in Tuskegee, Adams had been approached by two White Democrats prior to the election of 1880. They asked for his endorsement, since the traditional Republican Black vote meant a great deal in a district where White people were outnumbered by a large margin. Adams agreed—but only after extracting a promise that they sponsor a bill that would "establish a Normal School for colored teachers at Tuskegee."[5] All three men had gotten what they wanted when the two candidates won and then lived up to their word.

Despite the daunting task before him, Washington was pleased with the town and its setting. Tuskegee sat on a rolling landscape in the southernmost foothills of the Appalachian chain. It overlooked a broad coastal plain called the Black Belt after its rich, black topsoil. Before the Civil War, plantation owners had enjoyed the cool breezes in town, while enslaved field hands harvested the wildly profitable cotton crops below. Although the main railroad line had bypassed Tuskegee, it remained a market town, its population hovering around two thousand people. Washington found it reassuring that the nearest city, the state capital at Montgomery, was fully forty miles away. He believed that meant that the newly freed people of Tuskegee "had not, as a rule, degraded and weakened their bodies by vices such as are common in the lower class of people in large cities."[6]

On the day after his arrival, Washington reported back to Hampton. "The place has a healthy and pleasant location," he wrote. "Think I shall like it. Will open school 1st Monday in July."[7]

The deadline was ten days away.

Required by statute to begin with no fewer than twenty-five pupils, he went recruiting. Looking to find candidates, he spoke from the porches of sharecropper cabins and from the pulpit at both the Black churches in Tuskegee. He wanted no one under sixteen and preferably men and women who already were public-school teachers. Some who wished to enroll were a decade or more older than himself. He was amused to discover that when teachers and their students applied together, "in several cases the pupil entered a higher class than did his former teacher."[8]

He wrote to the business manager back at Hampton asking to borrow maps, globes, and library books. He even asked for a disused penmanship chart, designed to be hung on a classroom wall, which he recalled seeing in the back of a closet at Hampton.[9]

Finding a temporary home for his school was another challenge, and he had to settle for a humble shanty at Tuskegee's AME Church, with missing windows. And that wasn't the worst of it, as Washington later remembered:

> Both the church and the shanty were in about as bad condition as was possible. I recall that during the first months of school that I taught this building was in such poor repair that, whenever it rained, one of the older students would very kindly leave his lessons and hold an umbrella over me while I heard the recitations of the others.

His rooming house was no better: There, too, an umbrella was required on rainy days in order for Washington to eat his breakfast in peace.[10]

Yet he accomplished the near impossible, pulling the pieces together in order to conduct his first classes, as promised, on the first Monday of

*The Normal School for Colored Teachers, as Booker's little
educational experiment was known in its early days,
before its founder and his students transformed an
abandoned farm into the Tuskegee Institute.*

the month, July 4, 1881. The chairs were handmade and crude, the desks
were planks nailed to the seats in front. Tuskegee that summer was a mir-
acle of creation, and in the coming months, Washington would do everything as the school's head and the only teacher for its thirty students. The
little shanty in which classes met was just a way station: modest, remarkable that it existed at all—and the launching place for something vastly
greater.

## A CAMPUS OF THEIR OWN

Together with Lewis Adams, Washington plotted the purchase of a permanent campus. They found a hilly hundred-acre farm just outside of

*In order to look older, Booker Washington grew a mustache when he went to Tuskegee, an unspoken acknowledgment of how young he looked for a man tasked with such responsibilities: As one of the new school's trustees observed, "He looked like he was eighteen."*

town. The main house had been destroyed in a fire, but three crude agricultural buildings survived, along with fields, forest, and an orchard.

The five-hundred-dollar price for the property seemed fair, but Washington had nothing like that much in his pocket. Once more he reached out to friends back at Hampton Normal, and the school's treasurer, General J. F. B. Marshall, another former Union officer, agreed to make a personal loan to Washington himself for the two-hundred-dollar down payment. Afraid that one day the state might withdraw its support for the school, Washington insisted that the property be deeded to Tuskegee's trustees, assuring Tuskegee Normal's independence. By the end of the summer, the deal was done.

He would make this school in the image of Hampton. True to the work ethic he learned there, Washington wanted his new school to function on a "labor basis." After completing a day's class study at Tuskegee, which consisted of instruction in grammar and composition, arithmetic, history, geography, and hygiene, his students spent the remaining afternoon hours improving the new property: "We made it a rule that no student, however well off he might be, was to be permitted to remain unless he did some work, in addition to taking studies in the academic department."[11]

Booker Washington saw the dignity in work. Black men in the revamped social structure of the South were no longer technically the property of slaveholders; now they worked for themselves and for pay. Booker understood that under the new rules the Black laborer also had something to prove to the unfairly skeptical White man: "With few exceptions," he argued, "the negro youth must work harder and perform his tasks even better than a white youth in order to secure recognition." He also saw a silver lining in the Black laborer demonstrating his reliability and rigor: "Out of the hard and unusual struggle through which he is compelled to pass, he gets a strength, a confidence that one misses whose pathway is comparatively smooth by reason of birth and race."[12]

At Tuskegee, Washington and his students first took on the hard work of clearing some twenty acres for planting cotton to sell for much-needed cash. Any reluctance among the students to perform hard, physical work was overcome when the principal, an axe on his shoulder, led the work gang into the woods. "They couldn't say they were too good for that kind of work when Mr. Washington himself was at it harder than any of them."[13]

A henhouse and the stable became recitation rooms. The students, some of whom had carpentry experience, fabricated blackboards. Washington spent weekends recruiting, and students flocked to Tuskegee. Although many White people in the town regarded this educational experiment as doomed to failure, enrollment nearly tripled in the school's first six months.

Washington soon hired a second teacher. Miss Olivia Davidson, born enslaved in Virginia, in 1854, had been educated at a girls' school in Ohio and then at Hampton, where she graduated in 1879, the year Washington gave his postgraduate address. A wealthy Hampton donor had then paid for the young Black woman to attend Framingham Normal

School in Massachusetts. She had classroom skills beyond Washington's own, as well as experience in dealing with Northern philanthropists.

With Davidson's assistance, Washington would soon retire the debt for the new campus, helped by more than a hundred dollars from the Tuskegee community, including White and Black residents and the town merchants; he was making allies of neighbors. A new building was badly needed, one with a chapel, more classrooms, a library, reading room, school office, and laundry. The plan included sleeping spaces for men in the basement and for women in the attic. The estimated cost was three thousand dollars.

The Tuskegee Normal School held its first closing exercises on March 30, 1882. A total of 112 students attended Tuskegee in its first nine months, and a large crowd assembled for recitations, songs, speeches, and prayers. There were the students' families and friends, but there were White faces, too, including local officials and businessmen.

Although the fundraising was far from complete, the foundation for the new building had progressed enough that at 11:30 A.M. everyone marched to the construction site, where the county superintendent of education dedicated the cornerstone for what become Porter Hall, named for Brooklyn, New York, banker and benefactor Alfred Porter. Against the odds—deep in Confederate country, White people still regarded Blacks as their inferiors—Washington and his students were making a school, by themselves and for themselves, *and* building interracial bonds in the process.

The school on the town's outskirts represented not merely progress for its students; Washington also made sure the merchants in the town understood that the school served the business interests of the town, too. Growth on Washington's campus meant added prosperity for Tuskegee's citizens, whatever the color of their skin. Better-educated citizens would earn more and spend more, while construction projects added to the local economy. The message was received and even welcomed. As one Black pastor put it, "I have seen one who but yesterday was one of our

owners, to-day lay the corner stone of a building dedicated to the education of my race. For such a change let us all thank God." After the ceremony, everyone enjoyed a meal, "served in true picnic style, on the ground
under the trees, from bountifully filled baskets."[14]

In less than a year, Booker Washington was sending off teachers to
instruct the children of the formerly enslaved across Alabama and beyond. The students who came to him were hungry to learn, putting the
lie to the widely held attitude in his region that, as one columnist in *The
Atlanta Constitution* wrote, "the masses of the negro race are never so
happy as when in the cornfield or the cotton patch and being dependent
upon the white man for protections and advice."[15]

Washington was working to educate Black teachers in his classroom
*and* to open the minds of the White population around them. But he had
to work strategically, without endangering himself or his educational experiment.

# A CAUTIONARY TALE

While the Tuskegee Institute showed signs of immediate success, its principal knew he must not flaunt his accomplishments.

Across the South, the status of Black Americans was undergoing another change. The 1860s had brought emancipation. After the postwar
passage of the three so-called Reconstruction Amendments, numerous
Black men served as Republican members of Congress and helped enact
the Civil Rights Act of 1875, which prohibited discrimination at hotels
and theaters and on trains and other public transport.*

---

* The Civil Rights Act of 1875 was short-lived: In 1883, the Supreme Court declared
the law unconstitutional by a vote of 8 to 1. The freedoms granted by the legislation
were not fully restored until the Civil Rights Acts of 1964 and 1968.

Yet the momentum toward real equality slowed after the administration of Rutherford B. Hayes stopped enforcing the Reconstruction Amendments in the South. Democrats rapidly regained power in Southern legislatures, passing the first Jim Crow laws that made racial segregation legal once again. In Alabama, a new state constitution made interracial marriage punishable by up to seven years of hard labor. It also forbade White and Black children to attend the same schools.

In an increasingly racist climate, Booker Washington walked a tricky path. If he wanted to advance the interests of Tuskegee, he would have to maintain a low-enough profile not to upset unsympathetic White people around him. Even if Armstrong hadn't repeatedly warned him to stay out of politics—which Washington was becoming adept at doing—events in Choctaw County in August 1882 were a terrible reminder of how great the dangers were for Black men who dared to display their power.

The central figure was Jack Turner, a native Alabamian, born into slavery on a cotton plantation in the Black Belt. "Of pure negro blood, with a perfectly black skin," he was physically impressive at six feet and a solid two hundred pounds.[16] He had become a persuasive orator, gaining a following among Black voters. He was also not a man who cowered before anyone. His influence and his unapologetic independence made the self-assured and dignified Turner a target for rejuvenated White Democrats.

Turner managed during the 1870s to survive numerous run-ins with the law for misdemeanors that were some mix of real and imagined. By the early 1880s, he was a prosperous farmer, with clear title to eighty acres of land, putting him on a financial plane above most Black people—and many White citizens. During the election year of 1882, he turned his attention once more to politics, supporting a candidate for governor who, though the loser overall, prevailed over the Democratic candidate in Choctaw County that August. With congressional elections to follow in November, Turner was seen as a growing threat to Democratic control.

On August 17, 1882, five days after Alabamians had gone to the polls, Jack Turner, along with six other Black men, was arrested for conspiracy and locked in the county jail.

# A COMMITTEE OF SAFETY

A twelve-year-old boy named Herd Brown had found a bundle that seemed to have fallen from a rider's saddlebags on a country road near the gate to his father's farm. Still damp with morning dew, it was a sheaf of papers, bound together with strips of brown calico. When the handwritten sheets were examined, they appeared to be mostly minutes from recent meetings of an unnamed "club." Though garbled, ungrammatical, and hard to follow, the notes described a plot to attack a forthcoming religious gathering of White people at a fairground in nearby Desotoville. Some pages bore the signature of Jack Turner.

"We are com again to the Sec. War For our benfit in Choctaw County Ala and we are . . . ready now For our war and we . . . expect to kill all the white mans and women and Baby," read one entry. "We are going [to] take this County by Shedding Blood," said another, "and we going to slay from the young up to the oldes."[17]

Turner and his alleged coconspirators denied any knowledge of the papers or of any plot. But one of the men was taken to a nearby wood, where he was whipped, stabbed, and "more or less scourged." Yes, there had been plot, he told his torturers. And, yes, Jack Turner was the leader.[18]

On Saturday, August 19, 1882, a crowd of a thousand people assembled in the town square to decide Turner's fate. "Technically, it was a mob," New Orleans's *Daily Picayune* later reported, "but in reality, a committee of safety of the whole people." A motion was made to examine the documents to be certain the handwriting was Turner's; the motion was rejected 368 to 217. Despite the many incongruities of the story—*Why would the plotters have kept copious notes of such a dastardly plan? Wasn't the alleged plot to kill all the White citizens in the county preposterous on its face?*—the angry crowd, in its "primitive might and majesty," demanded a second motion be put before them. In the absence of any evidence beyond the dubious papers and a coerced confession, they voted 998 to 2 in favor of hanging Jack Turner.[19]

The composed and dignified prisoner was escorted from the jail to the courthouse square. There, despite professing his innocence one last time in a firm and unemotional voice, he was hanged from a tall oak.

The *Mercury*, a newspaper published in nearby Meridian, Mississippi, saw his execution as entirely just. "And thus died one of the worst of his race that ever lived," the paper reported. "The moderation of the citizens of Choctaw, under the circumstances is a marvel."[20] But Turner's violent end was news beyond Alabama and the South, and in many places, it was regarded as a travesty of justice. *The New-York Tribune* called "the alleged conspiracy . . . an invention of the bulldozers." Hanging Turner without a trial, the *Tribune* continued, "is only the beginning of another season of political terrorism."[21]

Turner's death was more than just a lynching, which were far from rare in the post-Reconstruction South. He had pushed the boundaries of race. His violent end was a message of intimidation to any Black person who dared to be an instrument of change, and the weight of this threat was a burden Booker carried, though he said little of it. In his public utterances, he took great care to keep his comments to home, acknowledging the mutual good will and good feelings of "the white men of Tuskegee" and the Black inhabitants of the model community he was creating just north and west of town.

# BRICKMAKER, BRICKMAKER

In May 1882, Booker Washington discovered the rules were different on the other side of the Mason–Dixon Line.

On his first fundraising foray to New England, he visited the western Massachusetts city of Northampton. There he spent hours trying to find "a coloured family with whom I could board."[22] At last, desperate for a room, he inquired about hotels—might there be one that would rent him a room? This led to the stunning discovery that the color of his skin did not automatically exclude him from all New England inns.

A second happy surprise was how many other doors opened to him. He met both the Merriam brothers, the publishers of the Webster Dictionary, in Springfield, and Homer Merriam gave him ten dollars. The local paper, *The Republican*, publicized his presence, leading to speaking engagements. He encountered generosity at almost every stop in increments of five dollars, ten dollars, and occasionally much more. A pair of Boston sisters made a four-hundred-dollar gift, the first of many that would amount to tens of thousands of dollars in the years to come. Between them, Washington and his lady principal, Olivia Davidson, who traveled separately to double the number of visits they could make, collected three thousand dollars in a month.

That summer, Washington felt confident enough in the future of Tuskegee Normal to make Fanny Smith his wife. She, too, was a native of Kanawha Salines and a graduate of Hampton. "From the first," Washington reported, "my wife most earnestly devoted her thought and time to the work of the school, and was completely one with me in every interest and ambition."[23] Barely nine months after their wedding, Fanny gave birth to a daughter, Portia.

In the winter of 1883, a generous donor from Connecticut underwrote the purchase of an additional forty acres of land.[24] Porter Hall had been

*Fanny Washington, mother of Booker's daughter, Portia, had grown up in West Virginia and followed her future husband to Hampton.*

completed, becoming the biggest building in town. Its cost was $4,550, without the assumption of any debt, thanks largely to Yankee philanthropists. But it would be just the first of almost twenty buildings that would be built almost entirely by Tuskegee students in the school's first two decades, including Armstrong Hall (1886), a men's dormitory, Teacher's Cottage (1887), and a foundry and blacksmith shop (1889).

Student labor was fundamental to Washington's educational philosophy:

> My plan was to have them . . . taught the latest and best methods of labour, so that the school would not only get the benefit of their efforts, but the students themselves would be taught to see not only utility in labour, but beauty and dignity would be taught, in fact, how to lift labour up from mere drudgery and toil, and would learn to love work for its own sake.[25]

Aiming to create an institution that would endure, Washington decided that building structures of brick, rather than of wood, would convey a sense of permanence. The geology of Macon County favored such an enterprise, with soils rich in kaolin; in fact, one bank of clay on the school's property had already been used for brickmaking. Establishing a brickyard made business sense, too, since Washington was confident of a continuing market for bricks in the town. He told General Marshall, "I feel sure that the yard will pay for itself within a few months."[26] Plus, it would add to the interdependence between the White town and the Black school.

Shifting to brick would mean Washington and his students had to learn *two* new and quite different trades about which he knew nothing: first, how to make and second, how to lay bricks. Undaunted by the challenge, Washington found a neighbor to donate unused molds, barrows, and other equipment. The students opened several clay pits seeking to find the best clay. Washington borrowed two hundred dollars from General Marshall to defray expenses, and the first bricks were being molded by late April 1883 at the rate of several thousand a day. The work was hard, requiring the brickmakers—among them Washington himself—to stand for hours knee-deep in mud.

Then Washington's well-laid plans went wrong. After burning the first 25,000 bricks, the novice brickmakers opened the kiln to find the masonry building blocks hadn't fired properly. Instead of solid bricks, they had a sodden mass of mud.

A second kiln proved no less successful.

A third collapsed into itself.

Washington was out of money, his students and staff out of patience, and they had no bricks to sell. Never one to give up, he took the train to Montgomery and pawned his gold watch, a gift from a New England widow. The fifteen dollars he received was enough to attempt a fourth—and this time successful—brick firing. In the years that followed, millions of bricks would be produced—HARD BURNT MACHINE MADE BRICK read newspaper ads—and both the school and the town would boast impressive masonry buildings. And Washington would tell the story of their sequence of failures many times, a Job-like morality tale about facing down adversity.

*At Tuskegee, Washington preached learning, work, and even entrepreneurship, as the school's kilns would produce bricks for use on campus and for sale to local builders beyond the bounds of campus.*

With the embrace of Tuskegee's bricks by the townspeople, the school full of formerly enslaved people had also begun to demonstrate it was an asset to the town. In April 1884, however, Washington was in Philadelphia seeking money for the school's continued expansion when a telegram arrived. His wife was very ill, and he hurried back to Alabama.

Pretty Fanny had been his hometown sweetheart and among his first students when he returned home to teach, and he had made it possible for her to attend Hampton. A woman with Black, White, and Native American ancestors, she had been devoted to Tuskegee after their marriage and become the mother of their daughter, Portia, not yet a year old. Booker managed to reach Tuskegee in time to be at Fanny's bedside, but at twenty-six, she died, leaving Washington to care for their young daughter.

"Nothing [she did] was done loosely or carelessly," he told friends at Hampton. "In this respect, she taught our students many valuable lessons."[27]

He kept his grief to himself, but had Booker Washington known Theodore Roosevelt in early 1884, the two might have shared words of consolation; in a matter of months, each experienced the profound loss of the death of a spouse.

## CHAPTER SIX

# LESSONS AND LOSSES

I would rather go out of politics having the feeling that I had done what was right than stay in with the approval of all men, knowing in my heart that I had acted as I ought not to.

THEODORE ROOSEVELT, MARCH 1883

With his club days at Harvard well behind him, Theodore Roosevelt joined a new fraternity that was different in almost every way. This one—the Twenty-First District Republican Association in Manhattan—would be pure politics.

Wellborn friends warned him that he would find himself surrounded by "saloon-keepers" and "horse-car conductors," men who would be "rough and brutal and unpleasant to deal with." But Theodore knew he wanted to be a member of the "governing class," and in 1880 and early 1881, he made the time, between his law studies, social obligations, and writing, to attend evening meetings of the Republican Association.[1] He found some of the members of the association unexpectedly affable, and began to feel confident he could speak their language. He also discovered that when he rose to speak, people listened.

Best of all, his timing was excellent. A shakeup in the club's leadership was brewing. A young captain in the Twenty-First, an Irish-born postal worker named Joe Murray, saw something in Roosevelt, nominating him for the local seat in the state legislature and volunteering to run Roosevelt's campaign. When a surprised but pleased T.R. agreed to run, he kept his pitch simple: He was, he told potential voters, "owned by no man."[2] The combination of that avowed independence, the Roosevelt name, and the power of the Republican machine with Murray at the controls won Theodore his first elective office, on November 8, 1881. He claimed it would be his last—"Don't think I am going to go into politics after this," he wrote to a friend a week later. "I am not."[3] Whatever his intentions then, however, events in his life, both public and private, would shape his career in ways he did not expect.

# REFORMER ROOSEVELT

Samuel Gompers and Theodore Roosevelt came from different worlds. Representing New York's wealthiest district in the State Assembly, Roosevelt felt comfortable in evening dress, wore silk hats and gold-rimmed glasses, and lived in a mansion just off Fifth Avenue. In Gompers's words, he was a "silk stocking."[4]

A Jew who grew up in poverty in London's East End, Gompers left school at age ten to apprentice as a cigar maker, a craft he continued to practice after his family emigrated to New York. Now in his early thirties, the short, stout, and mustachioed Gompers headed the strongest local in the Cigar Makers International Union. An 1881 bill he helped draft would bring him together with Roosevelt when the legislation was referred to the freshman assemblyman's city affairs committee.

Cigar-making was big business in New York City, with roughly a quarter billion handmade each year by immigrant laborers living and working in teeming tenements. Posing as a bookman selling the works of Charles Dickens, Gompers had conducted a survey. He found families living in squalor, "little children with their old-young faces" and "nothing in those tenements to stimulate cleanliness."[5] To meet their quotas, people were forced to work sixteen and eighteen hours a day. What Gompers saw propelled him to write the proposed bill, which would outlaw cigar-making in tenements.

On first reading, according to Gompers, Roosevelt's "attitude was antagonistic."[6] Roosevelt disliked unions and thought of himself as a laissez-faire man, opposed to government interference of most any sort. As he wrote in *The Century Magazine*, a prestigious publication to which he had recently begun to contribute, "In the long run, the only way to help people is make them help themselves."[7] Still, when Gompers offered to take him on a tenement tour, the ever-curious Roosevelt agreed.

As he recalled in his autobiography years later, he was changed by what he saw:

> I have always remembered one room in which two families were living. . . . There are were several children, three men, and two women in this room. The tobacco was stowed about everywhere, alongside the foul bedding, and in a corner where there were scraps of food.
>
> The men, women, and children in this room worked by day and far on into the evening, and they slept and ate there[,] . . . unable to speak English, except that one of the children knew enough to act as interpreter.[8]

After witnessing slum life in his own city, Roosevelt agreed to champion the bill. He made a powerful argument from the floor of the assembly, despite the fact his was no honeyed voice ("I always think of a man biting tenpenny nails when I think of Roosevelt making a speech," one journalist observed).[9] But he spoke from the heart in his squeaky twang, his pace fast-forward. He argued that what he had seen was a menace to public health, that such social and industrial conditions needed reform.

With his support, the bill passed in the assembly and, though it failed in the state senate, Theodore Roosevelt's public life had truly begun.* He and Gompers would not always see eye to eye, but for decades Roosevelt would look to the union man to be an on-again, off-again adviser as Gompers rose to national prominence, founding the American Federation of Labor and serving as its president for more than thirty years. In this early encounter, Roosevelt demonstrated his empathy for the less privileged, despite having previously known little beyond the bounds of the "best society." He was his father's son, the product of an upbringing that left him with a deep-seated sense of fairness and justice.

# PARADISE LOST

Alice often accompanied her husband to Albany during his first year in the assembly. He liked the give-and-take of politics more than he expected, and despite his youth, Theodore decided he would one day run for speaker. He and Alice even considered buying a house in the countryside near New York's upstate capital, but by the time she gave her husband the happy news, in July 1883, that she was with child, their thoughts had already shifted back to the village of Oyster Bay.

---

* When it came up for a formal reading before the session adjourned, the final version of the bill had gone missing, apparently pocketed by a tenement lobbyist serving as a legislative clerk.

When Theodore was a teenager, his father rented a summer home in the sleepy shore town on Long Island, less than thirty miles east of Manhattan. The family so loved their time there—horseback riding, sailing, relaxing, and reading on the expansive porch—that the house gained the name *Tranquility*. The mix of memories and the presence of Roosevelt cousins in the vicinity had persuaded Theodore to begin buying acreage on Cove Neck, and now, with a baby on the way, he hired two young New York architects, Hugh Lamb and Charles Alonzo Rich, to design stables, an entrance lodge, and a sprawling house. He, Alice, and the architects, as well as Bamie and his mother, surveyed his ninety-five acres and chose a building site atop Cooper's Bluff. It had a sweeping view of Oyster Bay, of Long Island Sound in the middle distance, and, on the clearest days, the Connecticut shore beyond.

Roosevelt knew in a general way what he wanted. "A big piazza," he insisted, "where we could sit in rocking chairs and look at the sunset; a library with a shallow bay window looking south, the parlor or drawing-room occupying all the western end of the lower floor."[10] There must be fireplaces—eight of them, in the end—and enough space for what he expected would be a large family. What emerged were plans for a twenty-two-room house, which he decided to call *Leeholm* in Alice's honor.

That autumn Theodore attended state assembly sessions, but his forthcoming fatherhood was never far from his thoughts. He raced home for weekends, and wrote often from Albany, sometimes twice a day. "I love you and long for you all the time," he told Alice in one letter, "and oh so tenderly; doubly tenderly now, my sweetest little wife."[11]

The baby was due on Thursday, February 14, 1884. That Monday, Alice wrote Theodore in Albany that she had seen the doctor. He was not to worry about her, she instructed, but then did add a worrisome note, reporting that his mother, Mittie, suffering from a cold for several days, was now running a fever. But Alice didn't seem to think the news alarming enough to dwell on, and she went on to talk about her excitement for her coming child. "I wish I could have my little baby soon," she confided.[12]

Her labor began the following day, and at 8:30 P.M. that Tuesday evening, she and Theodore became the parents of a healthy eight-pound baby girl. After word of the baby's arrival reached Albany by telegram, Theodore shared the news with his fellow assemblymen. One remembered him full of life and overjoyed as they offered their congratulations.

Just a few hours later, however, a second telegram brought darker news. After reading it, Theodore—son, husband, and new father—departed hurriedly, looking grim and anxious, headed for the train station. Alice's health had taken a sudden turn for the worse.

# "THE LIGHT HAS GONE OUT OF MY LIFE"

*The New York Times* called it "suicidal weather."[13] A dense fog blanketed the Hudson Valley as the train, slowed by days of heavy rain, rumbled toward Manhattan, a journey of almost 150 miles. At last, shortly before midnight, the worried and impatient Theodore reached the tall house on West Fifty-Seventh Street.

Elliott met him at the door. "There is a curse on this house!" his brother exclaimed. "Mother is dying and Alice is dying too."[14]

Far worse than a simple cold, Mittie had contracted typhoid, *Salmonella typhosa*, and her body was afire with fever. Theodore learned that Alice's kidneys were failing, and other organs, too, were showing signs of shutting down. The baby was fine, but the doctors had no good medical solutions to offer either woman.

After hurrying up the stairs to their third-floor apartment, Theodore found Alice barely conscious, dimly aware of his arrival. For two hours, he held her in his arms, able to do little but try to envelop her in his own vitality. When he learned his mother's fever was spiking beyond human endurance—she would not live long—he descended one floor to say goodbye. Within the hour, with her four children at her bedside, Mittie died. His sister Corinne remembered Theodore echoing Ellie's words in those minutes: "There *is* a curse on this house."[15]

His vigil was far from over. For eleven hours he held the woman who had agreed to marry him barely four years before, and at 2:00 P.M. on Valentine's Day 1884, Alice Hathaway Lee Roosevelt, aged twenty-two, stopped breathing. On that day's diary page, Theodore wrote, "The light has gone out of my life."

The days that followed would be a blur.

On Saturday, two horse-drawn hearses, side by side, rolled down Fifth Avenue. Many cried openly in the packed service at the Fifth Avenue Presbyterian Church, among them the minister, as he delivered a sermon over the pair of rosewood caskets. Roosevelt looked shell-shocked. His old tutor reported that "he does not know what he does or says."[16]

"Baby Lee," Theodore and Alice's daughter, was christened the day after, Sunday, February 17, 1884. Care of the golden-haired newborn—full name, Alice Lee Roosevelt—was given over to Bamie. At thirty, Roosevelt's older sister, a plain woman with a painful spinal defect, was unmarried and seemed destined to remain so.*

On Monday, Theodore returned to his seat in Albany. He said nothing of the double tragedy but worked harder than ever. "Indeed," he wrote from Albany that week, "I think I would go mad if I were not so Employed."[17]

---

* Bamie suffered from Pott's disease, a tubercular arthritis that left her stooped and in nearly constant pain.

Not wanting ever to return to the house of his sadness, Roosevelt immediately put his parents' Fifty-Seventh Street house up for sale; it was sold privately, and he left it to Bamie to clear the house of Roosevelt possessions.

Two weeks after his wife's death, he signed a contract for construction of the house at Oyster Bay that he and Alice had planned. His daughter Alice would need a place to grow up, but the name *Leeholm* was quietly set aside. In its place, Roosevelt would call his estate Sagamore Hill after a Native American chief, Sagamore Mohannis, whose tribe, he believed, had signed away its rights to the land in the seventeenth century.[18]

In June, Roosevelt went to the Republican National Convention, advancing his standing in the party. There he cemented a friendship with another Harvard man, Bostonian Henry Cabot Lodge, who became a lifelong confidant. But he chose not to seek a fourth term in the assembly.

"For very many reasons I will not mind going back into private [life]," he told the editor of the upstate *Utica Morning Herald and Daily Gazette.* "For the next few months I shall probably be in Dakota, and I think I shall spend the next two to three years in making shooting trips. . . . And there will be plenty of work to do writing."[19]

Theodore Roosevelt's adult life had begun with a winning streak. On his twenty-second birthday he married a woman he loved deeply. At just twenty-three, he gained a seat in the New York Assembly; at twenty-four, he published a much-admired first book. But his luck suddenly turned and, at twenty-five, the terrible events of February 12, 1884, left him an orphan and widower.

Roosevelt and Booker T. Washington were leading strangely parallel lives, both suddenly faced with the death of a wife, each left with a tiny daughter. They were contemporaries whose life events seemed to be moving in tandem although they still had not met.

# MAN VERSUS NATURE

Though a child of the city, Theodore Roosevelt was a passionate out-
doorsman. He had been a hunter since childhood, starting with his bird
specimens, which, like John James Audubon, he killed in order to mount
and examine them. During his college days, he traveled to the wilds of
Maine, and on one two-week trip, equipped with snowshoes, he made
his way through six-foot drifts, shot a buck, and trapped a lynx. Awed
by the northern woods in winter, he wrote his mother, "I have never
seen a grander or more beautiful sight."[20]

In 1880, he had taken his first trip west, although he and his brother
Elliott got no farther than Minnesota. Finally, in 1883, Theodore had
made it to what he called the "Far West" and what was then regarded as
the frontier, the Western Dakota Territory. He shot his first buffalo
there, but he saw more than game in the region known as the Badlands.

The unspoiled landscape spoke to him. The Little Missouri River
meandered north through what Roosevelt called "a chaos of peaks, pla-
teaus, and ridges [that] rose abruptly from the edges of the level, tree-
clad, or grassy alluvial meadows."[21] Over the eons the shallow river had
carved a looping series of cliffs, buttes, and ravines, revealing layers of
pale clay, deposits of red igneous rock, sandstone, and even lignite coal.
The area was one of America's great natural wonders, a midsize Grand
Canyon.

The Little Missouri region was also home to the vestiges of the last
great bison herd; once consisting of millions of the majestic animals, no
more than a few thousand still grazed on the western prairies. The arrival of the railroad had led to a vast slaughter, and the Badlands were
transitioning to a new business, with the first Texas longhorn cattle arriving by the tens of thousands. Although Roosevelt remained in country

just a few weeks in 1883, he was listening as well as looking. He learned that Easterners, as well as Texans, were buying cattle, men like him from New York and Pittsburgh and even Great Britain. The Roosevelts had long been men of business, and Theodore decided beef cattle would be a fine investment. He used $14,000 of his inheritance from his father to buy 450 head before returning home to his Alice, back in New York, where she had been growing heavy with child.

By the time he came back to the Badlands, in June 1884, Roosevelt had buried his wife and his mother. Riding the railroad to the West, he wanted distance from his busy urban life in the East. A man suddenly alone for the first time in his life, he hoped to "[lead] a free and hardy life, with horse and with rifle."[22]

He was at a personal crossroads. Although he had learned at the capitol in Albany that he could be an agent of change, his mourning heart left him bereft. He decided to leave New York to become a full-time Westerner, a cattleman, rancher, and hunter in the Dakota Territory. Unlike Booker Washington, with no enduring commitment to a cause he could throw himself into, Roosevelt, suddenly unmoored, was still looking for a larger purpose.

ON ARRIVAL, Roosevelt found that, despite a winter spent outdoors, his herd had prospered; he lost just two dozen animals to wolves while gaining 155 calves.[23] Within three days of arrival, he decided to double-down on his initial investment, purchasing another thousand head at a cost of $26,000.

By August he found a low bluff overlooking the Little Missouri River for his home base. Elkhorn Ranch, he decided to call it, and work was soon underway to build an eight-room, flat-roofed ranch house of hewn cottonwood logs. Although Roosevelt helped with construction, he relied on two outdoorsmen imported from Maine to do most of the work. A remark he overhead one evening reminded him his skills were limited.

Asked about the day's labor, one of Maine men reported he had chopped down forty-nine trees, his partner fifty-three. As for the "boss"? "Well . . . he beavered down 17." The amused Roosevelt took ownership: "Those who have seen the stump of a tree which has been gnawed down by a beaver will understand the exact force of the comparison."[24]

Roosevelt did, however, take full part in the roundups that defined the seasons in the Dakota Territory. With the disappearance of the bison, cattle now roamed untended, grazing on the nutritive bunch and buffalo grasses of the bottomland and valleys. Since neither North nor South Dakota had yet become a state, all the land in the territory was in the public domain. With no individuals permitted to hold title to the land—Roosevelt and everyone else were just squatters—there were no fences. That meant Roosevelt's herd dispersed over an area of several hundred square miles, his cows and bulls distinguishable from the thousands belonging to others only by the brand seared into the hide of an animal's rear hip. A roundup meant finding the mature animals in order to identify and brand the calves that trailed them.[25]

A typical roundup lasted five weeks. Eight or ten men together with a chuck wagon driven by a teamster set up camp along with other such teams. After breakfasting before sunrise, riders spent long days, often sixteen or eighteen hours, identifying which cattle belonged to their employers. Covering fifty and more miles in a day, Roosevelt rode as his men did, moving in a great circle, cutting out his animals, and then herding the bulls, cows, and calves back to camp, where the calves would be wrestled to the ground and branded. After a midmorning dinner, the cycle began again. At night, the cowboys took two-hour shifts as night guards, keeping the herd together. In the morning, the cycle would repeat, with the wagon moving along eight or ten miles to the next appointed camping place.

*Roosevelt, trying on life as a cattle rancher in the West, poses with his horse in the Dakota Territory, in 1885, the year after Alice died.*

Roosevelt looked the part of cowpoke, dressed like the rest in a flannel shirt, chaps, high-heeled boots, a broad hat, and a neckerchief. He carried his favorite rifle, a lever-action .45-75 Winchester, model 1876; a .45 revolver; and, when hunting game, a hunting knife, "short and sharp, but not too long with a round handle." And sometimes a shotgun.[26]

The work was exhausting—he often slept in his clothes—and there would be no bathing. But he thrived on it and gradually won the respect of the cowpokes around him. They laughed at his glasses, but one ranch foreman, after labeling Roosevelt a "four-eyed maverick," added, "He's sure a man to hold up his end."[27]

During his months in the Badlands, he found time for hunting between roundups. The duck, grouse, chickens, doves, rabbit, elk, and blacktail deer he shot were staples of the cowboy diet, but some of his hunting ventures covered hundreds of miles and required weeks on horseback. On one early venture into Wyoming's Bighorn Mountains, he and a guide came across the unmistakable tracks of a large grizzly.

Following its trail into in a dense thicket, the guide suddenly dropped to one knee. Ignoring the excited look on the man's face, Roosevelt cocked his rifle and strode past. Then he froze.

An enormous grizzly, weighing more than half a ton, had awakened at their approach. As the nine-foot-tall bear reared up, it saw Roosevelt, who stood, as Theodore recounted the story to Bamie, "less than twenty five feet off—not eight steps." No time could be wasted: "At that distance and in such a place it was very necessary to kill or disable him at the first fire."

Roosevelt coolly sighted along the blue barrel of his gun at the animal's great head, aiming between its "two sinister looking eyes." He pulled the trigger, and then, half-hidden by a cloud of gun smoke, jumped aside in case the bear charged. But there was no need. "As you will see when I bring home his skin," he told his sister, "the bullet hole in his skull was exactly between his eyes as if I had measured the distance with a carpenters rule."[28]

Roosevelt appeared to have everything he wanted amid the solitude of open country. From his favorite rocking chair on the veranda at Elkhorn Ranch—"I am very fond of rocking chairs"—not a neighbor could be seen, the closest more than ten miles distant. He had a great expanse of country to explore, the challenge of the hunt, a growing beef business, and his books, a writing room, a big fireplace, and even a rubber bathtub in which to bathe.

He would never be a great rider or roper; he admitted that. Roosevelt's poor eyesight meant that he had difficulty distinguishing cattle brands from any distance. Still, he began to feel deeply at home in the Badlands as he proved to himself that he could live a frontier life. It was man versus nature, and the man was winning.

As the months passed, however, he acknowledged something else that, in his heart, he had known from the beginning: The Dakota Territory could never be more than his home away from home. He broke up his time in the West with periodic visits to Manhattan before returning to the Badlands. He was working out how to restore himself to a central role in the much larger story of his life—and to understand what he could do for his country.

# A CHANGE OF HEART

Their brief encounter was unexpected. A temporary guest at Bamie's Madison Avenue house, he was in from the Badlands tending to some New York business. She had been living abroad, her mother having been left in reduced circumstances after the death of her alcoholic husband. Yet when Theodore Roosevelt came in the front door at No. 422, there was Edith Kermit Carow descending the stairs. The air was suddenly charged, accompanied by recollections of past flirtations.

His wife had been dead only twenty months, and by the standards of

*Roosevelt's second wife, Edith Kermit Carow Roosevelt. With six children to look after—as well as an exuberant husband with the enthusiasm of a child— a relaxed respite on the piazza with a parasol was no doubt welcome.*

Victorian morality, that was too brief an interval for a mourning man to even think of a second marriage. But Edith, a contemporary of his sister Corinne, was beyond eligible—at twenty-five, people were wondering whether she was on her way to spinsterhood—and Roosevelt, in pre-Alice days, had been infatuated with his sister's friend.

For her part, Edith saw a man much changed. Browned by the sun, his mustache long in the approved cowboy style, he looked very different. The physical demands of days on horseback and extended hunting ventures had hardened off the slender young widower. Toughened by a life exposed to the elements, Roosevelt's neck, shoulders, and chest were noticeably more muscular. The eager boy had become an imposing and confident man.

Neither Theodore nor Edith would leave a detailed account of their meeting that day; in all likelihood, it was proper, polite, and brief. But something was kindled. The two began seeing one another, privately at first, then publicly, and just a few weeks later, on November 17, 1885, she accepted his proposal of marriage. They agreed to keep their betrothal secret and to wait a year, but on December 2, 1886, they married in London.

The marriage made it official: Roosevelt would resume his old life in the city. For two and a half years he had called the Dakotas home, though during that time he had made many New York visits to pursue his writing career and to see daughter "Baby Lee," who, though in Bamie's good care, got only irregular attention from her father. He wrote several books based on his Badlands days, including *Ranch Life and the Hunting Trail*, and was writing a biography of the famous Missouri senator Thomas Hart Benton. There would be more books, too, including a multivolume history of the West.

He had never stopped giving occasional campaign speeches for other candidates. At the last minute, he had permitted his name to appear on the ballot as a Republican candidate for mayor of New York in 1886, but no one, including Roosevelt himself, had believed he could win—he finished third. But he managed to keep his hand in the political game during a time when he was distracted by other matters, including hunting. His now completed Long Island home, Sagamore Hill, was decorated with many game heads, trophies from his successful hunts in the West.

*The house that Theodore built on his estate, Sagamore Hill,*
*overlooking Long Island Sound, where he would expose*
*his children to the outdoor life he cherished.*

He had gone to the Badlands to seek solace. For the first half of his twenties, his good fortune had risen like a hot air balloon—he'd enjoyed the emotional highs of a joyful marriage, his elevation as a major writer and historian, and his growing mastery of the levers of political power in Albany. Then his happiness had crashed to earth on the day of two deaths.

Early in his Dakota time, he had begun to make his peace with the loss of Alice. Writing a few weeks after his arrival, seated at a crude table in a cabin, he composed a brief memorial. It read in part:

> Fair, pure, and joyous as a maiden; loving, tender, and happy as a young wife; when she had just become a mother, when her life seemed to be just begun, and when the years seemed so bright before her—then, by a strange and terrible fate, death came to her.[29]

These were among his final words, in public or private, concerning the wife he lost before he banished the painful memories for good. In writing *An Autobiography* three decades later, he omitted all mention of Alice Lee Roosevelt.

But now he was embarking on a new life: Both he and Edith wanted a big family, and they wasted no time. After the couple's wedding trip to England, France, and Italy, Bamie relinquished three-year-old Alice, at Edith's insistence, to her father and stepmother's care, and nine months after the wedding Alice gained a sibling. A son named Theodore, like his father and grandfather, would be the first of five children born to Edith and Theodore in a ten-year span.

Roosevelt's time in the Dakotas had involved an economic experiment, too, though one that ended badly when the brutal winter blizzards of 1887 wiped out two-thirds of his herd. He lost what to many men would be a fortune—to Roosevelt, it amounted to roughly 20 percent of his inheritance. "The losses are crippling," he reported on a brief visit to the Badlands to assess the damage. "For the first time I have been utterly unable to enjoy my visit to the ranch."[30] Yet he carried forth no permanent resentments; in fact, his time in the West nurtured what would become an enduring commitment to conservation of the West.

He treasured the connection he had made with people he met in the territories. He liked them, and they accepted the man they called "Old Four Eyes," despite the foreignness of his pedigree as a wealthy, Harvard-educated East Coaster who spoke with an odd accent.

> Not only did the men and women whom I met in the cow country quite unconsciously help me, by . . . enable[ing] me to get into the mind and soul of the average American . . . but they helped me in another way. I made up my mind that the men were of just the kind whom it would be well to have with me if ever it became necessary to go to war.[31]

That was an insight he stored away for another time.

# CHAPTER SEVEN

# "LIKE CLOCK WORK"

[Booker T. Washington] is blessed with extraordinary executive ability and the large institution over which he presides moves like clock work, without friction or difficulty, and he has brought it from nothing to be one of the foremost Education and Industrial Schools in the South.

*Montgomery Advertiser*, DECEMBER 13, 1890

A fter his wife's death, Booker, unlike Theodore, stayed put. He took comfort in the habits and rituals of striving to make Tuskegee Normal bigger and better. As he confided in General Armstrong, the first man who had recognized Booker's true potential, "*Faith* and *hard work* I find will accomplish anything."[1]

His school was no mere teaching academy; its catalog described a program that, in addition to "extended mental training," offered instruction in farming, brickmaking, carpentry, printing, and blacksmithing for men, "house-keeping" and sewing for women.[2] He got little help from the state of Alabama, financial or otherwise. But thanks to his labors as a fundraiser, an administrator, and perhaps above all, an inspiration to students, faculty, and supporters, Tuskegee was becoming a regional powerhouse.

Enrollment continued to rise. In 1883–1884, the total was 169 students; the count more than doubled in the next four years. Washington also operated a night school, as he had done at Hampton, to serve working adults. During the same time span, the staff grew, too, reaching two dozen. One new face was John Henry Washington, who arrived in 1885. After Booker helped him graduate from Hampton, John had taken over his younger brother's teaching job and worked on a U.S. Army Corps of Engineers project that built dams and locks along the Kanawha River. At Tuskegee, John rapidly became a man-of-all-work.

"Mr. J.H.," as the students called Tuskegee's other Mr. Washington, first built a sawmill to harvest the abundant trees on the school's expanding acreage. He managed the school farm as the acres in tillage doubled and then tripled, with fields planted in cotton, corn, wheat, and vegetables. John Washington became campus commandant—as a means of establishing discipline, male students took part in mandatory military drills—and managed construction of new buildings. When increased demand for water led to a shortage, Mr. J.H. found a spring three-quarters of a mile away and personally lay the pipe to provide the school with abundant fresh water. In time, he would start the school band and introduce beekeeping.

Booker was increasingly in demand as a speaker, and in the spring of 1884 received an invitation to speak to the National Educational Association. That summer at their annual meeting, in Madison, Wisconsin, he addressed a crowd of five thousand teachers from across the country, most of them White.

He took pains to explain his mission and how delicate was the balance he needed to strike:

Any work looking toward the permanent improvement of the Negro in the South, must have for one of its aims the fitting of him to live friendly and peaceably with his white neighbors, both socially and politically. In spite of all talk of exodus the Negro's home is permanently in the South, for coming to the bread and meat side of the question the white man needs the Negro and the Negro needs the white man. His home being permanently in the South, it is our duty to help him prepare himself to live there, an independent, educated citizen. In order that there may be the broadest development of the colored man and that he may have an unbounded field in which to labor, the two races in the South must be brought to have faith in each other.

Being in the North, he could also be a little more candid than he might have been in Alabama:

In regard to what I have said about the relations of the two races, there should be no unmanly cowering or stooping to satisfy unreasonable whims of Southern white men; but it is charity and wisdom to keep in mind the two hundred years of schooling in prejudice against the Negro which the ex-slaveholders are called on to conquer. A certain class of whites object to the general education of the colored man on the ground that when he is educated he ceased to do manual labor, and there is no avoiding the fact that much aid is withheld from Negro education in the South by the states on these grounds. Just here the great mission of Industrial Education, coupled with the mental, comes in. It kills two birds with one stone, viz., it secures the co-operation of the whites and does the best possible thing for the black man.[3]

Washington was all for cooperation, but he wanted to foster self-respect, too.

Booker distracted himself from mourning his wife with other travels, frequently for meetings with the school's benefactors, most of whom lived in the North. His lady principal had once shared that responsibility, but Olivia Davidson, always a woman of fragile health, had been left in a state of collapse from the pressures of her extensive travel and many other duties. After a stay in a Boston hospital and a period of rehabilitation, she had returned to Tuskegee but confined her duties to those of teacher and administrator.

The endless work took a toll on Booker, too, and in October 1885 he was so exhausted he had to leave his post temporarily. After a period of doctor-prescribed bed rest, he went back to work, but he would sustain another shock when his mentor, General Armstrong, suffered a heart attack. The general blamed "eighteen years hard steady work" and warned Washington it could happen to him.[4] Davidson was so worried that when she heard about a summer training course at Harvard for teachers and doctors, one that blended a physical fitness program with coursework on human physiology, she persuaded Washington to spend a summer in Cambridge.

She and Booker inevitably grew closer. Davidson was as devoted to the work of Tuskegee as he, and two years after Fanny's death, Booker asked Olivia to become his wife. They were married, in Ohio, at her family's home, in August 1886. She became pregnant soon after their wedding day, but once again her delicate health led her to go to Boston for special care. In May 1887, they become the happy parents of a healthy baby boy, Baker T. Washington.*

Olivia had become Booker's partner in all things. She was mother to Baker and to Portia, Booker's daughter with Fanny. When he was trav-

---

* Baker Washington would later change his name to Booker T. Washington Jr.

*As his "lady principal," Olivia Davidson helped Washington hone his fundraising skills in the North, where she had studied at a Massachusetts normal school. After the death of Fanny Washington, Davidson became the second Mrs. Washington.*

eling, Mrs. Washington kept her "Dear Husband" apprised of all that happened at home. Her more sophisticated education seeped into his public speaking: Previously satisfied with describing his own experiences in plain terms, he began to make references to Plato and Sir Isaac Newton and educator Horace Mann, the father of the normal school movement for public school teachers.

Booker T. Washington had an extraordinarily full life as he—and Tuskegee Normal—gained respect and recognition well beyond Alabama's borders.

# FIRE!

The year 1889 brought the best—and the worst—of times. On Wednesday, February 6, Olivia gave birth to a second son, Ernest Davidson Washington. Like her first, this pregnancy had been difficult, but a nurse sent by generous Bostonians had seen her through a healthy delivery in Tuskegee. Mother and child were well enough that the

*Booker Taliaferro Washington
posing as a public man. Note
the manuscript pages in his
hand, almost certainly the
text of one of his increasingly
famous speeches.*

next day Booker departed for the North on another quest for contributions.

In the wee hours that Friday night, however, the recovering mother awakened to the smell of smoke. Flames from a chimney fire licked through a faulty flue, igniting the wooden structure of the Washingtons' campus home. Although still convalescing from her trying pregnancy and giving birth just two days before, Olivia rose from her bed to run from the house into the cold winter night, her newborn and infant sons in her arms. The fire could not be stopped, and the house burned to the ground.

Everyone survived the blaze, but another tragedy loomed. Exposure to the elements and the shock of the fire had taken a toll on Olivia, and after a month of declining health, her worried husband took her to Boston. There she received the best care that her Boston admirers could buy at Massachusetts General Hospital. Washington heard from many well-wishers, one of whom recommended a stay in the Tennessee mountains to take the waters, where such minerals as limestone, iron, and sulfur might effect a cure.[5] But she was in no state to travel, and at her Boston bedside, Booker could only watch and hope for the best, reporting to General Armstrong in early April, "My wife is better but is still far from well."[6]

When he felt he could, he took brief trips to New York and other Northeast cities to pursue contributions. "Mrs. Washington was much more comfortable when I left her yesterday," he wrote back to Tuskegee in mid-April.[7] But for the most part, he remained nearby. Late in the month, he admitted to Armstrong, "As hard as it is I guess it is best for me to look the matter in the face and say that at present she is not gaining and without a change soon can not last much longer."[8] There were good days: On May 2, he noted that "Mrs. Washington I am glad to say seems to me stronger than when last I wrote and her condition seems a little more encouraging."[9] But a week later, Olivia America Davidson Washington was gone, dead at just thirty-four, on May 9, 1889. Booker had barely enough money to transport her home, where the epitaph on her tombstone would read "She lived to the truth."

Twice a widower and the father of three children under six, Booker acknowledged to Armstrong his sense of loss. "Few will ever know just what she was to Tuskegee and me. But I can not trust myself to write more now. I want to tell you about it all some time."[10]

Events left him brokenhearted—and the school short of money. Just to keep the doors open he had to borrow funds from old friends, among them Armstrong, but he was no less determined that Tuskegee would survive and thrive. He was on a mission, and money woes were nothing new at Tuskegee. Washington's bigger worry as he lay awake at night, anxious and uncertain, was that "if the Tuskegee experiment failed, it would injure the whole race in the eyes of whites."[11]

# THE THIRD MRS. WASHINGTON

Washington worked harder than ever. He was creating a movement as well as a school, and as the number of Tuskegee graduates swelled, so did the school's influence. Years before, he had organized the Alabama State Teachers' Association with an all-Black membership. In the absence of a state agency concerned with educating Black students, it placed teachers and planned curricula for rural schools.

The campus continued to expand. New construction projects added academic buildings and a chapel. In 1893, Tuskegee's enrollment exceeded five hundred students; by 1895, the student body neared eight hundred, with twenty buildings on 1,810 acres, with roughly a third of the land in cultivation.

New instructors were required, too, and Washington traveled regularly to Fisk University, in Nashville, Tennessee, a source of capable teachers. Like both Hampton and Tuskegee, Fisk had been founded immediately after the Civil War as a school for freedmen. Despite Olivia's recent death, Washington went to Nashville in the spring of 1889 to deliver a commencement speech. While there, he met one graduate in particular.

Margaret James Murry was seated across from him at the graduation dinner. Maggie Murray was five years younger than he, one of ten children born in Mississippi to a Black washerwoman and an immigrant Irish railroad worker. After her father's death she grew up in the household of a Quaker brother and sister; an able student, she herself became a teacher at age fourteen and taught school for five years before working her way through Fisk. A member of that year's graduating class, she was pretty, worldly, accomplished, and poised.

At the dinner, Miss Murray reminded Mr. Washington that she had written him about a position at Tuskegee. She already had a job offer

*Washington's third wife, Margaret Murray "Maggie" Washington: stepmother to his children, lady principal at Tuskegee, and an invaluable presence for the closing twenty-five years of his life.*

from Prairie View Normal College in Texas, but she was attracted to Washington's program and his cautious and conservative outlook. Impressed by her maturity, he offered her a teaching job. She accepted, and within a year, he appointed her lady principal. Then, in October 1892, they became man and wife. He would rely on the capable Maggie in many ways, just as he had on Olivia, particularly since his travels kept him far from Tuskegee and his children as much as six months of the year.

This marriage was perhaps less loving than Booker and Olivia's. Maggie and Mr. J.H. didn't always see eye to eye, and relations with Washington's first child, Portia, were often prickly. But Booker and Maggie's partnership would last as long as he lived.

POWERFUL AND INFLUENTIAL PEOPLE were coming to know the name Booker T. Washington. Collis P. Huntington, a ruthless rail magnate who helped complete the transcontinental railroad, gave Tuskegee a thousand dollars. That sum would be followed by numerous much larger donations from wealthy captains of industry.

The money was welcome, even if it had strings attached. "I am quite convinced that donations from the North in the future are going to be more largely than ever devoted to industrial education," Washington wrote in 1893.[12] He founded Tuskegee to teach teachers—but his bootstrap philosophy could also accommodate the desire of men like Huntington to develop a Black workforce with trade skills. Tuskegee men could step into factory jobs, while its women graduates might also find work outside the classroom. With his goal of preparing students for steady work that would translate into good wages and the chance for them to gain prosperity and respect, Washington had no choice but to accept that most Northerners regarded Tuskegee's Black students as best suited to manual labor.

While elevating the lives of Tuskegee graduates, maintaining peaceable relations with Southern conservatives was even more essential to sustaining his project. If he asked—or demanded—too much too fast, he would offend White sentiments. "Any movement for the elevation of Southern Negro," as he put it, "[depended] to a certain extent [on] the cooperation of Southern whites." And jobs in industry, work that White people regarded as proper for the "Colored Race"? That would be good for both Black man and the larger society: "Nothing else so soon brings about right relations between the two races in the South," he believed, "as the industrial progress of the negro."[13]

He tempered his goals because white supremacy ruled in the South of the 1890s. The governor of South Carolina helped set the intimidating tone, in 1892, when he stood beneath a tree from which eight Black men had been hung in the previous year, proclaiming "[I] would lead a mob to lynch a negro who raped a white woman."[14] An allegation of sexual assault, with or without any supporting evidence, came to be the default justification for hundreds of hangings. In some instances, thousands of bystanders assembled to watch a Black man murdered, but Washington remained silent on the subject of lynching even as the numbers rose to hundreds per year. He knew what happened to those who spoke up: They were invariably punished, often by banishment from their communities, and *that* he could not afford. Tuskegee was his life, his way of advancing the cause. He spoke up for his people when he felt he could, but with caution: To push for anything like equality of the races would be seen by many as nothing less than a threat to the social order, endangering him and others.

The local paper, the *Tuskegee Reporter*, laid out the unwritten law of the South very clearly. The wise Black man would do well "to keep in view that that this is a white man's country and that they intend to control it."[15]

*With images of Abraham Lincoln and George Washington looking down from the wall above the blackboard, Tuskegee students learn American history in this 1902 photograph.*

*Booker's educational philosophy at work; at Tuskegee,
classroom time was always paired with physical labor,
in this case, the upholstering of barrel chairs.*

CHAPTER EIGHT

# ROOSEVELT THE REFORMER

The only trouble I ever had with managing [Roosevelt] was he wanted to put an end to all the evil in the world between sunrise and sunset.

PRESIDENT BENJAMIN HARRISON

R oosevelt was a very long way from the Deep South in the autumn of 1888. September found him pursuing a favorite pastime, hunting in Idaho, but he returned to the Dakotas with a new plan. On the eve of his thirtieth birthday, he would sell his remaining cattle and make a career change.

After a single day back in New York visiting Edith, young Alice, and Ted, who had just turned one, he again boarded a train, on October 7, bound for Chicago—and back into the political fray. Though he was not running for elective office, Benjamin Harrison was, and Roosevelt was ready to give his best effort to the cause.

The Civil War general and former senator known as "Little Ben"—he was just five foot six—was giving incumbent president Grover Cleveland a real run for his money. Roosevelt had volunteered to be part of the last push to try and get a Republican back in the White House. Harrison himself would not leave Indianapolis, though he would deliver some eighty speeches from the front step of his home in a so-called front-porch campaign. That meant he needed surrogates to stump for him elsewhere, and over the course of the next twelve days, Roosevelt would woo crowds in Minnesota, Michigan, and Illinois.

The New Yorker enjoyed the campaign—the swags of red-white-and-blue bunting, the cheers, the attacks on Cleveland. He brought to the task, he admitted, "immense zest."[1] He was very effective, his fellow Republicans agreed, arguably the best of Harrison's surrogates, and the final outcome in November also pleased his fellow Republicans. The party won majorities in both branches of Congress, and though Harrison lost the popular vote—Cleveland swept the South, partly because new restrictions had begun closing the polls to Black voters—Roosevelt's candidate managed to prevail in the Electoral College. To the disappointment of Booker Washington and other Black voters, neither party had focused on racial matters, arguing instead about economic policy and, in particular, tariffs. Roosevelt, not yet attuned to such issues, was no exception.

With the election over, Roosevelt went back to finishing the book he was writing. But as the new administration prepared to take over after the inauguration in March, powerful friends pled the case for rewarding him. Roosevelt wrote to his friend Henry Cabot Lodge, who had just been elected to a seat in the House from Massachusetts, confiding that "I would like above all things to go into politics."[2]

Despite Lodge's lobbying, Roosevelt didn't get the job he wanted in the Department of State. "I fear he lacks the repose and patient endurance required in an Assistant Secretary," the incoming secretary of state told Lodge. "I do somehow fear that my sleep at [home in] Augusta or [on vacation] in Bar Harbor would not be quite so easy and refreshing if so brilliant and aggressive a man had hold of the helm."³

The words would prove true in time, but in the short term another position was found for the eager Roosevelt. The money wasn't much, a mere $3,500 per year. And as one of three civil service commissioners, his friends warned, he could get lost in the bureaucracy, "shelved definitely in a maze of routine."⁴ The agency was tiny—other than the commissioners themselves, it had a staff of four, one of whom was a messenger. Furthermore, such a job would be one in which it would be easier to make political enemies than allies.

Edith didn't want him to take the job. She was pregnant with the couple's second child and had no wish to relocate to unfamiliar Washington. But Theodore felt he couldn't refuse. He immediately accepted the post—and set about making up for lost time.

# THE CIVIL SERVICE COMMISSION

From Roosevelt's first moment on the job, everyone in the west wing of Washington's City Hall understood it wouldn't be business as usual at the commission. Even before he reached his new desk, on May 13, 1889, he announced loudly to everyone in earshot, "I am the new Civil Service Commissioner, Theodore Roosevelt of New York."

"Have you a telephone?" he demanded of the first clerk he saw. The man leapt to his feet, but recalled later that the sound of such certainty was "peculiarly pleasant" in what had been a sleepy agency. The clerk wasn't so much intimidated by Roosevelt as impressed by the "dazzling smile [that] seemed to mirror the wholesomeness and geniality of the man and it put me wholly at ease."⁵

The commission had been created by the Pendleton Civil Service

Reform Act of 1883. Starting with the presidency of Andrew Jackson a half century before, the unwritten rule "To the victor belong the spoils" had been standard operating procedure in the nation's capital. Like a victorious army, each new administration would replace old officeholders, in particular those in the lucrative positions of postmaster, with their own men. Most of the new appointees were partisan loyalists; an appointment was a reward for votes or cash. As the business of government had grown more complex, however, a large flaw in the so-called spoils system had revealed itself. Many appointees, with little or no expertise in their area of responsibility, performed poorly. The Pendleton Act set out to change that.

The law required that some jobs be filled on the basis of merit and a competitive examination. When Roosevelt arrived, however, only about one in four federal employees fell under the aegis of the commission, leaving 75 percent of government jobs still occupied by political appointees. There were loopholes in the Pendleton Act, too, as well as ongoing opposition in Congress to abandoning a proven and valuable political tool.

Roosevelt arrived as a believer in the importance of the cause, a reformer to his core. He had worshiped his father, who as a philanthropist had worked for social reform. During his own days in Albany, Theodore Jr. had crusaded for working-class improvements, like the banning of tenement workshops, and his inbred instinct for fairness was offended by the spoils system. He believed it was undemocratic. He argued that "the farmer's lad and the mechanic's son who had no one to speak for them should have the same shot in competing for the public service as the son of wealth and social prestige."[6]

Although he was the youngest of the three commissioners, Roosevelt immediately took charge. He issued reports. He checked his facts. He generated headlines with his investigations into the New York Customs House and the appointment of corrupt postmasters in other parts of the country. He wrote long, outraged letters. He testified at congressional hearings. And in time, he made progress, as several agencies were professionalized, their staffs made permanent. When he could not push politics out of the process, he could at least set policies that created some distance between politics and the civil service. One rule established that a federal worker "has an entire right to vote as he pleases, and to express privately his opinions on all political subjects."[7]

Above all, the pugnacious Roosevelt protected the Civil Service Commission. Many of his efforts to expand the merit system were resisted by politicians accustomed to dispensing favors and jobs the old way; to them, Roosevelt was a "ranting young humbug."[8] He wasn't bashful about going public and naming names, regardless of party affiliation, and his language was always colorful, quotable, and often critical. If some of the criticism ricocheted back on him, he didn't seem to mind.

When Democrat Grover Cleveland won back the White House in 1892, he unexpectedly retained Roosevelt; for two more years, Theodore continued his passionate pursuit of reform, seemingly above politics. His good work and the sheer power of his personality won him important friends in the Washington elite, men like Henry Adams, the descendant of presidents, whose famous "breakfasts" were always populated by powerful and influential people. Even Edith, once reluctant to make Washington her home, came to relish her duties as a hostess.

Roosevelt's six years as a civil service warrior was both humbling and empowering. He did what he could, but less than he hoped, and not as quickly as he would have liked. ("Roosevelt seemed to feel that everything ought to be done before sundown," President Harrison once observed.)[9] Roosevelt also gained administrative and management skills that he would put to good use in future elective offices.

He observed some key truths. Government is less about legislation than about administration. Good governing was possible only when one put the best people in the right places, then delegated responsibility and provided them with the support they needed. Knowing all the facts led to better decisions. These were lessons that he would rely upon later as president.

He continued to hone his personal philosophy. He came to believe that "each man, whether brain worker or hand worker, should do the best work of which he was capable"—and he saw it was "the duty of government" to make it so.[10] He did his work in his straight-ahead manner. He never stepped back from a fight. He valued honesty and insisted upon it.

The resemblance between the newly empowered Roosevelt and his future friend Booker Washington grew; Washington's bedrock principles and Roosevelt's mirrored each other, even if Washington too often had to pull his punches, in a way Roosevelt did not, as a matter of self-preservation.

Roosevelt's new friend Henry Adams, whose grasp of history was the equal of anyone's, compared Roosevelt to an express locomotive steaming toward an "inevitable destination."[11] That exact destination was not yet clear, but Roosevelt acquired respect and visibility in the nation's capital as he readied himself to take on a new challenge.

# REFORMING THE NYPD

In 1884, Roosevelt had been invited to run for mayor of New York. He had hesitated, afraid that a second loss might damn his political fortunes forever. Plus, Edith was strongly opposed. A move from Washington was the last thing she needed as the mother of five. She and Theodore now had three sons underfoot—Ted was seven, Kermit five, and Archibald an infant—as well as their daughter Ethel, three, and ten-year-old Alice. For once, Roosevelt listened and declined the offer.

He immediately regretted his decision, worrying that he might have passed up "the one golden chance that never returns."[12] He grew angry and resentful when a few weeks later William Strong, a businessman with no political experience, won the mayoralty. Still mourning his missed opportunity, Roosevelt decided he would stay in Washington another year, only to realize that, after five years on the Civil Service Commission, "I am nearly through what I can do here."[13] So he was open to a new job when Mayor Strong, in the spring of 1895, asked him to join the Police Commission back in New York.

The new assignment took him downtown to New York's Little Italy neighborhood, a world away from the mid-Manhattan of Roosevelt's childhood. The fortress-like police headquarters was surrounded by grim tenements and brothels. Millions of penniless immigrants continued to pour into Ellis Island, and many southern and eastern European arrivals remained in teeming neighborhoods like New York's worst slum, the Five Points, a short walk from police headquarters at 300 Mulberry Street.

On the day of his swearing in, Roosevelt got himself elected president of the four-man board. A ten-thousand-page report released the previous year had documented vast corruption in the NYPD, detailing millions of dollars in kickbacks from brothels, gamblers, and saloons. It found that many cops had bought their jobs in order to get in on the take. The force was famously crooked, brutal, and little interested in public service.

The new commissioner wanted to see for himself how the police operated, and one of those he turned to was Jacob Riis. A Danish immigrant who had arrived in New York with next to nothing more than two decades before, Riis had become a journalist, working the night shift for *The Evening Sun.* His beat was the police department. Roosevelt had known Riis for some time and greatly admired his first book, *How the Other Half Lives,* published in 1890. It was a portrayal, both in stories and photographic images Riis himself recorded, of the awful conditions among the New York poor. This man was much more than a reporter, and his book had moved Roosevelt:

> Jacob Riis had drawn an indictment of the things that were wrong, pitifully and dreadfully wrong, with the tenement homes and the tenement lives of our wage-workers. In his book he had pointed out how the city government, and especially those connected with the departments of police and health, could aid in remedying some of the wrongs.[14]

Together with Riis, Roosevelt began making unannounced night patrols around the city. On the day after Roosevelt's first inspection trip, Riis reported in *The Evening Sun* that they found nine of the ten patrolmen in the neighborhoods they visited missing in action. But Roosevelt wasn't going to accept what he found. He wanted things to change, even if he himself had to be the enforcer.

On one foray in the wee hours of the night, he crisscrossed the area one beat cop was supposed to patrol. The officer was nowhere to be found, but just as he was about to give up and return to the station house, Roosevelt spotted the uniformed man sitting in a bar on Third Avenue. In front of him was a plate piled high with oysters.

Roosevelt approached and asked why the cop wasn't out on patrol.

"What's it to you?" the man demanded. "And who are you anyway?"

"You've got a good nerve," the barman chimed in, "coming in here and interfering with an officer."

Roosevelt, his anger rising, identified himself, then ordered, "Now get out on your post where you belong!"

The unintimidated officer reached for another oyster. "Yes, you are," he told Roosevelt sarcastically. "You're Grover Cleveland and Mayor Strong, all in a bunch. *Move on now,*" he threatened, "*or else—*

*As police commissioner in New York City and later as governor of New York, Roosevelt was a muckraker, always looking to root out political corruption.*

But the barman interrupted. "Shut up, Bill," he whispered to the cop. "It's his Nibs, sure! Don't you see his teeth and glasses?"[15] Anyone who read the newspaper associated the name Roosevelt with the face in the political cartoons.

Roosevelt made allies with other reporters, and they followed him everywhere. He made good copy, and his very public work began to have an impact. "We have a real Police Commissioner," reported *The New York World*. "He makes our policemen feel as the little froggies did when the stork came to rule them. His heart is full of reform."[16] Roosevelt's veiled threats to investigate famously corrupt chief Thomas F. Byrnes led to the man's resignation. He opened a police academy and established the city's first police bicycle patrol (the automobile—and the police car—had yet to hit the New York streets). Officer dismissals doubled, as did arrests—and so did complaints, once citizens of the city realized that cops were no longer above the law.

By the fall of 1896, however, Roosevelt was ready for a distraction from the twelve-and-more-hour days he spent fixing the police department. He jumped at the invitation when it came: Remembering how effective Roosevelt had been in campaigning for Benjamin Harrison, party men wanted to enlist Roosevelt in William McKinley's run for president. Like Harrison, the folksy Ohioan would run a front-porch campaign, remaining at home with his mother and invalid wife, speaking to substantial crowds that came to him in Canton, Ohio. Could Roosevelt take his aggressive, fist-pumping style on the road to make McKinley's case?

He traveled across New York to the Midwest, his train often arriving just after the departure of Democratic candidate William Jennings Bryan, whom Roosevelt then attacked as a dangerous populist and socialist. The melded campaign worked so well that McKinley won in a landslide that November, and Roosevelt hoped there would be a payoff for him, too, namely a job in the new administration.

In New York, Riis and others had introduced Roosevelt, a man of inherited wealth, to the "other half," those born into poverty. As a police commissioner, he had thrown his considerable energies into "making the city a better place in which to live and work for those to whom the conditions of life and labor were the hardest."[17] He still wished to expand his reform efforts to benefit less privileged citizens; in time, he would indeed find that opportunity.

First, however, his quest to "mak[e] the best of himself" would take him on unexpected adventure in the Caribbean.[18] Only after donning a uniform, charging up an obscure Cuban hillside, and returning a hero would Roosevelt meet and make Booker Washington a partner in his quest to do good for the downtrodden.

# CHAPTER NINE

# THE SPEECH THAT ECHOED

*In all things that are purely social we can be as separate as the fingers, yet one as the hand in all things essential to mutual progress.*

BOOKER T. WASHINGTON, SEPTEMBER 18, 1895

B ooker Washington didn't set out to become famous. Yet that's exactly what happened. A child of whom nothing could be expected, born enslaved in a backwater Virginia town, Booker set off in search of an education. He became a teacher, then he founded a school. In his next phase, as an advocate for improving the lives of the Black men and women in his region and beyond, he emerged as a national and even international celebrity. Yet he also found that notoriety is double-edged: Some of the attention you gain will be from admirers, some from people who only want to knock you down.

In the North, Washington had found audiences willing to listen, and newspapers tended to treat him with respect. Yet even prestige magazines like *Harper's Weekly*, *The Atlantic Monthly*, and *The Century* ran cartoons, stories, and poetry that featured stereotyped Black caricatures, frequently disparaging their intelligence, work ethic, reliability, cleanliness, morality, and honesty. In Southern newspapers the demonization was much worse: It was so pervasive that an influential Black Methodist bishop in Atlanta was forced to acknowledge that "No white dares to speak in defense of the negro and command the respect of the whites."[1] One result was that opportunities for Southern Black people were so restricted that the vast majority still tilled the land, typically as sharecroppers on former plantations, usually on terms that guaranteed they would remain in poverty.

*As Booker's fame expanded, he filled stadium-size*
*venues with admirers, dressed in their best.*

Washington's influence in the African American community would expand greatly after he reached out to these farmers and others, convening the first Tuskegee Negro Conference in 1892. He aimed "to bring together . . . representatives of the masses—the bone and sinew of the race—the common hardworking farmers with a few of the best ministers and teachers."[2] He got what he wanted: After extending an invitation to seventy-five farmers, more than five times that many arrived.

The conference was a casual affair with no long speeches. The farmers took turns speaking candidly of their lives. Washington mingled freely, listening to these plain people as they spoke with "native eloquence, wit, and humor" about their hardscrabble lives. When Booker asked how many of the 425 attendees owned their land debt-free, just 23 raised their hands.[3]

From one year to the next, the Negro Conference would grow in importance. Maggie Washington set up a model home where she demonstrated good nutritional practices and sanitary housekeeping, which was no easy thing in dirt-floor dwellings with poor ventilation and no plumbing. A second day was added to the annual meeting for teachers' conferences. Attendance doubled in 1893, then rose into the thousands.

Although correspondents came from Northern newspapers to report on the conference, Washington chose not to document what was said. "We have not gotten to the point in the South, I fear, where we can

*As a speaker, Booker Washington could amuse, encourage, and command his listeners' attention.*

discuss the interests of the race . . . with perfect freedom," he told the U.S. Commissioner of Education, who asked to publish the conference proceedings.[4] Washington was sure that any criticism of Whites—and, inevitably, there was some, given how Blacks in the region were treated by their fellow citizens—would only cause trouble.

The appearance of Tom Harris on his doorstep with a mob in hot pursuit was a reminder of how carefully Washington had to walk and talk as an emerging leader in the Black community.

# A LAWYER OF COLOR

One Saturday in June 1895, Wylie Harris finished his day's work at his butcher shop in Tuskegee.[5] He headed home, but stopped at the post office, where he picked up a letter addressed to his father, Thomas A. Harris, Esquire. Wylie did not know it, but its message was chilling: A band of local vigilantes ordered his father, a Black attorney, out of town by six o'clock that very day. Making matters worse, by the time the elder Harris opened the letter, the moon was rising—and the chapel bells at Tuskegee Normal had already struck six.

A native Alabamian, Tom Harris had been his slaveholder's body servant during the Civil War. After emancipation, he attended Tuskegee and, later, passed the bar. At the time, the all-White examiners, who included a former Confederate general and an ex-governor of Alabama, declared him "an intelligent and well-behaved negro."[6] When Harris returned to Tuskegee, however, *The Tuskegee News* was less respectful, dismissing Harris as "an idle negro man, extremely unpopular with his own race on account of his airs of superiority." The report added that he was disliked by White people because of his "impudent utterances and insolent bearing."[7] Despite the harsh words, Harris settled into a law practice in Tuskegee—until he stepped across a racial boundary.

The trouble began when he invited a White itinerant minister from Ohio to stay in his home in late May 1895. Even a hint of equality between the races was automatically seen as a dangerous transgression, but the guest, a Reverend Kelly, put Harris in a truly perilous position when, walking home from church, he sheltered Harris's pretty young daughters beneath his umbrella. Their seeming intimacy smacked of unholy miscegenation, and an angry mob soon arrived to run the "yankee preacher" out of town.* On a Saturday night, two days later, Tom Harris opened the threatening letter demanding that he, too, leave Tuskegee.

In the twilight, a nervous Tom Harris headed across the street to seek the advice of a White neighbor, but he saw he was too late. Down the road, marching toward him, was a mob of townspeople, men in masks carrying lit torches and brandishing pistols.

"There they are now, coming to kill me!" Harris shouted.[8]

He ran toward his neighbor's house, hoping to race in the front door and then out the back to elude the mob. But the owner, fearing for his life and the safety of his own daughters, who watched from his front porch, wrestled with Harris.

And then the mob was there. One man raised his pistol, its muzzle a foot from Harris's head. As the gunman pulled the trigger, Harris feinted and the bullet whistled past, lodging in his neighbor's neck. Breaking free, Harris attempted to escape up the road, but more shots rang out. One struck Harris, shattering a bone in his lower leg. He slumped to the ground.

Harris lay there, howling in pain, but the mob didn't swarm. Instead, they hovered around the wounded White man, leaving Harris to be cared for by family members who emerged from his house. A physician

---

* The term *miscegenation*—interbreeding of people of different races—came into use during the Civil War. The term survives even today in white supremacist rhetoric in the United States and abroad, which favors "racial purity" and opposes the "mixing" of Europeans and non-Europeans. The label *yankee preacher* comes from *The Tuskegee News.*

present refused to treat Harris, but no one interfered when Wylie and his siblings dragged their father away from the melee.

Later, with no one else to turn to, Tom Harris arrived on Booker Washington's front step.

At 10:00 P.M., Washington answered the knock at his door. Roused from his bed, Tuskegee's founder and principal faced an impossible choice.

Standing before him, supported by son Wylie, was Tom Harris, seriously wounded and still in need of medical attention. Native instinct told Washington to summon the school's resident physician to treat the man's gunshot wound, to give him the care he needed.

In his mind's eye, however, he also foresaw what would happen if he permitted this man to cross his threshold. He knew Tom Harris was trouble, that he took foolish risks. Taking him in would surely bring down on Washington's head, as he put it, "the fury of some drunken white men."[9] Doing the right thing, he realized in that instant, might well jeopardize his life's work, his school, even his own life.

What to do?

Documents from the time bring us two versions of the story. As reported in the newspapers, Washington turned Harris away, refusing him refuge. According to the *Richmond Planet*, after explaining the dangers he and Tuskegee Normal could face,

> Booker T. Washington, the president of the Negro school [who] has ever conducted himself and his school in the most prudent and conservative manner, . . . told [Harris] that he could not be admitted there.[10]

Later, when he opened his door a second time, he was confronted by a band of angry and armed White men demanding he hand over Tom

Harris. Their anger was high: In their view, Harris, a Black man, had been the cause of a White man being shot and they were there to carry out a lynching. But Washington told the men he had turned Harris away, that he didn't know where he had gone. With Harris nowhere to be found, the mob disbanded.

The episode ended there—except it didn't. When the story reached the North, Washington was harshly criticized in the Black press, the papers published by African Americans to serve their communities, most of them in Northern cities like Boston, New York, and Philadelphia. One Washington editor condemned his conduct as "hypocritical and showing the natural bent of the man" when he denied Harris "the right of medical assistance."[11] He seemed not have stood up for his people, and an old friend in the nation's capital, the Reverend Francis J. Grimké, wrote to ask for an explanation. Only then did Washington—*for Grimké's eyes only*—confide the full story.

> I helped them [Tom and Wylie Harris] to a place of safety and paid the money out of my own pocket for the comfort and treatment of the man while he was sick. Today I have no warmer friends than the man and his son. They have nothing but the warmest feelings of gratitude for me . . . but I do not care to publish to the world what I do. . . . I simply chose to help and relieve this man in my own way.[12]

The true story remained a closely held secret for many decades; only when a Washington biographer came across the correspondence with Grimké long after all the participants were dead was the story told. That it was true was attested to by other correspondence, including letters from Tom Harris in which he expressed his appreciation for Washington's help. "I am ever your friend," Harris had written.[13]

The neighbor made a full recovery from his gunshot wound. Harris, having decided that being a "negro lawyer" was too dangerous a profession in a state hostile to Black advancement, asked Washington for a letter of reference when he applied for a job as a notary public elsewhere in Alabama. Business proceeded as usual at Tuskegee, the life of the school uninterrupted by the events of June 8, 1895. And Harris's name was conspicuously absent from the pages of Washington's later autobiographical writings.

For Washington, the Tom Harris incident was just another lesson in survival. He took the cascade of criticism from militant Black people in the North in silence; to defend himself with the truth would have enraged his White Alabama neighbors and put him at risk of much more than disapproval. If he wished to survive in a hostile and racist society, he saw no other choice but to live a life that was a strange mix of fact and fiction, one in which he would, at times, have to dissemble. Every audience to whom he spoke required that he tailor his words, often tempering what he really felt to avoid offense or to stay safe. His freedom to speak knew many boundaries.

He chose to rise above, following the wise words of Frederick Douglass, who had recently spoken at a Tuskegee graduation. "They cannot degrade Frederick Douglass," Douglass had told Washington after an episode where he had been forced to ride in a train's baggage car. "The soul that is within me no man can degrade. I am not the one that is being degraded on account of this treatment, but those who are inflicting it upon me."[14]

## "A NEGRO WHO HAS SENSE"

Washington was about to become the most influential Black man in America. His fame had expanded steadily among White Northerners following addresses to large audiences in Boston; Saratoga, New York;

Lincoln University in Pennsylvania; and other places. But his reputation grew more slowly in the South until a new door opened, in May 1894, when a telegram called him to Washington.

A year before, the World's Columbian Exposition in Chicago had been an immense success, drawing more than twenty-five million people. Hoping to attract similar attention to the South, a group of influential Atlantans were organizing the Cotton States and International Exposition for the following year. A delegation seeking congressional funding was traveling to Washington, D.C., and Booker was invited to speak at a hearing before the House Committee on Appropriations.

He raced to Washington, reaching the Capitol only minutes before the exposition delegates made their pitch. He listened for almost the entire two hours while they made their long-winded arguments, which left Washington, the last to take the floor, with just six minutes.

Referring to scribbled notes on an envelope in his hand, an earnest Booker Washington spoke plainly. He told the congressmen he wasn't a political man. In speaking to them, he said, he was breaking his own rule against political involvement, one he had maintained since founding his school almost fifteen years before. He had their attention.

He had come at his own expense and at short notice, Washington continued, because he believed in education and practical matters. He thought "the negro [should] acquire property, own his land, drive his own mule hitched to his own wagon, milk his own cow, raise his own crop and keep out of debt, and that when he acquired a home he became fit for a conservative citizen." He asked the committee to help the exposition because he wanted representatives of his race "[to] have the chance to give an account of its stewardship."[15] The unspoken message was that, at a time when the nation was again divided by racial matters, he was a reconciler, not an agitator. With neither party keen to refight the Civil War, his message of compromise and opportunity was welcome.

Washington spoke beyond his allotted time, talking for more than fifteen minutes. His fellow delegates were impressed—afterward they offered him hearty congratulations and thanks—as were the committeemen, who voted unanimously in favor of appropriating $200,000 for the exposition. A rare Black lobbyist in the halls of Congress, Booker was honored to shake the hand of the Speaker of the House. He had been heard as a spokesman for the Black South, one who could be trusted to tailor his words to make friends, not enemies.

## IN A TIGHT PLACE

His words to Congress led to what would be a career-defining moment for Booker T. Washington. It occurred back in the South, in Atlanta, at the opening of the Cotton States and International Exposition in September 1895. Initially, the fair's planners relegated him to a speech at the fair's Negro Building—where the Tuskegee Institute would be showcased—but an intense lobbying campaign led to a telegram, sent to him in Boston:

Congratulations. You are the Orator.[16]

The opportunity was extraordinary: He was about to reach a national, even international audience—*and* his sponsors were White Southerners. This would be a first, a symbolic moment for Black Americans. His speech was newsworthy even before Washington could open his mouth: A COLORED ORATOR HAS BEEN INVITED TO PARTICIPATE IN THE OPENING read a headline in *The Atlanta Constitution*.[17] But Washington had just three weeks to craft a speech that must do the nearly impossible. He felt compelled to advance the cause of the Black man and yet appease an audience filled with White people who accepted the idea, as the popular

Georgian Bill Arp put it in the pages of the region's best paper, that Black folk were "[a] restless, trifling, insolent, crime-loving class."[18]

When Washington spoke north of the Mason–Dixon Line, he could be frank. In 1891, for example, he told a Boston audience that that even if "legal slavery is dead, there is a mental, moral, and industrial slavery in the South that is not."[19] One big factor was the financial practice of mortgaging crops. The majority of Black farmers borrowed against their crops to buy fertilizer and foodstuffs until harvest, and then White store owners often marked up goods 40 percent and added interest charges of 25 to 30 percent.[20] The plain fact was that most Black farmers in the South could barely make ends meet. But that was a truth that Washington could not speak on his home turf.

Instead, the approach he would have to take was clear from his note to the exposition's director, when he thanked him for the honor of speaking. "It will be my aim," he promised, "to make my remarks of service to the exposition . . . and to both races in the South."[21]

He produced multiple drafts of the speech. He edited, elaborated, and deleted. He repeatedly reworked his phrasing. He worried, at times, that he would fail. He struggled to serve several goals—to give no offense to White people; to speak to the interests of his own race; and to say nothing that he did not feel in his heart to be true.

He read the speech to Maggie and, before leaving Alabama for Atlanta, he delivered it to the Tuskegee faculty. They approved. Then, accompanied by his wife and children, he headed for Tuskegee's rail depot to catch the train to Georgia. On the way he met up with a White farmer he knew, and in his autobiography, *Up from Slavery*, Washington remembered the encounter.

> In a jesting manner this man said: "Washington, you have spoken before to the Northern white people, the Negroes in the

South, and to us country white people in the South; but in Atlanta, tomorrow, you will have before you the Northern whites,
the Southern whites, and the Negroes all together. I am afraid
that you have got yourself into a tight place."

Though the man "diagnosed the situation correctly," Washington
wrote, "his frank words did not add anything to my comfort."[22]

## "A LEADER OF OUR RACE"

The long procession of dignitaries, bands, and marchers snaked through
Atlanta, taking three hours to reach the exposition grounds. Last came
the Black contingent, including Washington's carriage, so when he entered the hall where the opening ceremony was about to begin, he "found
it packed with humanity from top to bottom."[23] Thousands remained
outside, unable to squeeze in.

Georgia's governor and other officials took the stage to loud cheers
and clapping, but according to one observer, "when amongst them a colored man appeared, there was an instant cessation of the applause, and a
sudden chill fell upon the whole assemblage."[24] This scene was not usual
in Atlanta, Georgia, in 1895: Washington's speech would be the first ever
delivered by an African American to a racially mixed Southern audience.

The speeches began, interspersed with musical interludes. The crowd
greeted "The Star-Spangled Banner" with enthusiasm and "Dixie" with
loud cheers; "Yankee Doodle" got only respectful clapping. When Washington's turn came, Georgia's governor announced, "We shall now be
favored with an address by a great southern educator." The crowd ap-
plauded loudly—until, once more, the man they were welcoming proved
to be a Black figure rising from his seat. As Washington stepped to the

front of the stage, however, those in the Jim Crow section cheered wildly, more than compensating for the White audience that had gone quiet.

When he looked upon the crowd, Booker could barely distinguish their faces because of a blinding shaft of sunlight from a high window. To the audience, that same bright blast seemed to spotlight the speaker, who stood "with piercing eyes and commanding manner."[25] Yet this man was disarming, too, speaking with ease and confidence, his tone almost conversational.

For more than fifteen years, Washington had been polishing his arguments and developing a speaking style in his travels to the North and Midwest. He was a natural storyteller with a personal narrative that moved people when he recounted his rise from an enslaved childhood to freedom and the creation of Tuskegee Normal and Industrial Institute, which had become the school's formal name in 1891. But this speech had to be different. His audience included former Confederate and Yankee soldiers, one-time Klansmen and abolitionists, and both the formerly enslaved and past slaveholders.

He held a pencil in his hand, a tool of the teacher, as he told the crowd that members of the "negro race" constituted a third of the region's people.[26] He expressed appreciation to the exposition organizers for including him and spoke of his hope that the big gathering would "cement the friendships" between the races.

As he often did, Washington then related a parable. He told of a ship lost at sea for many days, its water supply exhausted. On spying another vessel at a distance, it signaled to the strange ship, *Water, water, we die of thirst.*

The response was unexpected: *Cast down your bucket where you are.*

Thinking his request had been misunderstood—salt water was of no use to parched seamen—the captain of the ship in distress signaled again but got the same response: *Cast down your bucket where you are.*

Finally, after four identical exchanges, the desperate captain did as instructed. When the bucket was raised, he tasted the water and made the happy discovery it was sparkling and fresh, part of the voluminous discharge from the mouth of a nearby river.

The lesson, Washington explained, was that the Southern Black man should "cultivat[e] friendly relations with the Southern white man" and cast down their buckets in "agriculture, mechanics, in commerce, in domestic service, and in the professions." The South was their home. They could and should stay, despite the problems. They could work and prosper.

To the White members of the audience, he offered a variation of the same theme. "I would repeat what I say to my own race: 'cast down your bucket where you are.'" The millions of formerly enslaved men and women in the South amounted to a vast labor pool, men and women who were known and could be trusted. Washington reminded his audience that unlike "those of foreign birth and strange tongue and habits," Black Southerners had proved their "loyalty to you in the past, in nursing your children, watching by the sick-bed of your mothers and fathers, and often following them with tear-dimmed eyes to their graves." He made a promise: "We shall stand by you with a devotion that no foreigner can approach."

According to a reporter for *The New York World*, Washington won the crowd over. "Within ten minutes, the multitude was in an uproar of enthusiasm, handkerchiefs were waved, canes were flourished, hats were tossed in the air. The fairest women of Georgia stood and cheered. It was as if the orator had bewitched them."[27]

The climax of the speech was to still come.

Washington, raising his right arm, held his broad hand high over his head, the fingers spread. Addressing the crowd, he said he foresaw a cooperative future for Black and White. "In all things that are purely social we can be as separate as the fingers, yet one as the hand in all things essential to mutual progress."

The words—the message—were quintessential Booker T. Washington. He spoke to what people called the "Negro Problem." He wanted simple acceptance, and he proposed a new way for White people to regard his brothers and sisters. In some two dozen carefully crafted words he accepted segregation and yet asked for acceptance. Coming from the circumstances he did, knowing the dangers posed by the Klan and other powerful Southern forces always ready to confront change with violence, he knew he could not demand equality. But he did appeal for opportunity, and the audience, Black and White, understood. As one, the crowd leapt to its feet and unleashed deafening applause.

When Washington finished—in his closing words he expressed his hope for a "material prosperity" that "will bring into our beloved South a new heaven and earth"—Black faces in the audience were stained with tears. But the acclaim seemed universal. He had managed to straddle the divide and later, as he left the building, Washington was mobbed by hundreds of admirers. The next morning he was recognized and congratulated on the streets of Atlanta. Across the country, his speech was widely published, and on his return trip to Tuskegee he was met by waiting crowds at almost every station along the route. He was inundated with letters and telegrams from well-wishers and with requests from editors for articles and lecture bureaus for appearances. Even President Grover Cleveland sent his congratulations. "Your words cannot fail to delight and encourage all who wish well for your race," Cleveland wrote from his Massachusetts farm.[28] A White editor at *The Atlanta Constitution* offered high praise, too. "It was an epoch-making talk, and marks distinctly a turning point in the progress of the Negro race, and its effect in bringing about a perfect understanding between whites and blacks of the South will be the immediate. The address was a revelation."[29]

The barefoot boy from Hale's Ford was achieving his great destiny as an agent of change for all Black Americans.

## A VOICE FROM THE FUTURE

One of the many letters of congratulation that Booker received after his Atlanta speech came from a brilliant young scholar, then teaching at Wilberforce University, a Black college in Ohio. The two men knew one another slightly, and Professor William Edward Burghardt Du Bois— better remembered today as W. E. B. Du Bois—was no doubt looking to connect with the suddenly very visible Booker Washington. Over time, however, he would emerge as more than an acquaintance. He became in the coming years Washington's chief competitor for the attention of Black Americans.

Like Washington, Du Bois (pronounced *Du Boyce*) was of mixed race, but otherwise their origins had been very different. A decade younger, Du Bois was born to free parents, on February 23, 1868. A great-grandfather had been a French Huguenot slaveholder, but Du Bois's ancestry was also African, Dutch, Haitian, and English. A maternal ancestor, though born in West Africa, had fought in the American Revolution.

Du Bois grew up in the North, in the western Massachusetts town of Great Barrington. His father abandoned the family when Will was still an infant; as a schoolboy, Du Bois had become his mother's close companion after a stroke left her lame. Despite her disabilities, however, she continued to work—and her determination that he get a good education helped drive her son to excel. His teachers recognized his high intelligence and grit very early. He was often years ahead of his peers.

Although his schoolmates at the local public school were virtually all White, Will was accepted as their social equal in the classroom, on the playground, and even in their homes. "I was a boy unconscious of color discrimination," Du Bois later wrote. He would be the first Black graduate from the town's high school.[30]

After his mother's death, in 1885, the seventeen-year-old Du Bois left rural Massachusetts, embarking on a long educational journey. That fall he enrolled at historically Black Fisk University, and in Nashville he confronted the "Negro Problem" for the first time. "I suddenly came to a region where the world was split into white and black halves, and where the darker half was held back by race prejudice and legal bonds, as well as by deep ignorance and dire poverty."[31]

He earned his first bachelor's degree at Fisk and then enrolled at Harvard, where he was awarded a second BA—Harvard had refused to honor his Fisk credits—then a master's degree in history. Europe was his next stop, when the John F. Slater Fund for the Education of Freedmen awarded the twenty-four-year-old a fellowship to study at the University of Berlin. During his two years abroad, he traveled extensively around the continent. He discovered Europeans were less concerned with the color of his skin than his fellow Americans back home. "I found myself on the outside of the American world," he remembered later. "With me were white folk—students, acquaintances, teachers—who viewed the scene with me. They did not pause to regard me as a curiosity, or something sub-human; I was just a man of the somewhat privileged student rank."[32]

When Du Bois returned to the United States in 1894, he had two dollars in his pocket. He wrote that summer to numerous institutions, describing his qualifications and asking for a teaching position. When an invitation arrived in August—Wilberforce University, an African Methodist Episcopal Church school in western Ohio, offered him a salary of eight hundred dollars a year to teach Latin and Greek—he promptly accepted. That September, Du Bois began what would be decades of life in academia and activism in African American affairs.

The note the young and cosmopolitan academic sent to Booker Washington was brief, reading in its entirety, "Let me heartily congratulate you upon your phenomenal success at Atlanta—it was a word fitly spoken."[33] But this flattering commentary would, in time, give way to harsher words concerning Washington's thinking. A wide chasm soon opened between the balm of Booker's pragmatic approach and Du Bois's biting and uncompromising rhetoric.

CHAPTER TEN

# AMERICA THE UNREADY

No triumph of peace is quite so great as the supreme triumph
of war.

THEODORE ROOSEVELT, NAVAL WAR COLLEGE, JUNE 1897

I n the days after William McKinley won the presidency—with
Roosevelt's help, in the election of 1896—Theodore surveyed the
employment possibilities. As a well-to-do and well-placed White
male, he could think big and make bold choices in a way that Washington never could. Roosevelt would later learn how fortunate he was, in
contrast even to the highly visible Booker, and as a rising power in the
Republican Party, he set his sights on exactly the job he wanted.

In a departure from his previous focus on domestic matters, in Washington and in his home state, Roosevelt shifted to thinking about his
nation's role in the world. He had spent eight years paying political dues
and accumulating skills in two bureaucratic jobs; now he hoped to work
in a new arena, one that he knew well from his writings and travels—
and that he cared deeply about.

If he were assistant secretary of the navy, he decided, he could transform the United States fighting force on the high seas. Broadening his portfolio would no doubt be of value to his future political career, too, but above all, the secretaryship would give him a chance to put to use his ideas and his passion for warships, old and new.

He reached out to Henry Cabot Lodge, asking for his help in getting the appointment.

Lodge, who had moved up from the House to his first term in the U.S. Senate, pitched his friend Roosevelt directly to McKinley, as did a number of other prominent Washingtonians. The president, all too aware of Roosevelt's reputation, needed persuading. McKinley had served as a sergeant at Antietam, one of the bloodiest Civil War battles, and he worried about Roosevelt's hawkish tendencies. "I want peace," McKinley observed, "and I am told that your friend Theodore—whom I know only slightly—is always getting in rows with everybody. I am afraid he is too pugnacious."[1] Eventually, the pleas of Roosevelt's many supporters wore McKinley down, and in April 1897, *The Washington Post* announced the appointment. "[Theodore Roosevelt] is a fighter, a man of indomitable pluck and energy," reported the paper. "A field of immeasurable usefulness awaits him."[2]

*Massachusetts senator Henry Cabot Lodge, pictured in 1898 with the nation on the brink of war, would be a close and enduring Roosevelt ally in the lead-up to the Spanish–American War and later during Roosevelt's presidency.*

Reading habits reveal much about a person, and Roosevelt read constantly. Despite long working days and his own writing—he published roughly a book a year along with a steady stream of magazine articles, in part to supplement his income—he managed to consume a book every day, sometimes two. But one in particular, which he had savored over the course of a weekend in 1890, had helped rekindle his passion for naval affairs.

As a noted naval historian himself, Roosevelt appreciated the merits of *The Influence of Sea Power upon History, 1660–1783*. Within days of publication, he wrote to its author, Alfred Thayer Mahan, praising it as "a *very* good book—admirable; and I am greatly in error if it does not become a naval classic."[3] He had recently met Mahan, a veteran of the U.S. Navy and president of the Naval War College, in Newport, Rhode Island, when he delivered a lecture there. But it was less their acquaintance than a shared worldview that drew Roosevelt.

In his own *The Naval War of 1812*, he had taken great pride in what the little U.S. Navy had done almost a century earlier. But he had also expressed outrage at the "ludicrous and painful folly and stupidity" of the Jefferson and Madison administrations in failing to prepare their nation adequately for war.[4] Roosevelt believed Jefferson's defensive naval philosophy in particular—the third president thought the navy's near-exclusive job was to protect its coastline—had been wrongheaded then. Many decades later, such thinking made even less sense to the new assistant secretary of the navy. In the view of Roosevelt and Captain Mahan, the United States, which now wielded great economic power, needed to build a fleet of warships, modern vessels capable of doing battle at sea. Furthermore, they believed, such ships should be deployed at key pinch points around the world in order to ensure both the unrestricted flow of global trade and national sovereignty.

When Mahan's book was published, the U.S. Navy was ranked a lowly sixth in the world, behind Great Britain, France, Italy, Russia, and

Germany. A slow shift was underway as Congress underwrote the first of the nation's steel-hulled, steam-powered battleships to replace antiquated wooden sailing ships. But even after the USS *Indiana* was commissioned in 1895 and the USS *Massachusetts* and USS *Oregon* were launched a year later, a large imbalance remained: The Royal Navy, for example, had fifty battleships to America's three.

Henry Cabot Lodge shared Roosevelt's and Mahan's thinking. The three were in the vanguard of those who wanted the United States to expand beyond its continental borders. They had big ideas that fit into a national master plan. They thought the U.S. should possess Hawaii, Cuba, and Puerto Rico, and that a canal should be dug across the isthmus of Panama. Superiority on the seas was essential if the United States was to achieve its destiny and become a dominant world power.

## "HOT-WEATHER SECRETARY"

After months of waiting for his appointment to come through, Roosevelt arrived in Washington, in April 1897, with a full agenda. He wasted no time in briefing McKinley about the movements of the Japanese Navy near Hawaii and a troubling conflict between Turkey and Greece in the Mediterranean. But the big bogeyman Roosevelt saw was on the near horizon. "We should keep the battleships," he advised the president, ". . . in readiness for action should any complications arise in Cuba."[5]

For more than two years, a civil war had raged on the island barely a hundred miles from the Florida Keys. Cuban freedom fighters had engaged their Spanish colonial rulers in a fight for independence, the latest confrontation in a deadly tug-of-war that had waxed and waned for decades. But this time Spain had declared martial law, which meant a third of the island's peasant population now lived in detention camps, where poor sanitation and nutrition were the rule and cholera raged. The country was a tinderbox, just a spark away from exploding, and Roosevelt saw an opportunity to end Spain's colonial presence in the American hemisphere. "I am a quietly rampant 'Cuba libre' man," he told his sister Bamie.[6]

On June 2, Roosevelt delivered his first speech as assistant secretary. Borrowing from George Washington, he fashioned his address around the proposition that "To be prepared for war is the most effectual means to promote peace." He warned that "no nation can hold its place in the world . . . unless it stands ready to guard its rights with an armed hand." He also used the word *war* more than *sixty* times in the speech.[7]

The man officially in charge at the Department of the Navy was Secretary John D. Long. A former governor of Massachusetts who had served as a congressman with McKinley, Long came out of retirement to run the department at his old friend's request. But Long, worried about his health, felt most comfortable at home on Boston's South Shore. He also found summer in the nation's capital intolerable, so when the miasma of the Washington heat settled in in July, he went north, where he would stay until September. That left Roosevelt with his boss's full authority to act "entirely independently." He took full advantage.[8]

He ordered keels laid for a range of new vessels, from torpedo boats to battleships. The armaments on existing ships were updated. He consulted with Captain Mahan. He rethought the procurement process. Construction was begun to enlarge dry docks, expanded budgets were developed, promotion lists evaluated.

Readiness to Roosevelt also meant strategy. He devised a plan for consolidating the fleet near the Florida Keys, meaning that, in the event of war, American warships could steam into firing range of Cuba within forty-eight hours. He proposed that four fast cruisers be readied to harass the Spanish at home, while a task force in the Pacific might be positioned to blockade Manila, capital of the Philippines, another Spanish colony. In Long's absence, he briefed the president on his plans during a pair of long carriage rides and a dinner at the White House.

The "hot-weather secretary," as Roosevelt called himself, even went to sea on maneuvers off the Virginia coast, where he was able "to satisfy myself definitely of the great superiority of the battleship as a gun platform."[9] He liked his new power: "The Secretary is away," he wrote to one of those who had lobbied McKinley on his behalf, "and I am having immense fun running the navy."[10]

As one early biographer would observe, "It is not easy to draw a line between Roosevelt's anxiety to build up the navy, which was legitimate preparedness, and his lust for war."[11] Yet as winter weather moved in, matters seemed a bit quieter in Cuba, and Roosevelt was able to celebrate the birth of his sixth and last child, son Quentin, born November 19, 1897.

# A CALL TO WAR?

Just when it appeared Spain might grant Cuba home rule, riots broke out in Havana, on January 12, 1898. Printing presses at a newspaper were demolished, and loyalists and rebels fought in the streets. In the United States, papers the next morning exaggerated the story, falsely reporting that American citizens had been assaulted. This was the era of "yellow journalism," when competing press barons like Joseph Pulitzer and William Randolph Hearst sensationalized the news to build circulation. Hearst's *New York Evening Journal* headline read like a command to the commander-in-chief: NEXT TO WAR WITH SPAIN!

When Roosevelt arrived at the Navy Department that Wednesday, he went to Long's office and closed the door. He was as hot under the collar as the headline writer of the *Journal*. According to Long's diary entry,

"[Roosevelt] told me that in case of war with Spain, he intends to abandon everything and go to the front."[12] Long told the impetuous Roosevelt he was a "crank," but there was no dissuading his assistant secretary from his plan. "The funny part is," the baffled Long concluded, "he takes the thing seriously."[13]

For the moment, cooler heads prevailed, and McKinley and Long decided to dispatch the USS *Maine* on a peacekeeping mission. The 324-foot-long armed cruiser soon sailed from Key West, and on January 25, dropped anchor off Morro Castle, the centuries-old fortress at the mouth of Havana Harbor. The white hull of the *Maine* made an impressive sight, a bright band afloat on the azure water, with a densely packed superstructure above. There were two masts—for emergency sail only—along with the upper decks and the bridge, two tall funnels, a conning tower, boat crane, and two large gun turrets. On Roosevelt's watch, the ship had been outfitted with new armaments, including four ten-inch cannons that could fire five-hundred-pound shells a distance of ten miles.

*The USS* Maine *in better days, prior to its sinking.*
*Her explosive end in Havana Harbor provided*
*the pretext for going to war with Spain.*

A crew of 355 manned the ship, operating its eight boilers, tending to more than two dozen guns. Despite the tensions, sailors went ashore as navy discipline permitted, enjoying the city's cafes and entertainments. Only time would reveal that the USS *Maine*'s destiny would not be as a messenger of peace.

THE NIGHT OF February 15, 1898, was overcast and quiet, the sultry air in Havana Harbor stirred by a gentle breeze. In his quarters in the ship's stern, Captain Charles Sigsbee completed a report for Assistant Secretary Roosevelt concerning a new weapon, the torpedo, which Roosevelt favored and the *Maine* could fire through its four torpedo tubes.

At 9:10 P.M., taps signaled lights out for most of the sailors aboard the USS *Maine*. His duty done, the captain began a letter to his wife. Sigsbee's pet pug, Peggy, slept at his feet. On finishing his letter, he placed the sheet in an envelope, but at that instant, without warning—it was 9:40 P.M.—an explosion obliterated the stillness of the night.

Sigsbee felt the ship tremble after another deafening "bursting, rending" roar. He heard the crash of metal and felt the deck drop beneath his feet. The lights went out, and smoke began to fill his cabin. "The situation could not be mistaken," he later wrote, "the *Maine* was blown up and sinking."[14]

From the shore and nearby ships, observers saw a column of flames rocket upward near the bow of the ship. The explosion spewed fragments of steel and wood, along with the bodies of crew members; debris and human remains hit the water as much as a mile from the *Maine*'s mooring. A great cloud of gray smoke formed over the ship, and by the time Sigsbee made it to the poop deck, groping his way along the dark, pitched passageways, the bow was down and a large fire blazed amidships. He could hear cries from the water and recognized that the white

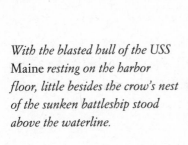

*With the blasted hull of the USS* Maine *resting on the harbor floor, little besides the crow's nest of the sunken battleship stood above the waterline.*

forms afloat were injured and drowning crewman. He ordered the manning of the lifeboats, but only three of the *Maine*'s were usable. Help arrived from other ships, among them Spanish military vessels, rescuing sailors in the water and aiding in the evacuation of the *Maine*.

True to tradition, Captain Sigsbee was the last to step off the deck of his ship into a waiting lifeboat. He was ferried to a nearby vessel, where he visited the wounded before retiring to compose a telegram to Washington.

The news, he knew, had to be framed carefully. He began with just facts. MAINE BLOWN UP IN HAVANA HARBOR AT NINE FORTY TO NIGHT AND DESTROYED, he wrote. MANY WOUNDED AND DOUBTLESS MORE KILLED OR DROWNED.[15] In fact, the numbers were worse than he knew: More than three-quarters of his crew were drowned, blasted, or trapped belowdecks. Two hundred and sixty good men were dead.

But he had been sent to Cuba because tensions between the United States and Spain had spiked. His job was to calm matters, not inflame them—and he grasped that some Americans at home might instinctively blame Spain for the night's catastrophe, even though he, on the scene, could draw no firm conclusions. He chose to add to the telegram that Spanish ships had come to his aid. In the last hour, Spanish officers had visited to him to express their condolences. Thus, in absence of any certainly as to what had happened, he added a suggestion: PUBLIC OPINION SHOULD BE SUSPENDED UNTIL FURTHER REPORT, he advised.

On the receiving end, in Washington, D.C., many took the captain at his word, among them Long and McKinley, who would make no rush to judgment. Theodore Roosevelt took a different view altogether.

# CASUS BELLI

*The New York Evening Journal* greeted the morning with the banner headline DESTRUCTION OF THE WARSHIP MAINE WAS THE WORK OF AN ENEMY.[16] Based on nothing, the lead article reported the cause of the blast was a "submarine mine, or fixed torpedo."[17]

*The Washington Star* took a gentler tack, reaching out to the best available authority on such matters. Philip Alger, a professor at the U.S. Naval Academy and an artillery expert, dismissed the claim of an explosive device. Though he, too, had seen no physical evidence, he told the *Star* that "no torpedo such as is known in modern warfare can cause an explosion as powerful as that which destroyed the *Maine*."[18] Instead, he proposed the likely cause was a spontaneous coal fire in a bunker adjacent to the ship's magazine, which, in turn, ignited the ship's stores of gunpowder.

Secretary Long was inclined to Alger's view—"My own judgement is [the explosion] was the result of an accident"—but Roosevelt tilted the other way.[19] Despite the presence on his desk of a memorandum from an officer aboard the *Maine* recommending that powder magazines on shipboard be better insulated, Roosevelt stressed to a Harvard friend in a letter that "the *Maine* was sunk by an act of direct treachery on the part of the Spaniards." In Roosevelt's willful view, the blast in Havana Harbor amounted to a casus belli, as his Latin tutor had taught him, an act or event that provokes or can be used to provoke war. What happened to the *Maine* demanded a response. "I would give anything," wrote Roosevelt, "if President McKinley would order the fleet to Havana tomorrow."[20]

The opinion that really mattered, however, was indeed McKinley's, and the president remained adamantly opposed to war.

A naval inquiry was convened; pressured by Roosevelt, the investigators did not call Alger to testify. The report eventually concluded on the thinnest evidence—an upward bend in the ship's keel—that the explosion had been caused by an underwater mine. Although the report supposed the explosion was of an act of sabotage, it stopped short of pointing the finger at Spain. Still, Roosevelt ordered the white hulls of the navy's ships be repainted battle gray. He had already, during Long's absence one late February afternoon, ordered Commodore George Dewey, stationed in Japan, to have his Pacific squadron in readiness, "in the event of a declaration of war with Spain," in order to keep Spanish forces in check near the Philippines.[21]

The supposedly secret report was soon leaked to the press. Fanned by the pro-war headlines, a burst of patriotism and war fever swept the country. The memorable rallying cry *Remember the Maine! To hell with Spain!* was everywhere—on many lips, in the papers, printed on matchbooks.

Congress deliberated at great length, with Lodge framing the argument. "We represent the spirit of liberty and the spirit of the new time," he told the Senate, "and Spain is over against us because she is medieval, cruel, dying. . . . That gigantic murder, the last spasm of a corrupt and dying society, which carried down our ship and our men, cries aloud for justice."[22] A joint war resolution eventually passed, and on April 24 and 25, respectively, Spain and the United States declared war on each other.*

President McKinley called for 125,000 volunteers, which would more than quadruple the regular army. One of them would be Roosevelt, who once again marched into Secretary Long's office. His visit was far from unexpected since Long had long since recognized Roosevelt as a hothead and "a bull in a China shop."[23] But the fact of his resignation on that rainy April morning still left Long both disappointed and doubtful. He confided as much in his diary:

> [Roosevelt] has lost his head to this unutterable folly of deserting his post where he is of most service and running off to ride a horse. . . . His heart is right, and he means well, but it is one of these cases of aberration—desertion—vainglory; of which he is utterly unaware. He thinks he is following his highest ideal whereas, in fact, as without exception everyone of his friends advises him, he is acting like a fool. And, yet, how absurd all this will sound, if, by some turn of fortune, he should accomplish some great thing and strike a very high mark.[24]

When Roosevelt saw something that needed doing, he knew only one way to respond: His commitment was clear and immediate. If men like Long thought he had blinders on, Roosevelt didn't particularly care:

---

* The cause of the explosion has never been established beyond a doubt, but no persuasive evidence ever emerged that the Spanish played a role in the loss of the USS *Maine*. The closest any of the numerous investigations came to deciding the matter was the one headed by Admiral Rickover, the so-called father of the nuclear navy, many decades later. It ruled the cause of the accident was the spontaneous combustion of coal dust in a fuel bin that, in turn, ignited the ship's powder stores. George Hyman Rickover, *How the Battleship Maine Was Destroyed* (Annapolis, MD: Naval Institute Press, 1976).

When he was in, he was all in. This was the man that Booker Washington would see for himself three years later, the straight-ahead, go-for-it Roosevelt.

First, however, Roosevelt needed to reach the pinnacle of power—and much later, Secretary Long would explain how, against the odds, he got there. "Roosevelt was right and we, his friends, were all wrong," he wrote in a postscript added to an 1898 diary entry. Roosevelt would demonstrate such extraordinary leadership on the field of battle that Long remembered his insistence on donning a uniform as a tipping point. "His going into the Army led straight to the Presidency."[25]

# CHAPTER ELEVEN

# THE MOSES OF HIS PEOPLE

I feel like a huckleberry in a bowl of milk.

BOOKER T. WASHINGTON,
HARVARD UNIVERSITY, JUNE 2, 1896

Booker Washington had already achieved national fame. Newspapers had begun calling him "the Moses of his People," although the label imposed a heavy burden by the late 1890s. At that historic moment, the idea that the United States of America was a "promised land" for Black citizens looked more absurd by the year. Just one day after the spectacular success of the Atlanta address, Washington's daughter, Portia, bore witness to an all-too-typical episode.

Booker had decided the twelve-year-old should continue her education in Massachusetts. The girl's relationship with her second stepmother remained distant—Portia confessed that, at times, she "[felt] like a motherless child"—and Northern schools had done very well by other women, Black and White, whom Booker admired.[1] To deliver her safely to school, the father entrusted his daughter to Robert Taylor, a well-spoken young

Tuskegee graduate who had gone on the school payroll two years before, doing double duty as a math instructor at Tuskegee and as a traveling agent for fundraising efforts in the North.

At 10:00 P.M., on September 19, 1895, Portia and her protector boarded a Southern Railway train headed north. They found facing seats, with Taylor occupying the one looking backward.

When the conductor came through to punch their tickets, he ordered Taylor to get up so the seat could be flopped, returning it to its front-facing position.

A frequent train traveler, Taylor told him that he preferred riding backward.

The White conductor grew angry. As he handed the tickets back, he told Taylor "in a very contemptuous and ungentlemanly way" that he couldn't care less about his "preference." Then, without warning, he grabbed for Taylor's collar.[2]

Taylor raised a hand, deflecting the conductor's attempt to eject him bodily from his seat. But the man managed to catch hold of Taylor's vest with his left hand. Three buttons went flying as they wrestled. With the ticket punch still in his grasp, the conductor then drove his right fist into Taylor's mouth, tearing his upper lip. Although Taylor got ahold of his attacker's arm before he could deliver further blows, the conductor commenced kicking Taylor, ceasing only when other passengers intervened.

Portia looked on in horror. Her chaperone's failure to show deference had been rewarded with bodily harm. Blood poured from Taylor's mouth, and the wound would leave his lip permanently disfigured. But this particular insult to a Black man peaceably riding a train was no rarity.

Even in Portia's short lifetime, the rights of African Americans, so recently guaranteed by the Reconstruction Amendments, had shrunk. In fact, the American railroad was about to be the setting for a United States Supreme Court decision that would codify legal discrimination on the basis of skin color.

# PLESSY V. FERGUSON

First in Florida, in 1887, then in nine other Southern states, laws had passed that required railroads to provide separate cars for White patrons.[3] The statute in Louisiana was typical. Although the bill claimed to be "an Act to promote the comfort of passengers," the real purpose of House Bill No. 42 was to establish a legal caste system, requiring railroads to provide separate cars "for the white and colored races."[4]

In New Orleans, few were fooled among the city's well-established professional class of educated Black people: This was railway robbery, and rights were boldly being taken from them. Money was raised, a committee was formed, and lawyers hired. The constitutionality of segregation would be tested.

The case that would decide the matter concerned Homer Adolph Plessy. A light-skinned man of mixed race (he described himself as

*Washington could break bread with captains of industry, but he never lost the ability to take a seat and tutor a student even by the roadside.*

seven-eighths Caucasian), he purchased a ticket in New Orleans, boarded a train bound for Covington, Louisiana, and took a seat in a coach designated "Whites Only." When the conductor asked Plessy to move to the Jim Crow car, he refused. He was quickly arrested and removed from the train without disturbance. Conductor, cops, and perpetrator all knew what was up. As one newspaper reported the following day, "It is generally believed that Plessy intends testing the law before the courts."[5]

The case slowly made its way to Washington, with Plessy as plaintiff. The legal proceeding evolved over a series of briefs, hearings, and appeals, and the case assumed its final form—*Plessy v. Ferguson* to the U.S. Supreme Court—after Homer Plessy sued a lower court judge named John H. Ferguson. Ferguson had ruled that the "equal, but separate" doctrine, as specified in the Louisiana state law, was not in violation of the Fourteenth Amendment to the Constitution, which expressly forbade states to deny "any person within their jurisdiction the equal protection of the laws." Thus, the central legal dilemma for the Supreme Court was, in simple terms, *Did Louisiana's requirement of "equal, but separate, accommodation for the white and colored races" meet the equal protection standard of the U.S. Constitution?*

The case took four years to be decided. On May 18, 1896, the Supreme Court ruled that the equal protection clause applied only to political and civil rights, such as voting and jury service. "Social rights," such as the right to choose which railroad coach to sit in, were not protected. The plaintiff, Homer Plessy, lost; the law would stand.

The majority opinion dismissed the Plessy argument, concluding it was not true that "enforced separation of the two races stamps the colored race with a badge of inferiority." The reasoning was that "If this be so, it is not by reason of anything found in the act, but solely because the colored race chooses to put that construction upon it."[6]

Simply put, the Court found that the fault lay not with the Louisiana law but with "the colored race." Any sense of inferiority Black passengers

*Although he was born into a slaveholding Kentucky family, Supreme Court Associate Justice John Marshall Harlan dissented from the majority in* Plessy v. Ferguson, *the case that legalized the racist separate but equal doctrine. He would be remembered as a seminal civil libertarian.*

felt riding in their "equal, but separate accommodations" was in their heads. Yet the reality, as any informed person knew full well, was that the conditions were rarely equal.

Only one member of the court, Associate Justice John Marshall Harlan, disagreed with this sophistry. In a scathing dissenting opinion, Harlan called the Plessy decision "pernicious." He compared it to the 1857 *Dred Scott* case that had ruled Scott, as "a negro of African descent" was "of an inferior order . . . so far inferior, [he] had no rights which the white man was bound to respect."[7] The comparison was bitter and ominous, since the *Dred Scott* case was among the recognized causes of the Civil War.

In Harlan's judgment, the majority ruling was just plain wrong:

> In view of the constitution, in the eye of the law, there is in this country no superior, dominant, ruling class of citizens. There is no caste here. Our constitution is color-blind, and neither knows nor tolerates classes among citizens. In respect of civil rights, all citizens are equal before the law. The humblest is the peer of the most powerful. The law regards man as man, and takes no account of his surroundings or of his color when his civil rights as

guaranteed by the supreme law of the land are involved. It is therefore to be regretted that this high tribunal, the final expositor of the fundamental law of the land, has reached the conclusion that it is competent for a state to regulate the enjoyment by citizens of their civil rights solely upon the basis of race.

Despite Harlan's persuasive argument, the majority ruling became law. Emboldened by *Plessy v. Ferguson*, states across the country passed new laws regarding separate—and rarely equal—facilities. New "Black Codes" required that schools, public bathrooms, cemeteries, and water fountains be segregated. Signage appeared specifying "Whites Only" and "Colored Only." Georgia's Black barbers were barred from serving White women or girls; White and Black Alabamians were forbidden to play billiards together.[8]

Booker Washington found himself caught in the middle. He insisted upon being heard—his voice was important, everyone knew that. But to influence the conversation, his had to be a voice of moderation, even if every part of him wanted to call out in outrage.

# THE VOICE OF THE PEOPLE

Since Frederick Douglass had emerged as a public figure in the 1840s, announcing his presence in electrifying speeches and the spellbinding story he told in his first autobiography, *Narrative of the Life of Frederick Douglass, an American Slave* (1845), his had been the leading Black voice in America. But just seven months before Booker Washington's Atlanta speech, in February 1895, Douglass died. His mantle dropped onto Washington's shoulders.

Like Washington, Douglass had been born into slavery. He taught himself to read and write and risked his life to escape a plantation in

Maryland for a new life in the North. In his thousands of speeches to abolitionist audiences, he had honed a vision of freedom for the enslaved. His argument and personal charisma had swayed Abraham Lincoln, a late and hesitant supporter of emancipation. Many years later, Booker Washington himself had invited the elderly Douglass to Tuskegee, where he had spoken of self-made men, his emphasis on education aligning with Washington's vision.

*The great Frederick Douglass made a pilgrimage to Tuskegee, too. In the spring of 1892, just three years before his death, he addressed the graduates. Booker reported that his words that day were "fully up to the high standard of excellence, eloquence and wisdom for which that venerable gentleman was noted."*

Although both had risen from bondage to great fame, their stories and personalities were very different. Douglass was a man of controlled fury: No one who attended a Douglass speech doubted his intensity. In contrast, Washington rarely raised his voice, speaking with his hands in his pockets as if engaged in a sidewalk chat. He spoke matter-of-factly, with few pauses, in short, declarative sentences. Though his was a passion veiled, he enthralled and persuaded audiences.*

For reasons of personal safety, Douglass, based at different times in Massachusetts, Rochester, New York, and the nation's capital, rarely ventured south; in contrast, Washington lived in the Deep South. Douglass was a man of the mind, a deep thinker who made a legal and philosophical case for freeing the Black man based on his reading of the U.S. Constitution and the Declaration of Independence. Washington was a quiet man of action, whose dogged determination had, in a period of fifteen years, established a successful, growing institution that was bettering the lives of hundreds upon hundreds of Black graduates. Yet after Atlanta, his new visibility and Douglass's disappearance from the scene meant he had a new role.

*Booker rarely relaxed but when he did, fishing was a favorite pastime.*

* A recording made of Washington speaking survives in the Smithsonian Folkways collection. Listen at https://www.youtube.com/watch?v=aHnkzMZuq2A&t=41s.

As Douglass's heir, he faced pressure to be more visible and more outspoken on the national stage. Timothy Thomas Fortune, editor of the most widely read Black newspaper of the day, the *New York Age*, told Washington, "You are our Douglass and I am glad of it." African Americans needed a leader, he continued. *"We must have a head*, and it ought to be in the South."[9] Fortune made a public case, too, asking in an article for New York's *The Sun*, a newspaper read primarily by White people, "Is He the Negro Moses?"[10]

In the months and years after his Atlanta speech, Washington received a constant stream of requests to address Black and White audiences. That meant more and more time on the road, sleeping on trains or waking up in unfamiliar hotel rooms. It meant taking on national issues well beyond the provincial concerns of the Tuskegee Institute.

After the *Plessy v. Ferguson* decision, Washington felt the need to go on the record concerning the "equal, but separate" doctrine.

> This separation may be good law, but it is not good common sense. The difference in the color of the skin is a matter for which nature is responsible. If the Supreme Court can say that it is lawful to compel all persons with black skins to ride in one car, and all with white skins to ride in another, why may it not say it is lawful to put all yellow people in one car and all white people, whose skin is sun burned in another car. Nature has given both their color; or why cannot the courts go further and decide that all men with bald heads must ride in one car all with red hair still in another.[11]

The ruling was a disaster, an insult to the American notion of fairness, and Booker, grasping its plainspoken dishonesty, turned the argument on its head.

In June 1896, Harvard University awarded Washington an honorary degree. Speaking to college alumni, he began as he often did with quiet humor. Looking out upon a roomful of the nation's most powerful men, he observed, "I feel like a huckleberry in a bowl of milk."[12] After the laughter died out, he made his case, asking Harvard's movers and shakers to "feel and see the need of the spirits in the lowliest cabin in the Alabama cotton fields or Louisiana sugar bottoms." By dint of hard work and study, he told them, "We are crawling up, working up, yea, bursting up."[13]

In May 1897, he returned to Massachusetts to speak at the unveiling of the Robert Gould Shaw Memorial on historic Boston Common. This time he stood outdoors, where the fine sculpture, executed by the nation's most admired sculptor, Augustus Saint-Gaudens, faced the rising steps of Massachusetts State House just across Beacon Street.

During the Civil War, the young White colonel had commanded one of the first all-Black regiments, the Fifty-Fourth Massachusetts Volunteers. Shaw had died fighting bravely at the Battle of Fort Wagner, and on Memorial Day 1897, many of the Black enlistees who survived the brutal fight near Charleston, South Carolina, stood behind Washington as he spoke of them, their commander, and the Union victory they personified.

Washington took care to honor both the White and Black warriors, but his words would prove strangely prophetic in the months to come. "One of the wishes that lay nearest Col. Shaw's heart was, that his black troops might be permitted to fight by the side of white soldiers."[14] Barely a year later, Black soldiers—Buffalo Soldiers, as they were called—would accompany their White brothers, including Theodore Roosevelt, to the island of Cuba, again in defense of a people's freedom. They would fight bravely indeed in the combat to come.

# CHAPTER TWELVE

# A SPLENDID LITTLE WAR

I am going to Cuba. I will take all the chances of meeting
death by yellow fever, smallpox or by a Spanish bullet just to
see the Spanish flag once on a battlefield.

THEODORE ROOSEVELT

E dith had been gravely ill since Quentin's birth in the fall of
1897, but Theodore was going to war—no matter what. His
father's failure to don a Union uniform still stung, while the
exploits of his Bulloch uncles still inspired him. Besides, Edith's problem, a large abscess near her hip, had been surgically removed. She remained weak but recovering when, after war was declared, Theodore
was offered command of the First United States Volunteer Cavalry.

Without hesitation he said yes. Unexpectedly, however, his was a
qualified yes. Though he had lobbied hard for a commission, when the
secretary of war offered him the rank of colonel to lead the brigade,
with Captain Leonard Wood as second in command, the enthusiastic
Roosevelt demurred.

I told [the secretary] that after six weeks' service in the field I would feel competent to handle the regiment, but that I would not know how to equip it or how to get it into the first action; but that Wood was entirely competent at once to take command, and that if he would make Wood colonel I would accept lieutenant-colonelcy.[1]

Roosevelt never doubted he was up to the fight, but he was a practical man who recognized that success in war depended as much on logistics as on bravery. He wanted an experienced soldier who could organize an altogether new unit from the ground up.

A Harvard-trained doctor, Wood was also President McKinley's personal physician. When they met a year earlier at a Washington dinner party, Wood and Roosevelt found they had much in common, including a passion for physical exercise. The two men had sparred in the boxing ring, hiked in Rock Creek Park, and skied cross-country together. Their shared affection for the West added to their bond, and Roosevelt greatly admired Wood's conduct there.

During the Apache Wars, Wood had earned the Medal of Honor for taking command of an infantry regiment whose officers had been killed. He was tall, well muscled, and a certified hero, a man who, in Roosevelt's eyes, "had every physical, moral and mental quality which fitted him for a soldier's life and for the exercise of command."[2] The two friends, Roosevelt believed, could command the volunteers together. The secretary of war agreed.

After his appointment, Wood spent two days completing requisitions for ordnance and other supplies in Washington, including cartridges, revolvers, clothes, tents, and horse gear. He made an in-person plea to President McKinley to make sure his brigade got the best guns, Krag-Jorgensen .30-40 bolt-action rifles, which fired cartridges charged by smokeless powder. He telegrammed several retired officers he knew and trusted, inviting them to join the brigade before he himself headed to San Antonio, where the regiment would muster. That the south Texas city had been the site of another battle with Spanish colonial forces was lost on no one. As Roosevelt pointed out, "The Alamo commemorates the death fight of Crockett, Bowie, and their famous band."[3]

Having promised Secretary of the Navy Long he would carry out his duties until his replacement arrived, Roosevelt stayed behind in Washington. There he was inundated with mail—twenty-seven great sacks arrived in his office with the first of tens of thousands of applications from men who wanted to be among the 780 enlistees and officers in the First U.S. Volunteer Cavalry.* The newspapers had made much of Secretary Roosevelt, always a magnet for press coverage, and the new brigade was the focus of nationwide attention. These applicants, men of all sorts from all over, wanted to be a part of this great adventure.

At the Navy Department, Roosevelt also was among the first to hear of naval action in the Pacific. Commodore Dewey, his ships well armed thanks to Assistant Secretary of the Navy Roosevelt, had sailed to the Philippines after the war declaration. At 5:41 A.M. on May 1, Dewey had ordered the first American shells fired into Manila Bay. By lunchtime that same day, the battle was over, the harbor strewn with Spanish ships either sunk or on fire; the U.S. Navy lost not a single vessel. The next day's *New York Evening Journal* said it all: "VICTORY!! Complete! Glorious!" Dewey become famous overnight. People named their newborn boys for him, and both Democrats and Republicans spoke of the commodore—soon to be admiral—as a potential presidential candidate in 1900.

Roosevelt ordered a uniform from Brooks Brothers, complete with special pockets sewn in for backup pairs of pince-nez, the style of eyeglasses he favored. Finally, at 10:00 P.M. on May 12, 1898, he boarded a

---

* The total was soon increased to 1,000.

*A drawing of T.R. in his Rough Riders uniform, complete with sword, spurs, gloves, and spectacles.*

train, together with Edward Marshall, his valet, a Black cavalry veteran. After taking the oath to defend the Constitution against all enemies, Roosevelt had officially become a soldier and an officer. Despite his subsequent presidency, he would, at his own insistence, be known forever after as *Colonel* Roosevelt.

## THE ROUGH RIDERS

By the time he reached San Antonio, his brigade already had a name: A sign at the rail station instructed *"This Way to Camp of Roosevelt's Rough Riders."*[4] His destination was the city's fairgrounds, which consisted of six hundred open acres surrounding an exhibition hall.

Boot camp would be short, so the volunteers needed to be battle-ready, if not battle-hardened. Roosevelt wanted men like himself, athletes and outdoorsmen, men with a strong sense of duty. While still in the capital, he had reached out to fellow clubmen and graduates of New England's best schools. He wrote personally to police officers he knew in New York, three of whom would enlist. In the end, he got more than forty Harvard men plus others from Princeton, Yale, and Columbia. But on arrival at Camp Wood, as the place was officially known, he found the eastern seaboard men were vastly outnumbered by those from the New Mexico, Arizona, and Oklahoma territories.

He welcomed the Southwesterners warmly, knowing their kind from his Dakota years. "There could be no better material for soldiers," Roosevelt later wrote, "than these grim hunters of the mountains, these wild rough riders of the plains. They were accustomed to handling wild and savage horses; they were accustomed to following the chase with the rifle. They were hardened to life in the open and to shifting for themselves under adverse circumstances."[5] A handful of Native Americans had joined up, too: Cherokee, Pawnee, and Chickasaw, along with two soldiers named Crockett.

From a champion broncobuster to Harvard's football captain, each of the enlistees shared with Roosevelt the belief they were the reincarnation of the American citizen-soldier, men who heard the same drumbeat as the revolutionaries at Lexington and Concord. They were patriots who, at no small personal risk, were going to fight for justice and liberty. They were sympathetic with the Cuban freedom fighters; they were men who joined up out of love for their own free nation and belief in its destiny.

Roosevelt and Wood set about transforming their varied volunteers into a unified fighting force. Military discipline had to be instilled. Guard duty was established. Colonel Wood laid down the law regarding high standards of hygiene, and Roosevelt gathered the entire regiment and read them the Articles of War, then led them in a hymn. Some men shed tears.

They drilled during the day, under Roosevelt's watchful eye, and officers' school met at night. There were long marches in the hot sun and mounted drills where the troopers formed up and wheeled, advanced, and re-formed. Soon the three freshly disciplined squadrons began practicing maneuvers, with skirmishing and firing.

The men's respect for Roosevelt grew. There was no officer's tent or mess; he slept and ate as they did. They learned to overlook his glasses. In return, Roosevelt took great pride in his men at evening dress parade, now dressed in slouch hats, brown trousers, blue flannel shirts, leggings and boots. "With handkerchiefs knotted loosely around their necks," he noted, "they looked exactly as a body of cow-boy cavalry should look."[6] The kerchiefs would be their trademark.

Roosevelt and Wood were whipping the Rough Riders into fighting shape—and none too soon. On May 25, after less than a month of training, a telegram arrived from the Department of War, asking when the First U.S. Volunteer Cavalry would be ready to ship out to their next staging point, the Florida city of Tampa.

With war whoops echoing as the news spread across the camp, the two elated commanding officers "embraced like schoolboys."[7] Roosevelt danced a little jig while Wood wired back, sending a terse, two-word answer to the question when they could be ready: "At once."

# TO TAMPA!

For Roosevelt, a man who had spent many years waiting to prove himself in combat, it was a frustrating time of hurry up and wait.

After breaking camp before dawn on Monday, May 30, the troops worked until midnight, loading rail cars with 1,200 horses and pack mules plus saddles, baggage, and other equipment—only to have to bed down in the brush until nearly dawn, waiting for more passenger cars to arrive. Riding in last of the seven-train convoy, Roosevelt didn't leave San Antonio until Tuesday afternoon.

The hot and monotonous eleven-hundred-mile journey across the Gulf Coast took three and a half days. There were frequent and interminable delays, plus regular stops to feed and water the livestock. But at almost every pause a crowd greeted the volunteers, bringing them jugs of milk, watermelons, tobacco, cakes, vegetables, and even flowers. For Roosevelt, this show of support was remarkable: Here he was in Confederate country, and among their stops were the towns of New Iberia, Louisiana; Mobile, Alabama; and Pensacola, Florida, places where children were nurtured on stories in which the Union was the evil enemy. "[But] everywhere we saw the Stars and Stripes, and everywhere we were told, half-laughingly, by grizzled ex-Confederates that they had never dreamed in the by-gone days of bitterness to greet the old flag as they now were greeting it, and to send their sons, as now they were sending them, to fight and die under it."[8] He saw a country coming together—and everywhere he heard chants of "Teddy, Teddy, Teddy!" He and his Rough Riders were famous.

When the brigade finally reached the pine flats near Tampa, on the evening of June 2, the troops covered the last six miles on horseback, arriving well after taps at the encampment of the Fifth Army Expeditionary Force. Under Wood's direction, the rows of tents, kitchens, and latrines were meticulously arranged—unlike the rest of the encampment, which was, in Roosevelt's view, "a perfect welter of confusion."[9] The whole installation was home to some 25,000 men, mostly regular army, the largest assemblage of American troops since the Civil War.

Tampa was a mile away, a sleepy townscape of sandy streets and weather-beaten wooden houses. A decade earlier the rail magnate Henry Plant had built a single rail line to Tampa Bay, hoping to create a vacation destination for the rich. His five-hundred-room Tampa Bay Hotel, known as "Plant's Folly," was a strange sight on the horizon, with its thirteen silver minarets topped with onion domes.

With the army in town, the hotel's covered veranda had become a gathering place for army officers, newspaper correspondents, and foreign military attachés, many occupying bentwood rocking chairs, sipping iced tea, and quaffing champagne in the ninety-degree heat. Among the newspapermen was Richard Harding Davis, star reporter for the *New York Herald*. He and Roosevelt knew each other from Roosevelt's days as police commissioner in New York, and although they weren't exactly friends, Roosevelt gave him access to the camp. Davis knew full well what good copy this man Roosevelt was—as he said to one just-arrived British captain, "Good heavens, you don't know Theodore Roosevelt? . . . He is the biggest thing here and the most typical American living."[10] As for Roosevelt, he knew someone had to tell the story from the inside. If Wood was his invaluable partner in military matters, when it came to sharing the story of this military adventure with the world, Davis was destined to be Roosevelt's best collaborator.

After dark, Theodore joined Mrs. Roosevelt at the hotel; she had arrived to see her husband off to war. "I am writing in my thinnest nightgown," Edith confided in her sister, "in a comfortable room with a bath room adjoining."[11] In his role as physician to powerful people in Washington, Leonard Wood had tended to Edith during the early days of her post-pregnancy illness; as Colonel Wood, in Tampa, he gave his second-in-command permission to share her bed. Each morning, though, Roosevelt would rise in time to rejoin his troops for reveille.

# BUFFALO SOLDIERS

The Tampa military camp wasn't always peaceful. Asking 25,000 young and impatient men to behave like churchgoers was impossible; fights and drunkenness were ongoing problems, especially as days of waiting turned into weeks. Adding to the volatile mix were Black soldiers: Despite the fact that Booker Washington's offer to help recruiting efforts had been declined by the War Department, some four thousand Black regular army infantrymen and cavalry were billeted in and around Tampa.[12]

Most were veteran soldiers, enlistees from the West, but the War Department wanted them there because of the prevailing—though mistaken—belief that "the Negro" possessed a "natural immunity" to such tropical diseases as yellow fever. These so-called Buffalo Soldiers were also elite fighters, many of them having served with distinction in the Indian Wars. Like the Rough Riders, they had been met en route to Florida by crowds that cheered, raised their hats, and waved their handkerchiefs—until, that is, they reached Tennessee, where the cheering abruptly stopped.[13]

Upon arriving in Tampa, they expected to be treated the same as White soldiers, just as they had been in Nebraska and other Northern states. Instead, they were shocked to encounter the bigotry of Jim Crowism. They were refused service at taverns and barbershops. At times, the resulting tension led to violence.

The worst episode unfolded when a unit of intoxicated White soldiers snatched a two-year-old Black boy from the arms of his mother, then dangled him upside down as a target for a test of their marksmanship. The boy was unhurt (a rifleman whose bullet tore a hole in the child's sleeve was declared the winner), but pent-up anger surged among the Black troops. A riot resulted, leaving blood in the streets. Twenty-seven Black soldiers were seriously wounded, along with several members of the Georgia regiment dispatched to quell the violence.[14]

The sooner this army went to war, the better.

# THE ROCKING-CHAIR PERIOD

These were days that *New York World* correspondent Davis called "the rocking-chair period of the war."[15] Planners in Washington had long since decided that the American expeditionary force should land on Cuba's southern coast. In theory, a U.S. Navy blockade would shield the troops going ashore, and the Americans would bring the Cuban rebels needed supplies—*and* send a message to Spain. This was no holiday in the making: It was an invasion of enemy territory. Men would die. The mission could fail. But to Roosevelt, ever impatient, the larger matter was *When?* And the answer seemed always to be *Not yet.*

The particulars of the plan changed almost daily. Pressured by the public and the press, President McKinley and his advisers were now firmly in favor of the attack, but the generals were cautious. Was there enough ammunition? What about transport? No, not enough of either was at hand, so a decision was made that not everyone could go. The ranks of the Rough Riders would have to be cut by a third. Then word came that too few ships meant only a fraction of the horses and mules could be accommodated; in an instant, Roosevelt's Rough Riders were no longer riders at all but an infantry unit.

A further delay was the result of the mystery of the Spanish Atlantic Squadron. Though the enemy flotilla had set sail from the Cape Verde Islands off the West African coast in late April, its subsequent where-abouts were unknown, making it a potential danger to any invasion effort. Finally, at the end of May, a report reached Washington that the Spanish fleet had anchored in the harbor of Santiago on Cuba's south-eastern coast. Two cruisers, the USS *New York* and the USS *Oregon*, were dispatched to keep it there, and finally, on June 7, a telegram from the White House arrived in Tampa: YOU WILL SAIL IMMEDIATELY.

The Rough Riders might not have gone at all if it hadn't been for

Roosevelt's quick thinking at Port Tampa, eight miles south of the town. A chaotic scene at the single dock left him competing with other officers for space on a ship. He managed to hustle his men aboard the *Yucatan*, a converted passenger ship. But unidentified ships were sighted in the sea lane, possibly enemy vessels lying in wait. Only after six stinking days, with animals standing in their own manure and dropping dead in the hold, was the all clear sounded.

Thus, on June 13, the invasion force finally weighed anchor. It consisted of thirty-two transports, carrying almost seventeen thousand men, and an escort of a dozen warships. "Today we are streaming southward through a sapphire sea," wrote an ecstatic Roosevelt to his sister Corinne. "It is a great historical expedition, and I thrill to feel I am part of it."[16]

The sense that he and his Rough Riders were on a virtuous mission was widely accepted, not only at home but abroad. Even Great Britain's staid *Manchester Guardian* offered its endorsement:

> One thing should be said at the beginning: it is predominantly the humanitarian instinct which has led "the plain people of the United States"—to use Lincoln's phrase—to acquiesce in the war with Spain. The dominant aim of the American people is not to avenge the loss of the Maine, not to annex Cuba, but to do a bit of stern work in the interest of humanity.[17]

# INTO THE HILLS

Six more days passed aboard ship. During that time, back in Washington, a bill to annex Hawaii passed the House of Representatives, another advance in the country's embrace of expansionism. After Roosevelt and the men aboard the *Yucatan* finally spied a string of blue mountain peaks looming up to starboard, the U.S. Navy guns cleared a landing zone with twenty minutes of sustained artillery fire. On the morning of Wednesday, June 22, the army began going ashore.

The scene was chaotic. Two of the Buffalo Soldiers drowned after a boat capsized. Horses were unceremoniously dropped into the water to swim to shore, and one was reduced to ground meat when, caught in the wake of a departing ship, it was drawn into the propeller of another. Boats ferried men to the beach at the mostly empty village of Nueva Salamanca, at the mouth of the Daiquiri River. Home to a defunct iron-works, little of the town remained beyond rusting corrugated shacks and a single rotting dock. "The Star-Spangled Banner" echoed across the water, played by a military band, and Old Glory soon waved from a blockhouse on a rocky hill overlooking the harbor. The Spanish had re-treated into the mountains.

A few Cuban insurgents appeared to join forces with the Americans, but they were hardly recognizable as soldiers. Their clothes were ragged, their bodies emaciated—for years, they had lived a scavenger existence, hiding in the hills. More shocking was that the Cuban force was integrated, with white- and black-skinned solders serving side by side—*plus* some of the rebel officers were Black. The ethos of this force—*We are not Black or White, we are all Cubans*—reverberated among the Americans; in the U.S. Army, even Black units were led by White officers.

The primary military objective was Santiago de Cuba, twenty miles west. On Thursday afternoon, as the rest of the army landed, the six thousand soldiers who were already ashore, among them the Rough Riders, began the trek to Santiago. They marched along the Camino Real, the rutted "royal road." The route was deceptively picturesque. "There is no country on earth more beautiful," wrote one correspondent, "[and] we were almost embowered by the rising Cuban jungle" of towering groves of coconuts and palms.[18] But the day was blisteringly hot, and Colonel Wood had to urge some of his tired cowboy soldiers, men more accustomed to sitting in the saddle than trudging on foot, to keep pace. As the Camino narrowed and entered the jungle, the troops passed exhausted men who had dropped out of the vanguard, lying in the roadside. But the Rough Riders pressed on, eager to be at the forefront of the coming fight.

Finally, after five hours, the brigade reached a beach town called Siboney. Night had fallen, and following a hurriedly prepared meal, the men grabbed a few hours' sleep in a driving rain. Roosevelt lay beneath a makeshift shelter of palm leaves.

While his soldiers rested, Colonel Wood rendezvoused with other commanders. Cuban rebels had been attacked that day by Spanish troops just north of Siboney. The two sides engaged in a bloody fight at Las Guásimas, a crossroads town sheltered by the plentiful tall hardwood trees for which it was named. With one man dead and several wounded, the rebels had retreated—but the American officers had gained the essential intelligence that, though Santiago was just eight miles ahead, an estimated 1,500 enemy troops lay in wait in the hills around Las Guásimas.

Wood summoned Roosevelt and his other commanders. Before dawn, he told them, the Rough Riders would climb a steep slope to reach a narrow trail that wove its way along a ridgeline some five hundred feet above. The rest of the brigade would continue along the valley trail. The two routes met where the main road rose to a mountain pass and became a wagon road to Santiago. At that junction the enemy awaited, protected by stone breastworks.

At last, Roosevelt thought, he was about to see action.

## SKIRMISH AT LAS GUÁSIMAS

Reveille awakened the men before sunrise, but Roosevelt, "as lively as a chipmunk," despite not having slept, "seemed to be in half a dozen places at once."[19] By six o'clock, with breakfast consumed and the mule-train packed, 574 Rough Riders broke camp and struggled up a steep slope to reach the trail above.

Led by a Cuban guide, they marched along the high path. An occasional distant vista opened but the palms soon closed in again. The heat was oppressive; still, the men pushed on. Ever the naturalist, Roosevelt took in the scarlet flowers decorating the acacia trees. He noted the "cooing of the doves."[20]

When Colonel Wood recognized the call of the cuckoo, however, he became uneasy. The Spanish were known to use its easily imitated syllables as a signal.

"Silence in the ranks!" ordered Wood.

The sound of the cuckoo resumed after a pause, but none of the Rough Riders could distinguish either bird or Spaniard in the surrounding walls of vegetation. The men were ordered to ready their rifles, and up and down the line the mechanical sounds of clicking magazines were heard.

The column marched on, passing an abandoned mansion. Once cultivated fields were now overgrown, and barbed wire lined the soldier's path. When the marchers paused for a rest in the sultry heat, Roosevelt's eye fell upon a length of wire that was no longer taut between posts. He examined the woven metal end that had fallen to the ground.

"My God, this wire has been cut to-day," he said quietly. "The end is bright, and there has been enough dew, even since sunrise, to put a light rust on it."[21] A mule thrashing along the path nearly drowned out his words—but not the first shot from a Spanish sniper, nor the volley that followed.

Two men in the advance guard fell. Bullets were zinging audibly, "making a noise," reported Roosevelt, "like the humming of telephone wires; but exactly where they came from we could not tell."[22] Sometimes the hum was followed by "the strange noise which soldiers in their trappings make as they go down. . . . It is a combination of the metallic jingle of canteens and guns, and the singular, thick thud of a falling human body."[23] The Rough Riders were firing back, but blindly, the enemy unseen.

Volley followed volley. His brigade now arrayed along the trail, Wood walked along the line of men, back and forth, urging them to keep firing, still uncertain where the Spanish soldiers, armed with German Mauser rifles and firing smokeless power, were hidden. He ordered Roosevelt and his men to advance into the woods.

*Roosevelt saw his first real military action in the*
*Battle of Las Guásimas, on June 24, 1898.*

Every soldier wonders how he or she will react under fire. In 1754, a twenty-two-year-old Virginia colonist named George Washington had relished the adrenaline rush that accompanied the ambush of a detachment of French soldiers in the conflict remembered as the French and Indian War. "I heard the bullets whistle and, believe me, there is something charming in the sound," he confided in his younger brother Jack.[24] The man who would be the twenty-fifth heir to Washington's role as president had much the same reaction a century and a half later when he first saw combat.

According to a war correspondent present that day, on crossing the barbed wire line into the dense wood, Roosevelt "became the most magnificent soldier I have ever seen. It was as if that barbed-wire strand had formed a dividing line in his life . . . and [he] found on the other side of it, in that Cuban thicket, the coolness, the calm judgement, the towering heroism, which made him, perhaps, the most admired and best beloved of all Americans in Cuba."[25]

Though Roosevelt was half-protected by a tall palm, a bullet that struck its trunk send a burst of dust and bark splinters into his eye. But it was the correspondent Richard Harding Davis who finally identified the whereabouts of the Spaniards who were using the Americans for target practice: In the first nine minutes of the fight, nine Rough Riders had gone down.

"There they are, Colonel; look over there; I can see their hats near that glade," he called.[26] With the enemy in their sights, Roosevelt's men delivered a heavy fire, and the Spaniards were soon abandoning their trenches and retreating into the jungle. American spotters observed another Spanish force at a greater distance, but they, too, seemed to melt away, the jungle vegetation providing perfect cover.

When the sound of cheering reached him, Roosevelt knew the day was won. The Rough Riders and the regulars on the Camino had met. The fight—the ambush—had lasted ninety minutes. The casualties were counted: eight Rough Riders dead, thirty-four wounded. But 1,000 advancing American troops had driven 1,500 entrenched Spaniards from the road to Santiago. Roosevelt was pleased with the events of June 24, as he wrote to his friend Senator Lodge.

> Well, whatever comes I shall feel contented with having left the Navy Department to go into the army for the war; for our regiment has been in the first fight on land, and has done well.[27]

Lieutenant Colonel Roosevelt had gone to war, fought bravely—and lived to fight another day.

# CHAPTER THIRTEEN

# THE CROWDED HOUR

It is a great historical expedition, and I thrill to feel that I am a part of it. If . . . we are allowed to succeed (for certainly we shall succeed if allowed) we have scored the first great triumph in what will be a world movement.

THEODORE ROOSEVELT, 1898

A mong those laid to rest the next morning were "Indian and cow-boy, miner, packer, and college athlete."[1] The bodies of the dead went into a shared grave, but two of the Rough Riders assembled cairns after the trench was filled, leaving small stacks of stones to mark the burial places of each lost soldier. In unison, the regiment sang the hymn "Rock of Ages."

Back home, news of the fight would spread rapidly. In San Francisco, one paper reported "the Spaniards were no match for the Roosevelt fighters. The Western cowboys and Eastern dandies hammered the enemy from the path."[2] *The Washington Bee*, the capital's leading African American newspaper, expressed its pride, too. "The Tenth United

States Cavalry,—the famous colored regiment . . . side by side with Roosevelt's men they fought—these black men. Scarce used to freedom themselves, they are dying that Cuba may be Free."[3]

There was talk in Washington of making Roosevelt a general, and in New York, a group of Republicans announced their intention to nominate him for governor in the autumn. All of which was premature, as the fight in Cuba was far from over.

Yet the commanding generals seemed in no hurry to take the fight to the Spanish. After a day's rest, the Rough Riders set up camp just west of Las Guásimas where, for five days, Roosevelt and Wood worried less about the enemy than tropical diseases and feeding their men. Marshall, Roosevelt's body servant and a Buffalo Soldier, was already ill. The entire force endured a daily drenching in tropical rains. Sanitation was poor, and the men consumed meagre foodstuffs, consisting of hard tack, salt pork, and coffee. After agreeing to pay the cost himself, Roosevelt did manage to requisition beans that had been designated for the officers' mess, but drinking water was growing more putrid by the day.

Finally, on the last day of June, a council of war was convened atop El Pozo, a hill overlooking the Camino Real. From the summit, the officers saw the challenge posed by the topography below. To reach Santiago, they would have to follow the muddy Camino though dense jungle as it snaked across a river valley, a distance of roughly a mile and a half. On the far side, the track then opened into a grassy clearing before climbing to another line of hills. And there the Spanish waited. Just over the top of freshly dug trenches, enemy sombreros were visible from El Pozo through field glasses. The Americans would have to march through the broad valley, ford a river, and charge across open ground before climbing the steep San Juan Heights, all in the face of Spanish gunfire.

The fight would be costly with the American soldiers terribly exposed. But Cuban scouts reported Spanish reinforcements would be arriving in the vicinity over the next several days. The U.S. forces needed to capture the heights, the Spaniards' last major line of defense between the Americans and their key objective, the city of Santiago. The invaders had little choice but to attack now, before the odds against them got worse.

That afternoon a plan took shape. A division of regulars would attack El Caney, a fortified hill town to the north that was also the source of Santiago's water. Meanwhile the Fifth Army, which included the Rough Riders, would move at dusk along the Camino Real before camping for the night at the foot of El Pozo, and thereby be in position for a frontal assault in the morning. But before the troops moved out, Roosevelt and Wood got some unexpected news.

Two senior officers had fallen ill with tropical fever, and Wood was immediately promoted to commander of the Second Brigade, with the rank of brigadier general. Roosevelt—to his "intense delight"—got sole command of the Rough Riders and his full colonelcy.[4] This time, he felt ready.

Dark had fallen by the time Roosevelt's troops moved out. They pitched camp at nine o'clock, and with the sentries set, Roosevelt lay down, protected by a saddle blanket and a raincoat. When he rose at dawn, he displayed no fear to the men around him, calmly shaving beneath the majestic palms and a cloudless sky. Looking back at July 1, 1898, more than two decades later, he would remember it as "the great day of my life."[5]

# BLOODY FORD

The fighting began with a costly mistake. Four artillery pieces rattled in at sunrise, dragged by horses and mules. After establishing a position on a rise immediately in front of the Rough Riders' camp, the crew manning the small-bore cannon began firing at 6:00 A.M., signaling a day of warfare ahead.

General Wood, seeing the billowing clouds of black-powder smoke drifting lazily above, realized that, if the Spanish hit back, he and his men were in the line of fire. An instant after he confided his concern in Roosevelt, a shell whistled in and exploded overhead. More followed, and a shard of shrapnel struck Roosevelt's wrist, raising a bump the size of a hickory-nut. He was more fortunate than a nearby soldier, whose leg was torn off. Leaping onto his horse, Roosevelt hustled his regiment downhill where they scattered into the thick underbrush.

After the artillery fire ceased twenty minutes later, the Rough Riders re-formed into a column, four men across, and headed up the Camino. In places, the road was just wide enough for a horse cart, creating a bottleneck that at times brought the march of the seven-thousand-man assault force to a standstill. But Roosevelt's men had no trouble keeping track of their commander. Riding tall on his horse, Little Texas, he wore yellow suspenders and a blue polka-dot bandana that hung from the rim of his sombrero, protecting the back of his neck from the tropical sun.

The dense vegetation of the jungle opened up at the San Juan River. Just as the Rough Riders prepared to ford the shallow waters, Roosevelt glimpsed a U.S. Signal Corps balloon in the open sky above. Its purpose was aerial reconnaissance—on an open battlefield, the spotters aboard such a craft were to communicate the whereabouts of enemy guns to the infantry on the ground—but this hovering hot-air craft had the opposite effect in the Cuban jungle: It telegraphed the *troops'* location. Once again, the air was suddenly alive with Spanish shells and bullets. Roosevelt and his men found a sunken lane where they kept their heads down, but the Spanish guns took a terrible toll on the soldiers still spilling out of the woods. "Man after man in our ranks fell dead or wounded,"

Roosevelt later wrote. The wide streambed rapidly became a human pile-up, destined to be remembered as the "Bloody Ford."[6]

Lying low with his men, Roosevelt was impatient. When the balloon, its bag punctured by artillery shells, finally collapsed into the treetops, some of the troops cheered. But the shells kept coming, as did rifle shot from the treetops where Spanish snipers, camouflaged by their green uniforms, targeted the American ranks.

Roosevelt dispatched a junior officer back to get orders. His troops hunkered down as best they could, but with the Camino clogged behind them, they could not retreat. Roosevelt thought they would do better to fight their way up the San Juan Heights into the teeth of enemy guns than to stay where they were, peppered by Spanish rifle shot. He wanted authorization to attack, to carry this fight directly to the enemy.

One of Roosevelt's favorite regimental captains, William "Buckey" O'Neill, was striding along the ranks of his huddled men, smoking a cigarette. O'Neill, who had resigned as mayor of Prescott, Arizona, to join the Rough Riders, believed that an officer ought never to take cover. He was an inveterate gambler, a natural leader who had gone west for adventure, but even his men thought this bravura display was too risky. One urged him to take cover.

"Captain, a bullet is sure to hit you."

O'Neill laughed as he took the cigarette from his mouth and expelled a cloud of smoke.

"Sergeant," he assured the man, "the Spanish bullet isn't made that will kill me."

Moments later a bullet hit him in the mouth then burst out the back of his head. Buckey O'Neill was dead before his corpse hit the ground.[7]

Meanwhile, Roosevelt was playing out the battle to come in his head. Roughly a half mile ahead lay open ground and the first two hills in the San Juan Heights. A fortified blockhouse looked down from one, while the other was occupied by a hacienda and what looked like a giant kettle, most likely for boiling sugar cane. Impatient at the death and carnage around him, Roosevelt considered advancing without waiting for the command. But, at last, in the early afternoon, an officer arrived with word from the brass.

"The instant I received the order I sprang on my horse," he wrote in his account of events, "and then my 'crowded hour' began."[8]*

## KETTLE HILL

At first, Roosevelt rode in the rear, "the position," he said, "in which the colonel should theoretically stay."[9] His Rough Rider volunteers were supposed to play a supporting role while the regulars led the assault. But all would be forgotten in the heat of battle.

Colonel Roosevelt urged his men forward, cajoling and joking and sometimes reprimanding. Seeing one man still on the ground, half hidden behind a bush, he mocked the soldier from his seat in the saddle. "Are you afraid to stand up when I am on horseback?" Before the man could answer, he fell forward onto his face. A bullet, one likely aimed at the high-riding Roosevelt, killed the soldier who had been cringing the bushes.[10]

The advance was far from orderly. Roosevelt and his men moved up in the battle order as they marched along the Camino, passing other units. After emerging from the jungle, they came upon two brigades of U.S. Army regulars, one of White men, the other Buffalo Soldiers, sheltering in a line of trees well below the Spanish intrenchments.

---

* The quote, which Roosevelt knew from a citation in a novel by Sir Walter Scott, came from a poem by Thomas Osbert Mordaunt named "The Call": "One crowded hour of glorious life / Is worth an age without a name."

"Why aren't you attacking?" Roosevelt asked. The commander of the Ninth Cavalry told him he had no orders to advance. But Roosevelt had his.

"Then let my men through, sir," Roosevelt instructed.

The Rough Riders pushed on, and as they did, enlisted men and officers from the two brigades of regulars, both Black and White, jumped up and followed them into battle.

"I waved my hat," Roosevelt recalled simply, "and we went up the hill with a rush."[11]

The slope was steep, the ground uneven, and his horse struggled to keep its footing. Roosevelt had intended to attack on foot with the rest of his force but, given the hundred-degree heat and high humidity, he had decided that morning to conserve his energy. Now, however, the only mounted man on the field and well ahead of his troops, he was by the far the most obvious target for Spanish riflemen.

A bullet nicked his elbow; another hit Little Texas, opening a flesh wound. But Roosevelt rode on, fully aware that, as one newspaperman observed, "a leader on horseback, brandishing his sword and going like the devil up that hill, would be easier for the men to follow, and more inspiring to them, than a leader walking."[12] The polka-dot bandana fluttered behind him, a unofficial ensign signaling his men to follow.

Two of the Buffalo Soldiers opened a gap in a fence for Roosevelt and the troops to stream through. A Pawnee soldier unleashed a blood-curdling battle cry.

From across the valley, reporters on El Pozo watched as an uneven line of men took shape. Other commanders and their units were joining Roosevelt's Rough Riders, now reduced to some four hundred men, forming a spontaneous wave of soldiers that expanded as it ascended the hill. Three more regiments joined the flow, then a fourth. This wasn't a coordinated attack—it was a mad rush, a mass of disorganized humanity moving like a swarm of bees. From above, Spaniards in trenches fired at the oncoming soldiers.

The Americans, running and stumbling up the ever-steeper hill, were all following the one man on horseback. As Richard Harding Davis reported,

> Roosevelt . . . charging the rifle-pits at a gallop and quite alone, made you feel that you would like to cheer. . . . It looked like foolhardiness, but as a matter of fact, he set the pace with his horse and inspired the men to follow.[13]

The soldiers ran, stopped to take aim, fired at the enemy position, then ran again. Some men dropped to the ground, wounded or dead, and remained where they were.

There were cheers as Roosevelt, crisscrossing the field, urged the men forward.

*The artist Frederic Remington is remembered as a chronicler of the American West, but in 1898, he went to Cuba as a war correspondent. In this painting he captured some of the drama of the moment, with Roosevelt leading the charge in the face of volleys of enemy fire.*

His wire-rimmed glasses were jarred off his nose. He fumbled and found another pair in a pocket.

Coming upon another barbed-wire fence that ran across the slope just forty yards from the brow of the hill, Roosevelt jumped off Little Texas and turned him loose. His orderly, seeing two Spanish soldiers approaching his commander, now on foot, shot both with his revolver.

Spaniards ran out of the crude ranch buildings just ahead, no match for the much larger American force that was almost upon them. The closing skirmish on Kettle Hill lasted no more than ten minutes—but the fight for the ridge wasn't over as Roosevelt's men continued to get shot, targeted by Spanish soldiers in the trenches on the other hilltop less than a third of a mile away.

Roosevelt saw a mix of American forces charging up that hill, too. "We had a splendid view of the charge on the San Juan block-house," Roosevelt later remembered.[14] In another whirl of events, Roosevelt decided to join the attack even as a new sound added to the cacophony of battlefield shots and screams. The rapid *rat-a-tat*, *rat-a-tat* came from just below.

"It's the Gatlings, men, our Gatlings!" Roosevelt called out. A detachment of three of the ten-barrel machine guns that had trailed the infantry was now firing a dozen rounds per second at the Spanish, as their American crews worked the Gatlings' hand cranks, pouring shot into the Spanish line.

Roosevelt and his men swept across the hollow from Kettle Hill. As the attackers reached the crest of San Juan Hill, the Spaniards again abandoned their trenches and retreated down the far side, some of them sprinting for Santiago. But not all.

Two enemy soldiers were fleeing some twenty-five feet from Roosevelt, firing wildly in his direction. Out of instinct, the colonel's revolver came to hand; fittingly, the weapon had been salvaged from the

*The Buffalo Soldiers in action in Cuba in a chromolithograph, published in 1898, titled* Charge of the 24th and 25th Colored Infantry and Rescue of Rough Riders at San Juan Hill, July 2nd, 1898.

wreck of the USS *Maine.* As the two men turned to run, "I closed in and fired twice, missing the first killing the second."[15]

The second hill, too, was theirs. In the madness of combat the White and Black regulars and the Rough Rider volunteers, whether trained as infantry or cavalry, had become a single fighting force. Securing the hilltop, they found few wounded Spaniards in the trenches; instead, there were many dead bodies with "little holes in their heads from which their brains were oozing"—the deadly work of the Gatling guns.[16] On the far side of the ridge there was a clear view of Santiago.

For Roosevelt, his courage under fire signified something. At one level, it erased the stigma of his father's decision to send a substitute to fight in his place more than three decades earlier—but Theodore's performance on July 1, 1898, meant much more than that. He had risen to a challenge as a man; he fought, he led, he faced the fire of battle; he looked death in the eye and he had killed rather than been killed. On behalf of his nation and his beliefs, he had risked his life, done his duty without hesitation, and when he looked back, he understood that "all men who feel any power of joy in battle know what it is like when the wolf rises in the heart."[17]

He was also aware that his actions on that day had a public significance.

## BACK IN THE U.S.A.

The Rough Riders were not the first to come ashore, but the many spectators who jostled one another on the beach at Montauk Point, New York, were there for one reason. On the morning of August 15, they wanted to see the victorious return of the famous Colonel Roosevelt and his volunteers.

After the capture of San Juan Heights, the fight for Santiago had become a slow-motion siege. The American blockade kept the Spanish fleet in the harbor until the outnumbered and outgunned fleet decided to fight for its national honor and steamed out of port. The outcome on the morning of July 3 had been a disaster for Spain, with the flagship *Infanta María Teresa*, a trio of battleships, and a pair of destroyers set afire, sunk, or driven aground.

Even then, however, weeks had been required for the Spanish to surrender and for the parties to wrap up long-distance negotiations.* That delay had exacted a tall price. While the diplomats and generals talked,

---

* The peace accord had only just been signed on August 12, during the Rough Riders' sea journey home from Cuba. Subsequently, Cuba would, after three years of American control, gain its independence on May 20, 1902.

Roosevelt's troops confronted yellow fever, a new and even more deadly enemy. Within days of the sprint up Kettle Hill, many soldiers in the jungle had begun falling ill, spiking fevers and vomiting blood. Makeshift hospital wards were quickly established, but three times as many American men would die of fever in those weeks than were felled by Spanish bullets.

Many of the caregivers in the hospitals had been Buffalo Soldiers. These Black Americans were now returning to their country with new respect, having agreed to tend the sick after White regiments refused, thereby extending their life-and-death duty beyond the battlefield. But the "Smoked Yankees," as the Spanish called Black soldiers, had won admiration for their fighting, too. According to correspondent Richard Harding Davis, "Negro soldiers established themselves as fighting men."[18] They won some unlikely admirers along the way, among them one son of the South who had fought side by side with Black men at the Battle of San Juan Hill. "I am not a negro lover," he said, "but the negroes saved that fight."[19] Roosevelt himself observed that the "smoked Yankees . . . we came to know . . . were an excellent breed of Yankees."[20]

Now, a full six weeks after the big victory, which had been headline news across the country and even around the world, the Fifth Corps was coming home to recuperate, to celebrate, and to quarantine at the east end of Long Island. The sea of tents at Camp Wikoff, named for the first officer to die in the Cuba campaign, would be the temporary home for the Fifth Corps, which included the Rough Riders and the Buffalo Soldiers of the Ninth and Tenth Cavalry, as they prepared to return to civilian life.

Keeping the onlookers a hundred yards from the water's edge, U.S. Cavalry troops cordoned off the eager crowd. As her cables made the steamship *Miami* fast to the pier, a military band played the familiar Civil War anthem "When Johnny Comes Marching Home Again." The ship's rails were lined with the returning heroes of the Battle of San

Juan, some emaciated, ill, and wounded. The steamship's gangplank was lowered, and the air filled with a rising crescendo of cheers.

In response, the returning warriors chanted:

*Rough, tough, we're the stuff,*
*We want to fight and we can't get enough,*
*Whoop-ee!*[21]

Then Roosevelt appeared. The sun glinted off his spectacles. Dressed in a fresh brown uniform, deeply tanned, thinner but toughened by his weeks bivouacked with his men, he wore a cartridge belt with his heavy revolver hanging to the rear.

"How are you feeling, Colonel?" a voice called.

"Well, I am disgracefully healthy," he replied. "Really I am ashamed of myself, feeling so well and strong, with all these poor fellows suffering and so weak they can hardly stand. But I tell you we had a bully fight. This is a fine regiment, all a lot of crack-a-jacks."[22]

Then someone asked the man of the hour the obvious question. And he deflected.

"Will you be our next governor?"

"None of that," the colonel insisted. "All I'll talk about is the regiment. It's the finest regiment there ever was."[23]

# FROM RADICAL TO WARRIOR

As demobilization began around him at Camp Wikoff, Roosevelt shifted quietly back to political mode. McKinley came to visit the heroes—even the president of the United States wanted to associate himself with the Rough Riders and the commander of the volunteer regiment, who had become a shooting star. Six months before, Roosevelt had been a

Washington bureaucrat whose saber-rattling speeches made McKinley nervous. But against the better judgment of many, Roosevelt had walked away from the Navy Department, donned a uniform, and gone and made himself, in the course of a July day, perhaps the most admired man in America.

Roosevelt remained in uniform just 133 days, and three days after his discharge, on September 14, he acknowledged he wanted to be governor. The Republican Party promptly made him its nominee. When he hit the campaign trail, he reminded voters of his recent adventures: A bugle call saluted his arrival for each speech, and he took the stage along with an entourage of Rough Riders in uniform.

A small victory in Cuba had amounted to something much larger. It symbolized a redefinition of the nation's goals. The Spanish–American War announced the arrival of the United States military as a world power, ready to play an essential role in what would come to be called the American Century. Long isolationist, the United States seemed poised to lead the world. As Roosevelt himself put it, "If we are to be a really great people, we must strive in good faith to play a great part in the world."[24]

The Battle of San Juan Hill had been an audition for Teddy Roosevelt—and he wowed everyone, showing the world he was a natural leader for post-frontier America. That November, voters in New York State embraced him, and Roosevelt, having just turned forty, was elected governor of the Empire State. It was the climax of six months of "bull luck . . . first, to get into the war, then to get out of it; then to get elected. I have worked hard all my life," he told a friend, "and have been particularly lucky, but this summer I *was* lucky, and am enjoying it to the full."[25]

Perhaps Lady Luck played a role. For certain, however, so did Roosevelt's bedrock determination to do right by his nation and his countrymen. He had found himself—more accurately, he had *put* himself—at the center of an extraordinary venture. With him at the head, an army of Harvard men and Confederate generals, cowboys and Native Americans, Yankees and Southerners, Black men and White men, ballplayers and gentlemen had fought side by side. Their success had also made Roosevelt's political rise now seem inevitable.

# CHAPTER FOURTEEN

# MAN IN THE MIDDLE

Until we thus conquer ourselves, . . . we shall have, especially in the Southern part of our country, a cancer gnawing at the heart of the republic.

BOOKER T. WASHINGTON, NATIONAL PEACE
JUBILEE ADDRESS, OCTOBER 16, 1898

A s Americans reveled in the rapid victory in the Spanish–American War, a disturbing wave of mob violence spread across the South. Somehow, however, Tuskegee managed to remain in its own bubble: Washington's institution continued to thrive, with its student body rising to a thousand and its faculty reaching one hundred.

Though he needed to raise a $100,000 annually to cover Tuskegee's expenses, Washington was a remarkable fundraiser, as grateful for the five-dollar donations as for the tens of thousands he solicited from rich and powerful people. Among those who were willing to open his deep pockets to Washington's cause was John D. Rockefeller, whose holdings in Standard Oil made him the richest man in America. Booker's manner was the same with Alabama farmers and new donors like banker J. Pierpont Morgan: polite, respectful, forthright, and insistent. Railroad man Collis Huntington remained a Tuskegee supporter, in part out of admiration for Washington himself. "My dear Sir," he wrote Washington in October 1898, "[Tuskegee] is doing much for the negro race, and the credit for it is due to the practical sense of its guiding spirit—yourself."[1]

Step by step, such men also brought Washington closer to powerful political figures. A new board member at Tuskegee, William H. Baldwin Jr., an executive at the Southern Railway, knew the freshly famous Theodore Roosevelt personally. But the occasion of the National Peace Jubilee brought Washington directly to the top man. As a featured speaker on the opening evening of the Chicago jubilee, Washington shared the public eye with no less a personage than the president of the United States.

With the Treaty of Paris in final negotiation—hostilities had ceased on August 12—the Spanish–American War was effectively over. This was to be celebrated: The upstart United States had won a big victory over Spain, which had ceded control of Cuba, Puerto Rico, and the Philippines, bringing Spain's imperial days to an end. Other cities, among them Boston and Philadelphia, would hold their own victory parties, but the city of Chicago went all out.

Streetcars were dressed in bunting. Sixteen triumphal arches of wood and canvas spanned downtown avenues, some of them fifty-feet high. For the seven days of the festivities, the streets were lined with flags. There were parades and banquets, with the city illuminated after dark with red, white, and blue lights. Tens of thousands of people gathered in Illinois for an outpouring of public pride and patriotism at the outcome of the war with Spain.

The president of the University of Chicago had invited Washington to deliver an opening address at the magnificent Auditorium Theatre. On Sunday evening, October 16, Washington stood before a packed house of thousands, with as many more unable to gain entry. He stood beneath a set of immense ceiling arches decorated with 24-carat gold leaf. McKinley and his entourage occupied a box overlooking the stage; also in attendance were much of the president's cabinet and an array of military officers, veterans of the Spanish fight.

The audience might have expected Washington to speak of the war—and he did—but his reference points would not be the Rough Riders, Admiral Dewey, or Colonel Roosevelt. On this "important occasion," he began, he would speak first of the "American Negro."[2]

Black Americans had submitted to slavery, Washington told the crowd, yet in 1776, they had chosen to side with the colonists in the War of Independence. During the War of 1812, the Black man again fought on the American side, and "General Andrew Jackson himself testified that no heart was more loyal and no arm more strong and useful in defense of righteousness." During the Civil War, "the Negro was asked to come to the rescue in arms," Washington continued, "and the valor displayed at Fort Wagner and Port Hudson and Fort Pillow, testify most eloquently again that the Negro chose the better part."

He abruptly brought the history lesson to an end, shifting to the recent war with Spain to secure the "safety and honor of the Republic." Again, Washington said, the Black man came willingly:

We find the Negro forgetting his own wrongs, forgetting the laws and customs that discriminate against him in his own country, again choosing the better part. And if you would know how he deported himself in the field at Santiago . . . let [Roosevelt and the generals] tell how the Negro faced death and laid down his life in defense of honor and humanity, and when you have gotten the full story of the heroic conduct of the Negro in the Spanish–American war—heard it from the lips of Northern soldiers and Southern soldiers, from ex-abolitionist and ex-master, then decide within yourselves whether a race that is thus willing to die for its country, should not be given the highest opportunity to live for its country.

Washington was laying the groundwork for stronger words: "Let us be as generous in peace as we have been in battle," he suggested. "Until we thus conquer ourselves, I make no empty statement when I say that we shall have, especially in the Southern part of our country, a cancer gnawing at the heart of the republic."

The metaphor was harsh. Coming from the ever-cautious educator, "*a cancer gnawing at the heart of the republic*" was uncharacteristically vivid, even threatening. But Washington, perhaps emboldened by the presence of the president, demanded his listeners look deeply at themselves.

He turned to face the president's box and spoke directly to McKinley.[3] "I want to present the deep gratitude of nearly ten millions of my people

*Booker T. Washington addressing a packed house at the Chicago Jubilee, on October 16, 1898, where he spoke proudly of the bravery of the Buffalo Soldiers on the field of battle.*

to our wise, patient and brave Chief Executive for the generous manner in which my race has been recognized during the conflict. A recognition that has done more to blot out sectional and racial lines than any event since the dawn of freedom."[4]

The thank-you for acknowledging the Buffalo Soldiers, coupled with the demand for justice, transfixed the crowd. The audience rose to its feet, applauding, waving their hats, kerchiefs, and canes. The cheers grew so sustained that McKinley stood, too, then bowed to the Black man on the stage in appreciation and acknowledgment. "This kindled anew the enthusiasm," Washington noted later, and McKinley bowed to him a second time, to swelling cheers.[5]

Washington had spoken truth to power. He owned the Chicago crowd, the largest he had ever spoken to. But his appeal for racial fairness would soon enough be widely dismissed in the South—two days later, *The Atlanta Constitution* called Washington a "colored agitator" who was "talking to the grand stand."[6] And in the weeks and months that followed, the "gnawing cancer" he spoke of would radically corrode the rights of the Black American.

# THE MASSACRE AT WILMINGTON, NORTH CAROLINA

Lynching was a commonplace horror, yet the murder of individuals, appalling as they were, had less significance than the election in Wilmington, North Carolina, in November 1898. What happened then and there opened the door to white supremacists looking to end Black political influence in the South.

In the late 1890s, Wilmington, a prosperous port on the Cape Fear River, was a majority Black city. Prior to the 1898 election, the biracial city government included a number of Black men, including three members of its board of aldermen, numerous police officers, the justice of the peace, and the city coroner. Some White city residents didn't approve of sharing power—for one, the editor of the *Wilmington Messenger* routinely referred to John Campbell Dancy, who held the prominent post of customs collector, as "Sambo of the Customs House."[7] But with more than 120,000 Black voters still on the rolls in North Carolina, African Americans remained a potent electoral force, a rarity in the region after other states enacted legislation to disenfranchise Black men. Georgia had been among the first, instituting a poll tax in 1877; Florida followed soon after. Mississippi was next, in 1890, with a new constitution that required both a literacy test and payment at the polls in order to vote.

Because a Republican-Populist coalition held sway in much of North Carolina—Black and poor White voters had come together in common cause—that fall opposition Democrats launched a no-holds-barred campaign to "reestablish Anglo-Saxon rule."

Hoping to raise White resentment, Democrats exaggerated Black corruption and aired conspiratorial lies, including the nonexistent danger of "Negro domination." But sexual fearmongering, as expressed by white supremacist Rebecca Felton, superheated matters when the Wilmington *Weekly Star* reprinted a speech she gave in Tybee, Georgia. "If it needs lynching to protect woman's dearest possession from the ravening human beasts," she had told the Agricultural Society, "then I say lynch, a thousand times a week if necessary." No one needed help in reading between the lines: She was warning that the virtue and virginity of White women (their "dearest possession") was forever at risk in the presence of Black men ("the ravening human beasts").[8]

Though she lit the match, a Black newspaperman unintentionally turned it into a torch with an editorial in the town's Black newspaper, the *Wilmington Daily Record*. This wasn't a Black problem, wrote *Record* editor Alex Manly; he saw no difference between a Black man meeting secretly with a White woman and a White man seeking the company of a Black woman. He himself was the product of an interracial union. His father had been a governor of Georgia, his mother enslaved.

"Tell your men," he advised Felton in the pages of the *Daily Record*, "that it is no worse for a black man to be intimate with a white woman than for a white man to be intimate with a colored woman."

To many White readers, this was blasphemy, and unfortunately for the Black citizens of Wilmington, Manly's words provided fresh ammunition for the mix of former Democratic officeholders and Confederate officers who wanted to win back political control. Working with sympathetic newspaper editors, these white supremacists put the widely published editorial to use, claiming that the Black editor defamed White women.

Then a fresh news story rendered the debate explosive.

# NOVEMBER 1898

At the end of October 1898, a posse of White men lynched a Black North Carolina farmhand who had run off with a White woman.[9] In the view of many Democrats, this was fitting punishment for the crime of interracial love. The newspapers across the state ran such headlines as ELOPED WITH A NEGRO MAN and REAPED WHAT HE SOWED.

Racial tensions ran high, and in Wilmington intimidated Black voters stayed home on election day, Tuesday, November 8. Though the Democrats dominated at the polls, they would not be content with a peaceable transition of power, and the following day issued a "White Declaration of Independence." It called for White domination in the city, asserting that "the intelligent citizens of this community owning 95 percent of the property" should be in charge.

They also resolved to end publication of the *Daily Record*, and on Thursday, more than a thousand men, many armed, formed up into military columns. They marched to the paper's offices at the corner of Seventh and Nun Streets, where mayor-elect Alfred Waddell knocked on the door. When no one answered—fearing for his life, the editor had left town the day before—the mob broke in and systematically destroyed the press, furniture, and printing supplies. Hanging lamps were knocked to the floor, kerosene splashed about liberally. In less than an hour, the two-story wood-frame building was reduced to a smoking ruin.

*Members of the Wilmington, NC, mob that set fire to the offices of the town's Black newspaper in front of the charred ruins of the* Daily Record's *offices.*

White townspeople stood by as a Black fire company prevented the spread of the fire to other structures. With small bands of armed White men patrolling the streets, the city was eerily quiet as people went about their business, but that was the calm before the storm.

Shortly after eleven o'clock, shots echoed near the Fourth Street bridge, which led to Brooklyn, Wilmington's traditionally African American neighborhood. Several Black people were wounded and killed. That was the beginning of the rampage, and soon "Hell broke loose," as one journalist put it.

White people in a streetcar fired into Black homes and businesses along Castle Street. A half dozen Black men were shot and killed at the corner of Fourth and Harnett Streets. When a White man was shot in the chest, his supposed shooter, Daniel Wright, was caught after his pursuers set his house afire. One member of the crowd suggested he should be summarily hung from a nearby lamp post, but someone else suggested he be given a chance to run for his life. Wright covered a distance of about fifty yards before some forty guns were fired at his back. Despite thirteen gunshot wounds, he survived the night, only to die before dawn.

Gunfire echoed throughout the city. A machine gun owned by a coalition of white supremacist organizations was hauled to Brooklyn and at least twenty-five Black men were killed at the intersection of Sixth and Brunswick.

The bloodbath in Wilmington would be inconsistently reported. *The New York Times* numbered the dead at eight; the actual count was much greater, perhaps as high as three hundred. Witnesses reported seeing wagons piled high with cadavers.

"I'll tell you things are stirred up," wrote one witness, "and I am glad to say I am still living but we have not killed enough negroes—two or three white men were wounded and we have not gotten enough to make up for it."[10]

In a matter of days, the city government was entirely White. Wilmington lost its Black majority. More than a thousand Black citizens became refugees, fleeing the city permanently, their homes and livelihoods destroyed. The city center, once home to many Black businesses, became a White enclave. No Black newspaper would come off the press in the city for more than a decade. Aligning its laws with those of other states in the South, North Carolina soon restricted Black voting, codifying the racial caste system.

Much of the violence on November 10 was the work of militia groups. One had been a statewide white supremacist organization called the

*Much of the loss of life in the Wilmington massacre was the result of a mobile machine gun that opened fire upon citizens in Brooklyn, the city's predominantly Black neighborhood.*

"Red Shirts"; when they went into action, they were typically masked, on horseback, and armed with rifles, shotguns, and pistols. Another group that contributed to the violence in Wilmington consisted of White veterans of the Spanish–American conflict who proudly called themselves the Rough Riders. This branch of Roosevelt's ad hoc brigade had conveniently put out of their minds the bravery of the Buffalo Soldiers who fought beside them in the hills of Cuba.

# THE PRESIDENT COMES
# TO TUSKEGEE

In the days after the Wilmington massacre, Washington got wind of President McKinley's plan to come to Atlanta for that city's peace jubilee.

The educator hurried to Washington to ask the president in person to visit Tuskegee while he was in the region. He told McKinley that the events at Wilmington and elsewhere—the massacre in North Carolina was hardly an isolated incident—had left "the colored people greatly depressed."

The president was sympathetic: "I could perceive his heart was greatly burdened," Washington observed.[11] McKinley accepted the invitation of the man people had begun to call "the Wizard of Tuskegee."

The president arrived on December 16, 1898, accompanied by Mrs. McKinley, much of his cabinet, several of the commanding generals from the Cuba expedition, and the governor of Alabama. The distinguished visitors were greeted by the entire town, Black and White, and the main street had been elaborately decorated in McKinley's honor. Washington had also carefully choreographed a parade involving floats that displayed the work of the institute's many departments in agricultural and industrial training. While the guests watched from a platform of stacked hay bales, the student body of more than a thousand students marched past, each carrying "a stalk of sugar-cane with some open bolls of cotton fastened to the end of it."[12]

After escorting the visitors to Tuskegee's new chapel, Washington told them how honored he was at their presence—but he didn't lose sight of his purpose:

> We welcome you all to this spot, where without racial bitterness, but with sympathy and friendship, with the aid of the state, with the aid of black men and white men, with southern help and northern help, we are trying to assist the nation in working out one of the greatest problems ever given to men to solve.[13]

In response, McKinley, the nation's postmaster general, and the secretary of the navy all expressed their thanks. They spoke admiringly of

the school and, in particular, of its founder. "He has won a worthy reputation as one of the great leaders of his race," said McKinley, "widely
known and much respected at home and abroad as an accomplished
educator, a great orator, and a true philanthropist."[14]

*As President William McKinley watched from the reviewing stand, a long
procession of Tuskegee Institute students paraded by on December 16, 1898.*

Yet neither McKinley's words of admiration in Tuskegee nor the sentiments of the others would have much impact on the anti-Black climate
in the South. In 1899, at least eighty-five Black men would die by the
noose. One execution, just four months after the presidential visit, occurred fewer than a hundred miles from Washington's home base when
a farm worker from Palmetto, Georgia, named Sam Hose was tortured
and burned alive. What made the gruesome events doubly shocking was
the crowd of two thousand people who cheered Hose's departure from
life. Many had traveled on specially scheduled excursion trains from
nearby Atlanta to witness mob justice as its most grotesque.

# THE KINDNESS OF FRIENDS

Washington lived in limbo in Alabama. His was a day-to-day struggle to maintain a cooperative, respectful peace with White Tuskegee, but that also meant he could not say what was on his mind. To condemn the killers of Hose, for example, could—no, almost certainly *would*—invite retaliation, putting him and the experiment at Tuskegee in danger. Thus, to the frustration of some Black opinion makers in the North, such as Calvin Chase, editor of *The Washington Bee*, Chicago minister Reverdy Ransom, and W. E. B. Du Bois, Washington kept largely mum, saying very little in the weeks after Sam Hose's death. Even if his far-away critics didn't feel it, this incident was so close to home the perils of speaking out seemed almost palpable.

The stress of this enforced silence exhausted Washington: The dreams he carried for Black progress were under intense fire; wounded hopes seemed to surround him like wartime casualties. Maggie confided in friends that her husband was worn out and near collapse, but worried supporters in Boston soon came to the rescue. In May 1899, Maggie and Booker embarked on an all-expense-paid European vacation. The generous friends also enabled Washington to depart with the peace of mind that came with knowing that the same people would see to it that Tuskegee had enough money to operate, even as he took a break from his nonstop fundraising.

Though they traveled on a steamship line that promised the Washingtons would be treated the same as the White passengers, it hardly mattered to Booker. He slept fifteen hours a night during the ten-day Atlantic crossing. Once in Europe, though, the grand tour invigorated him.

The efficiency and beauty of Dutch farms wowed the Wizard of Tuskegee. He saw many lessons of real value to his school's agricultural curriculum. "I have a seen a whole family making a comfortable living by cultivating two acres of land, while our Southern farmers, in too many cases, try to till fifty or a hundred acres and find themselves in debt at the end of the year."[15]

In Paris, he visited the studio of Henry Ossawa Tanner. Two years before, Tanner's painting *The Resurrection of Lazarus* had been acquired by the French nation, destined to hang in the Louvre, perhaps the greatest treasure house of them all, after the artist's death. The canvas was among the first by an American artist to be so honored (*Arrangement in Grey and Black, No. 1*, better known as "Whistler's Mother," had been the very first). Washington was no art connoisseur, but he relished the Black artist's success. "Here in France," Washington wrote home, "no one judges a man by his color."[16] For that reason, in fact, Henry Tanner would choose to live out his life in France, rubbing shoulders, as he himself said, with "Muscovites and Tartars; Arabs and Japanese; Hindoos and Mongolians; Africans and South Sea islanders, all working earnestly and harmoniously with students of the Caucasian race."[17] As both men knew, such equality would not be on offer in the United States anytime soon.

Crossing the channel to England, Washington gave speeches, shook hands with statesmen, and visited the House of Commons. He was welcomed at the country homes of titled and distinguished Englishmen. He and Maggie took tea with eighty-year-old Queen Victoria at Windsor Castle; among the other guests was Susan B. Anthony, the great women's rights activist. In London, Booker met another fellow American, Sam Clemens; Booker and the author of *Adventures of Huckleberry Finn* launched an enduring friendship.

Even four thousand miles from home, Washington never stopped thinking about the individual rights of both Black and White Americans. He talked with English abolitionists, who impressed him with their "deep interest . . . in the cause of freedom" in the United States.

Although he thought the genteel life of the English country house was nearly perfect, he wondered about the servant class. The butlers, footmen, and maids seemed content with life in service; in comparison, Washington observed, "in our country the servant expects to become, in a few years, a 'master' himself. Which system is preferable?" he wondered. "I will not venture an answer."[18]

# THE FUTURE OF THE AMERICAN NEGRO

When the couple returned in the autumn, one task awaiting Booker was the editing of his speeches and various articles, which he had agreed to publish. Revised into chapter form, the various writings, under the title *The Future of the American Negro*, would go to press in October 1899.

Washington found that his time in Europe had freshened his view of the American scene. On his departure for the Old World, the Sam Hose murder had been the subject of a national debate and too hot for Washington to touch; by the time he returned, he felt the time was right for him to address once again the subject of lynching and its consequences.

The heart of his argument echoed the hand-and-fingers metaphor he made four years earlier in Atlanta, that the Black and White races were connected. "We are one in this country," he wrote.

> The question of the highest citizenship and the complete education of all concerns nearly ten millions of my people and sixty millions of the white race. When one race is strong, the other is strong; when one is weak, the other is weak. . . . No race can wrong another race simply because it has the power to do so, without being permanently injured in its own morals. The Negro

can endure the temporary inconvenience, but the injury to the white man is permanent. It is for the white man to save himself from this degradation that I plead. If a white man steals a Negro's ballot, it is the white man who is permanently injured. Physical death comes to the one Negro lynched in a county; but death of the morals—death of the soul—comes to those responsible for the lynching.[19]

His tone was less angry than sad, his words more a lament than a condemnation of the White vigilantes. "Never shall I forget the remark by a little nine-year-old white boy, with blue eyes and flaxen hair. The little fellow said to his mother, after he had returned from a lynching: 'I have seen a man hanged; now I wish I could see one burned.' Rather than hear such a remark from one of my little boys," Washington concluded, "I would prefer to see him in his grave."[20]

# CHAPTER FIFTEEN

# THE NEW CENTURY DAWNS

You have already shown that a man may be absolutely honest and yet practical; a reformer by instinct and a wise politician; brave, bold and uncompromising; and yet not a wild ass of the desert.

JOHN HAY TO THEODORE ROOSEVELT, 1898

Booker and Theodore had yet to meet—they would in a matter of months—and life in the North was a world apart from Tuskegee. In Roosevelt's home state, Black people were fewer in number and, though they had little status, violent episodes were much rarer than on Washington's turf. New York's battles were less likely to be life-or-death and more often fought over who wielded political power.

With Roosevelt at the head, the Republican ticket had swept New York's election in November 1898. Though now the nominal head of the state, governor-elect Roosevelt, savvy in the ways of New York politics, knew very well that his next matchup would be with a man named Thomas C. Platt. He was the face of machine politics in the Empire State.

Elected to his first political office the year Theodore Roosevelt was born, Tom Platt had known Abraham Lincoln and every president since. He was genteel, his voice soft and low. But he had a rigid grip on the party's purse strings, and Roosevelt saw "Boss" Platt, not the Democrats, as his chief obstacle to changing business as usual in Albany.

Even before Roosevelt took the oath of office, Platt asked him to call on him at the Fifth Avenue Hotel, where Platt, then serving in the U.S. Senate, resided when in New York.* The sixty-five-year-old man who greeted the governor-elect was "physically feeble," Roosevelt noted. Hunched in his chair, his frame frail and his skin parchment-like, "he looked more like a New England college professor or a retired clergyman [than] a seasoned political warrior."[1]

Platt immediately turned the conversation to the appointment of a new superintendent of public works.

A scandal concerning the expansion of the Erie Canal had led to the departure of the previous occupant of the office after allegations surfaced that millions of taxpayer dollars had been mismanaged. Platt greeted Roosevelt with the news that he had just filled the very important job of directing such projects. "The senator informed me," Roosevelt reported, "that he was glad to say that I would have a most admirable man as Superintendent of Public Works."[2] Then Platt handed him a telegram, sent by a veteran Republican politician, accepting the job Platt had offered him.

This was unwelcome. Such appointments were the governor's to make, and the underlying message was clear: Platt had no intention of relinquishing to a rookie governor any of his powers as the party's chief puppeteer.

---

* Platt is remembered in New York City for his major role in the consolidation of the five boroughs into the City of Greater New York; until 1898, the city of Brooklyn, Queens County, and the towns of Staten Island had been independent.

Confident that he was right, Roosevelt took a firm stand.

"I told the senator very politely that I was sorry, but that I could not appoint his man." He had a good reason. Although Roosevelt held the candidate in high regard, he came from Syracuse, a city along the canal, which would give his appointment the appearance of a conflict of interest. Even more important, Roosevelt noted in his autobiography years later, "It was necessary to have it understood from the outset that the Administration was my Administration and no one else's but mine."[3]

The confrontation did not end there. Roosevelt soon chose his own candidate, but the man refused the job. A second did the same, as did a third. The unspoken explanation? The post required approval by the state senate, a body firmly under Platt's control, and no up-and-coming political appointee wanted to risk the embarrassment of an inevitable rejection engineered by the Boss.

In the end, Roosevelt found a path to compromise. He chose four good men and presented the list to Platt. The latter approved of one, an engineer and Civil War veteran, who went on to run the office of Public Works with admirable efficiency.

During his term as governor, Roosevelt and Platt would breakfast most Saturdays at the Fifth Avenue Hotel's so-called Amen Corner. It was the meeting place where New York Republicans famously went to talk over the issues and seek Platt's approval (to which one generally said *Amen*). But Roosevelt was the exception, achieving a level of independence far greater than anyone expected.

He found ways to avoid political dead ends. In a party under the sway of wealthy and powerful interests, he established the Tenement House Commission; it would lead to legislation requiring landlords to improve housing conditions in poor neighborhoods. Significant labor legislation was enacted on his watch. Always a passionate advocate for wilderness, Roosevelt persuaded the state legislature to set aside tens of thousands of forested acres in the Adirondack and Catskill Mountains.

His biggest accomplishment was to levy taxes on public service cor-porations. Electric power was replacing horse power, and the franchises that operated the new street car lines paid no taxes. But Roosevelt mus-cled a bill through, despite Platt's opposition, which changed that.

This signal accomplishment, like most of the others, was inspired by one idea. Roosevelt saw that corporations had too much power, that their political contributions bought them "favoritism, a favoritism which in many cases was unquestionably secured by downright bribery, [that] led to all kinds of trouble."[4] Such an imbalance simply didn't serve all the people, in particular the regular folks of the sort he had come to know and love during his time leading the Rough Riders. Seeing the im-mense inequities of capitalism, Roosevelt would make fighting for the little man a guiding priority in later, higher offices.

Notable, too, was Roosevelt's style of governance. He was unexpect-edly transparent; as he liked to say, he would rather play the game on the table than under it. Twice a day he invited reporters into his office for fifteen-minute meetings. "He has torn down the curtain," reported *The New York Times*, "that shut in the Governor and taken the public into his confidence."[5]

Each of his successes, however, fed the anger of his enemies, among them the outflanked Boss Platt. The New York machine began devising a scheme to make Governor Roosevelt go away, and they quickly settled on a solution. *How about if he became vice president of the United States?* With him far away in the nation's capital, political life in Albany could go back to business as usual.

## "I RATHER LIKE HIM"

Neither man left a detailed account of their first meeting, but Roosevelt crossed paths with Booker Washington sometime during his brief governorship. Their introduction may have been arranged by another New York, Timothy Thomas Fortune, editor of the *New York Age*, the city's most-read African American newspaper, and a Washington confidant. After Fortune and Roosevelt met for the first time, on October 1, 1898, Fortune wrote immediately to Washington. They both knew Roosevelt was a man on the rise, that an association with the just-returned war hero and likely soon-to-be governor might be valuable.

"I had a long chat with Col. Roosevelt this morning on general topics," Fortune reported. He did not see a man all puffed up by his new fame and accomplishments. "He seems to be a very open and honest man," he told Washington. "I rather like him."[6]

Before meeting in person, Roosevelt and Washington corresponded. Theodore, always a voracious consumer of newspapers and magazines, knew Booker by reputation. As someone who had remade himself as a child, he admired Washington's pluck and courage as a man who had overcome vastly greater odds to reach a pinnacle of success as an educator and spokesman—and having done it amid a sea of doubters and even haters. Roosevelt was impressed: Washington was exactly the sort of man he admired most and wanted on his team.

At the time, the interests of Tuskegee's founder and New York's governor overlapped very little. Roosevelt was governor of a Northern state, Washington no more than an occasional visitor to New York. But the two admirable men, though living in different orbits, were drawn to each other.

When they did meet in the months that followed, Washington found Roosevelt unexpectedly forthright. "While other people are thinking around a question," Washington recalled, "he thinks through it. He reaches his conclusions while other people are considering the preliminaries. He cuts across the field, as it were, in his methods of thinking."

"One never wins a battle," Roosevelt told Washington, "unless he takes some risks."[7]

Perhaps more surprising, very early in their acquaintance—most likely mere months into his governorship—Roosevelt told Washington "in the frankest manner that some day he would like to be President of the United States."[8]

On a fundraising junket to the North soon after, Washington was welcomed as a guest of the Roosevelts at Sagamore Hill. A friendship was brewing.[9]

# HAMLET ON THE HUDSON

Roosevelt's military fame, now enhanced by his new role as New York's governor, led to a groundswell of talk about the presidency. Or, more immediately, the vice presidency.

After the legislature in New York adjourned for the year, in May 1899, Roosevelt headed west. His ultimate destination was Las Vegas, New Mexico, and a reunion of the Rough Riders on the first anniversary of the Battle of Las Guásimas. Along the way cheering crowds seemed to appear from nowhere at virtually every rail stop. In Kansas, he found time during one such pause for a chat with a newspaperman named William Allen White.

White's *Emporia Gazette* had a large following—he was, some said, the voice of the Middle West—and the editor himself had a deep admiration for Roosevelt. When the then assistant secretary of the navy had taken him to lunch in Washington two years before, White had come away awed, "afire with the splendor of the personality that I had met."[10] This time, Roosevelt's train had barely left the station after their meeting when White announced, "There is no one in America today whose personality is rooted deeper in the hearts of the people than Theodore Roosevelt." White then went further: "He is more than a presidential possibility in 1904, he is a presidential probability . . . he is the coming American of the twentieth century."[11]

Talk of a presidential run seemed premature, and out of respect for McKinley, Roosevelt quickly went public expressing his support of the sitting president for another term. On the other hand, the vice president, Garret A. Hobart, was rumored to be in poor health, and Roosevelt's confidant, Senator Henry Cabot Lodge, asked the obvious question. After talking the matter over with Edith, Theodore decided the job of vice president, "honorable" though it was, had little appeal. "I should like a position with more work in it," he told Lodge.[12] For the time being Vice President Hobart made the matter moot, announcing he had no intention of resigning.

Then, in November, Hobart died.

Lodge immediately wrote to encourage Roosevelt to throw his hat in the ring to fill the now empty office. Theodore told Bamie he "did not want and would not take the Vice Presidency." He insisted he had a job to finish in Albany, but he also hedged his bet. "Of course," he told his sister, "were my renomination [as governor] out of the question I should accept the Vice Presidency were I offered it."[13] Soon enough Platt weighed in, too, telling Roosevelt that he "ought to take the Vice-Presidency both for National and State reasons."[14]

By the time the Republicans met in Philadelphia, in June 1900, Lodge had persuaded McKinley to let him gavel their party's national convention: Lodge wanted to clear the path for his friend onto the ticket. Roosevelt continued to plead that the vice presidency would mean only idleness, that he would be nothing more than a "figurehead."[15] But he did agree to attend the convention as a delegate at large.

White's friends in Kansas were the first to get in line behind Roosevelt's nomination, followed quickly by the delegates from Pennsylvania. There were prolonged cheers when Roosevelt entered the hall. He delivered a powerful speech that met with an even greater ovation. Another man in Philadelphia summarized the momentum of events perfectly.

"Roosevelt might as well stand under Niagara Falls," observed Tom Platt, "and try to spit water back as to stop his nomination."[16]

As popular as Roosevelt was, however, not everyone was keen on putting him on the ticket. He was in too much of a hurry, some thought. His ideas were too radical. At forty-one, he was too young. Since he had been in the vanguard that took the nation to war, people worried about his impulsiveness. At the convention, one of McKinley's closest advisers and the chair of the Republican Party, Mark Hanna, put that into words in an unguarded remark: "Don't any of you realize that there's only one life between this madman and the presidency?"[17]

When the delegates voted, however, the momentum had swung Roosevelt's way. The Republicans wanted to win—and Roosevelt's national popularity would help ensure that happened. The tally was 925 to 1; the lone *nay* was Roosevelt's own.

And Mark Hanna's words would prove prescient.

## UP FROM SLAVERY

As the "madman" was preparing for his run for the vice presidency, Booker Washington was becoming an author.

New York, New York, was the nation's unofficial publishing capital. Publishers Row was lined with newspaper offices, where editors and reporters alike followed the exploits—and aspirations—of Governor Roosevelt. Manhattan was also home to virtually all the nation's best magazines, among them *The Outlook*, a journal of social and political issues. Years later, Roosevelt would become a frequent contributor, but in December 1899, its editor was more interested in Booker Washington.

Lyman Abbot had read *The Future of the American Negro*. After publishing an admiring review, he wrote directly to Washington to make a proposal on behalf of his highly respected weekly. In his letter of December 9, 1899, the minister turned editor began by expressing admiration for Washington's work. "No one in America has thrown so much light or exerted so beneficent an influence upon what we call the negro problem," declared Abbot. Then he got down to business.

Would Washington write an "autobiography or autobiographical reminiscences"? Abbot wanted the "story of your life," he told Washington, and he promised to publish it, in serial form, in his magazine. He suggested they meet "when next you come to New York."[18]

The idea was not new. Several years earlier another editor, this one in Boston, had suggested the narrative of Washington's life in book form might be of interest to the prestigious firm of Houghton, Mifflin.[19] Washington liked the idea, but hoping to bring his uplifting story to Black readers, he had opted for a little-known Illinois concern, J. L. Nichols and Company, which had a substantial Black sales force that went door-to-door. He hired Edgar Webber, a young Black journalist with degrees from Fisk and Howard University Law School to assemble the manuscript.

Then things had begun to go wrong. The busy Washington had little time to help or supervise, leaving Webber to work from scrapbooks and old speeches. He was slow, sloppy, and "in a nutshell," commented one Tuskegee teacher, "[Webber] does as little as he can and complains as much as he can."[20] The publisher was no better, and when *The Story of My Life and Work* was hurriedly printed, the text was full of typographical errors and even blank pages at the end of some chapters. It was a "book of the cheapest character," commented *The Nation* magazine.[21]

Thus, Washington was more than happy to start again, and Abbott struck him as much better collaborator. This time Washington tasked his recently hired public-relations man, a White Vermont native named Max Bennett Thrasher, to be his ghost. Thrasher brought years of travel, journalism, and school administration experience to the task, as well a firsthand knowledge of Washington and the Tuskegee Institute. Booker also made it a personal priority to keep a watchful eye over every step. He dictated notes to Thrasher, who accompanied him on his travels. He and Lyman Abbott corresponded, and the editor critiqued the manuscript, chapter by chapter, as it emerged. "I would like to know very much more of your boyhood life in the slave days," he wrote to Washington early in the process. "[Reconstruction] is generally looked upon wholly from the white man's point of view. . . . How did it seem then to the Negroes, and how does it seem now to one who has the interest of his race at heart?"[22] Washington, who had read Frederick Douglass's autobiography on his return voyage from Europe, saw the wisdom in what Abbott said.

Abbott offered insights throughout the process. "I have the impression that this manuscript has been dictated," he told Washington. "If you were to go over it carefully, you would condense it somewhat by cutting out some repetitions."[23]

Second time around, the Washington story, bearing the far more evocative title *Up from Slavery*, hit the mark. Reviewers in *The New York Times*, *The Atlantic Monthly*, and the *North American Review* admired its directness and eloquence. U.S. Commissioner of Education William T. Harris's reaction was typical:

> Mrs. Harriet Beecher Stowe wrote "Uncle Tom's Cabin" and thereby produced a civil war in the Nation. You have written a book which I think will do more than anything else to guide us to the true road on which we may successfully solve the problems left us by that civil war.[24]

People said *Up from Slavery* belonged on the shelf with Benjamin Franklin's autobiography, and in the coming years it came to be regarded as an American classic, destined to be widely read and never go out of print.

# FRENEMIES

The acclaim for *Up from Slavery* was general—but not quite universal. One man who took issue with the book—and with Washington's view of Black education—was W. E. B. Du Bois.

The two men had corresponded since Du Bois's note of congratulation to Washington, written at the time of the Atlanta speech, shortly after Du Bois himself had completed his dissertation on the slave trade (which earned him the first Harvard PhD ever awarded to a Black man).[25] In 1896, they exchanged letters about a possible job at Tuskegee, but Du Bois chose instead an appointment at the University of Pennsylvania, where he conducted research into systemic racial discrimination. The resulting book, *The Philadelphia Negro*, was published in 1897.

*Professor William Edward Burghardt Du Bois, in a photo taken in 1900 in Paris, where he curated an exhibition titled* American Negro. *The judges there awarded him a gold medal for his display of almost four hundred photographs of diverse Black Americans. Du Bois's goal had been to disprove the racist notion that all Blacks were alike and inferior to Whites.*

In late 1899, Washington again dangled a job offer, this time inviting Du Bois to establish a department at the Tuskegee Institute to carry on his research into Black life. Du Bois wrote back, wondering whether his work might be "ornamental" and "not quite in consonance with the fundamental Tuskegee idea?"[26] Eventually he turned down the job, though he did agree to conduct a sociological survey at the 1900 Tuskegee Conference.

Just to see them standing side by side said a great deal. On the road, Washington wore a baggy suit that often looked as if he had slept in it; on campus, he favored farmers' overalls. In contrast, the cosmopolitan Du Bois dressed with great care, carried a decorative cane in a gloved hand, and affected a neatly trimmed Vandyke beard and mustache.

Washington was a down-to-earth spokesman for Black America, the most admired man of his race in the country. Though less famous, by 1900, Du Bois had become indisputably America's most respected Black intellectual. Washington's practiced oratory delighted large crowds; Du Bois, an academic sociologist who believed in close observation and study, reached a smaller, more refined audience via the printed word in books and highbrow magazines.

If Washington was a man of action, Du Bois was a man of the mind. At age twenty-five, the former had founded a school for manual laborers; at the same age the latter was a student pursuing an Ivy League doctorate to add to his other degrees. Because he lived in the South, Washington lived by his region's racist rules; residing in the North or within the confines of academe—he would spend thirteen years cloistered at Atlanta University—Du Bois enjoyed more freedom to speak his mind.

They shared a profound desire to improve the lives of Black men and women. Each recognized that economic discrimination was the biggest obstacle, but as Du Bois's thinking matured, he disagreed more and more strongly with Washington's hopeful view that assimilation was the answer. To confront Jim Crow, Washington counseled patience. They

*In a private moment at home, the
unassuming Booker engages the
camera with his thoughtful gaze.*

should proceed slowly, he believed, and work to gain in education and business, thereby growing in influence.

Even at age fifteen, though sheltered and naive, Du Bois had begun to shape his vision of an independent Black American. Writing as a correspondent for the African American weekly *New York Globe* as a high school junior, he argued that Black people needed to band together. We must "act in concert," he wrote then, if Black Americans wished to "become a power not despised."[27]

He came to think that "Negroes . . . are the first fruits of this new nation . . . [the] people whose subtle sense of song has given America its only American music." He lay claim to a deep sense of spirituality, too. He believed in "race organization," in "race solidarity"—in short, in a collective Black identity, one that "could soften the whiteness of the Teutonic to-day."[28]

Du Bois and Washington also differed in educational philosophy. Du

Bois thought that talented Black students could and should pursue the same curriculum as White students, including Latin and Greek, while Washington favored a much more rudimentary mix of basic schoolwork and manual training. Du Bois was brilliant, a man who could hold his own with intellectuals at home and abroad, and he focused in particular on identifying other exceptional Black men he believed could guide the race to a better place. Washington's was a bottom-up view: He offered hope to the humble that they might raise themselves.

In a review of *Up from Slavery* that he wrote for *The Dial*, a prestigious journal of politics and literature, Du Bois stated his differences with Washington more clearly than he ever had. "Educated and thoughtful Negroes everywhere are glad to honor him and aid him, but all cannot agree with him," wrote Du Bois. He and others on the vanguard, he continued, "respect the Hampton-Tuskegee idea to a degree" but also "believe it falls far short of a complete programme."

In Du Bois's view, Washington was too willing to accommodate. Du Bois wanted more, believing in "self-assertion and ambition . . . and in the right of suffrage for blacks on the same terms as whites."[29] Washington wanted the same outcome, but thought Du Bois's demands unrealistic, even dangerous, at least in the South. The gap between the two men would only increase in the years to come.

## MR. VICE PRESIDENT

While Booker was selling books, Theodore hit the campaign trail.

T.R. was never a man who could sit still, drinking a gallon of coffee a day, with a half dozen spoons of sugar in each cup. As governor of New York, he arrived at the capitol long before official working hours. Ignoring the elevator, he bounded up the 150 steps to his office two at a time. He ran his busy day on a tight schedule, meeting assemblymen and senators, political supplicants, and members of his administration. He stayed late, energized by the work and the challenges.

He brought the same energy to the presidential race of 1900. McKinley again ran a front-porch campaign, remaining at home in Ohio, while Roosevelt, in the several months leading up to the election, delivered nearly seven hundred speeches in twenty-four states. The strategy worked, and McKinley and Roosevelt won going away.

After the inauguration, on March 4, 1901, however, Vice President Roosevelt found, as he feared, that he had next to nothing to do. His primary responsibility as presiding officer of the U.S. Senate ended when the upper body adjourned, on March 8, 1901, concluding his duties in the Capitol until the Senate reconvened, in December, after its usual nine-month recess. So Roosevelt retired to family life back at Sagamore Hill, abandoning Washington for the spring and summer.

He had ample time to think about the future. He and Senator Lodge exchanged letters that summer, talking about a possible run for the presidency in 1904. And he thought aloud to Booker Washington, "outlin[ing] to me how he wanted to help not only the Negro, but the whole South, should he ever become president."[30] But that all seemed far away as a bored Roosevelt contemplated putting his underutilized brain to use by returning to his law studies. Years later, in fact, looking back in the pages of his autobiography, he devoted not so much as a sentence to his tenure as vice president.

Thanks to an anarchist named Leon Czolgosz, however, his vice presidency lasted just six months and ten days.

# CHAPTER SIXTEEN

# DEATH OF A PRESIDENT

I saw a guide coming out of the woods on our trail from below.
I felt at once that he had bad news.

THEODORE ROOSEVELT, *An Autobiography*, 1913

W hen McKinley and Roosevelt won in November 1900, Washington telegraphed his congratulations. "Your telegram gave me peculiar pleasure," Theodore replied, before adding an invitation. "When you come up North next I particularly want to see you."[1] Washington obliged, and they met briefly a few weeks later, at New York City's prestigious Century Club.

Roosevelt now had very good reasons to be interested in regions well beyond the boundaries of New York State. He could read the arithmetic of politics. When the new presidential election cycle rolled around, in 1904, he would need a Southern strategy to gain his party's nomination if he wanted to win the presidency in his own right. No Southern state was likely to vote Republican in the election itself, but so-called Black and Tans, a biracial mix of Republicans in the South, could add crucial votes to the tally at the party's nominating convention.

Washington's star was continuing to rise. *Up from Slavery* was a big success. The autobiography even found an eager audience in Oyster Bay. "Mrs. Roosevelt is as much pleased as I am with your book," Roosevelt told Washington, in March 1901. He also signaled that he wanted to continue their conversation. "I wish I could see you to talk with you more at length."[2]

Washington needed no one to explain to him what an alliance with the executive branch could mean to Black Americans. And they needed all the help they could get—with death by lynching now normalized in the South, a Black man died at the hands of his fellow citizens *every other day*. The stench of racial injustice was in the air.*

Once again, Washington made the asked-for meeting happen, and on April 1, 1901, they sat down together at Roosevelt's Madison Avenue office.[3] Equally keen to grow their connection, Booker invited Theodore to come to Tuskegee. The idea made sense: *Up from Slavery* had cemented Washington's status as the leading Black American. Governor and war hero Roosevelt had been elevated to vice president. Their mutual admiration—and influence—could surely benefit both.

Washington's people began talking quietly to Roosevelt's people. Would the vice president's old friend Jacob Riis, himself now famous as a photographer and social reformer, like to join the traveling party? He would. Washington inquired whether the vice president might wish to make stops in the state capitals of Atlanta and Montgomery? Roosevelt quickly agreed, adding that he wanted to add a detour to Bulloch Hall, "my mother's old home at Roswell," not far from Atlanta.[4]

---

* A count kept by the *Chicago Tribune* found that 2,516 individuals were lynched in a sixteen-year period.

A November time frame was established since Roosevelt's Washington obligations would resume when Congress reconvened in December. Roosevelt was entirely in sympathy with the goals of enabling "the Colored man to shift for himself and of establishing a healthy relation between the Colored man and the white man who live in the same state."[5] Washington looked forward to learning what Roosevelt might bring to the table.

# THE PAN-AMERICAN EXPOSITION

Two bullets, fired almost as one, changed everything—for the nation, for Vice President Theodore Roosevelt, and for Booker T. Washington.

On that particular Friday, September 6, 1901, President William McKinley stood at the head of a receiving line in Buffalo, New York. He enjoyed pressing the flesh, priding himself on his ability to shake more than one voter hand per second. Maybe he should have realized he was moments away from confronting his mortality—after all, his secretary had tried to persuade the nation's twenty-fifth chief executive to cancel the reception and avoid this crush of people.

"Why should I?" McKinley had replied. "No one would want to hurt me."[6]

The setting was grand, the crowd milling beneath the towering dome of the Temple of Music. The ornate building had been constructed for the occasion of the Pan-American Exposition, an international fair designed to display progress in the western hemisphere. The scene had a soundtrack, too, with a Bach cantata being played on one of the largest pipe organs in the country. But those gunshots were about to be heard.

A man known as Fred Nieman—he had chosen the alias because, in German, it translated as "Fred Nobody"—would fire the pistol.

One of eight children of Polish immigrant parents, Leon Frank Czolgosz (*jowl-gosh*) had already faced his share of hardships. He grew up poor in Detroit. His mother died when he was ten, and by his mid-teens he worked in a factory. At age twenty, after the bosses at the steel mill cut wages in the economic downturn of 1893, Czolgosz joined a strike and got blacklisted, requiring him to assume his pseudonym to get work. He saw vast inequalities in a country where the wealthy industrialist, aided and protected by the government, made millions while the common worker was expected to be a mindless drudge laboring in a dangerous workplace. His mind opened to radical ideas, he joined a socialist club and, after meeting the famous Emma Goldman, became a committed anarchist.

Now twenty-eight, he was angry and alienated, but as he waited his turn to meet President McKinley, Czolgosz seemed "pleasant-faced and mild-mannered," in the words of one bystander.[7] Thin, of medium height with light-colored hair, he was indistinguishable from many others whom McKinley greeted.

The reception was ending. The music had stopped by 4:07 P.M. when Czolgosz's turn came. On facing him, McKinley noticed the man's right hand was wrapped in a swatch of fabric—*Was it a handkerchief? A bandage?* In that instant, the veteran politician did as he had done many times before. Supposing the right hand was injured or deformed, McKinley thoughtfully reached for the left. The careful choreography of the receiving line that McKinley knew so well then went suddenly, terribly wrong.

Czolgosz stepped closer, raising the shrouded right hand to McKinley's chest. In the next instant, he fired a .32 caliber revolver, which he had purchased four days earlier. The first shot hit the president's breastbone; a second ripped into the soft tissue of McKinley's abdomen.

The man next in line, James B. Parker, a tall and broad-shouldered

Black man, reacted, and hammered his massive fist into the assassin's neck. The stunned shooter crumpled to the floor, but the pistol remained in his grip. Before he could discharge it a third time, another blow from Parker knocked the pistol away. His next punch crushed Czolgosz's nose.

McKinley, too, had collapsed to the floor. Blood bloomed on his shirt, but the president managed to speak. "Be easy with him, boys," he said as Secret Service agents got hold of "Fred Nobody" and dragged him away. McKinley, too, soon departed the scene, carried to the Exposition's infirmary, a first-aid facility better equipped to treat bee stings than bullet wounds. But he was alive and conscious.

As for the hero of the day, James Parker walked away, proud and honored to have helped. "Just think," he told an *Atlanta Constitution* reporter, "Old father Abe freed me, and now I save his successor from death, provided that bullet that he fired into the President don't kill him."[8]

At that moment, that begged the big question: *Had Czolgosz killed McKinley?*

# VICE-PRESIDENT-IN-WAITING

A few months before, McKinley's second-in-command had complained, "The man who occupies [the vice presidency] may at any moment be everything, but meanwhile he is practically nothing."[9] In the early evening of September 6, 1901, the truth of those words came shockingly to life for the man who wrote them, Vice President Theodore Roosevelt.

In six months as McKinley's backup, the vigorous New Yorker gave an occasional speech but had few official duties. This particular Friday was no different. The forty-two-year-old was in Vermont, at the estate of the lieutenant governor, preparing for a reception. Among the other guests was another early-career politician, a British member of parliament named Winston Churchill.

Roosevelt was called to the phone. His first reaction to the words he heard of the attempted assassination was disbelief, but the gravity of the situation rapidly sunk in. "As soon as he realized the meaning of the terrible news," reported one observer, "a dazed expression followed by a look of unmistakable anguish came to his face, and tears immediately filled his eyes."[10]

Meanwhile, the doctors were at work in Buffalo. Shortly after the attack, McKinley himself had reached into his shirt and fingered a foreign object. Handing it to the Secret Service agent at his side, he said, "I believe that is a bullet."[11] The first physicians to examine the wounded president recommended emergency surgery to recover the second slug. Dr. Matthew Mann was summoned, a gynecological surgeon chosen more for his nearness to the exposition grounds than his training.

Barely an hour after the shots rang out, Dr. Mann administered ether to put McKinley out, and he did his best under difficult conditions. He made a long incision in the patient's stomach to gain access to his organs, but he had no retractors to clamp the abdominal cavity open. The lighting was so poor a hand mirror was used to help illuminate the procedure in the fading light of the day. In the end, Dr. Mann failed to find the bullet and settled for suturing the wound shut.

In Vermont, Roosevelt received an update via telegram: McKinley's wound had not taken his life. The vice president briefly weighed his options, finding himself in a "most delicate" position. He did not want people to think he was eager for McKinley's demise—*Would going to his bedside suggest a deathwatch?*—but he liked the man personally and to go at once to Buffalo seemed the "natural thing."[12] Before the sun had set, he was aboard a special train steaming toward the shores of Lake Erie.

On arrival the next day, he found the patient on the mend. McKinley's pulse was close to normal, his elevated temperature dropping, and his pain manageable. After talking to the president's doctors, Roosevelt wrote to Lodge. "I become confident of the President's recovery," he told his friend. "[His] splendid inherited strength, the temperate life he has led, and his singularly calm and equable temper of mind all count immensely in his favor."[13]

With the president apparently recovering, Roosevelt waited at the Buffalo Club. Nearby, it was business as usual at the Pan-American Exposition, and Roosevelt wrote to Washington to assure him the planned Tuskegee trip was still on. He offered assurances regarding McKinley, too. "Before you receive this, the president I am sure will be out of danger."[14]

# SUMMONS TO GREATNESS

After three days in Buffalo, Roosevelt concluded it was safe for him to retreat to the Adirondack Mountains. There he joined Edith and the six children for "expeditions and adventures."[15]

On Friday, September 13, he was taking in the grand vista from atop New York's highest peak, Mount Tahawus, named for the Indigenous word for *cloudsplitter*.* From more than five thousand feet above sea level, the view was forever as he lunched on sandwiches. But his midday respite was about to be interrupted.

A hiker came into view, emerging from the fog below and moving at

---

* Although he probably never visited his namesake landmark, the 5,343-foot peak is today known as Mount Marcy, after New York governor William Learned Marcy. In another oddity, its other name, Mount Tahawus, was applied not by Native Americans but by an obscure American poet named Charles Fenno Hoffman. Sandra Weber, *Mount Marcy: The High Peak of New York* (Fleischmanns, NY: Purple Mountain Press, 2001).

double-time. As the man got close, Roosevelt noticed a flash of yellow in the ranger's hand. "I felt at once he had bad news," Roosevelt would note, "and, sure enough, he handed me a telegram saying the president's condition was much worse."[16]

Without a word, Roosevelt packed up his lunch and shouldered his pack.[17] Four hours later, a hurried mountain descent had got him back to his accommodation, a clapboard house near the base of the mountains, where he ate dinner with the family as night fell. At nine o'clock, with no update regarding the president's condition, an uncertain Roosevelt retired for the night, tired from his climb up and down the mountain.

In Buffalo, McKinley's condition worsened. On Thursday, his pulse had spiked. After his physicians administered digitalis and strychnine, his condition stabilized, but by noon on Friday his heartbeat had become dangerously weak. The doctors tried adrenaline and nitroglycerin. And whiskey, brandy, and such remedies as camphor, clam broth, and coffee. During the vice president's mountain descent of Mount Tahawus that afternoon, the Buffalo medical team at the opposite end of the state resorted to oxygen; as Roosevelt dined in the early evening, the doctors dosed McKinley with morphine. Nothing worked. Although he regained consciousness and mumbled a few words of "Nearer, My God to Thee," his favorite hymn, the president was dying. His organs, damaged by the second gunshot, were shutting down.[18]

Roosevelt was awakened around midnight by a rap on his bedroom door and an update on McKinley's dire condition. Although he knew he must hurry to Buffalo, guides and other locals counseled that he should wait for dawn before embarking on the forty-mile journey to the closest rail station. Recent rains had muddied the roads, making travel by horse and buckboard perilous. But Roosevelt insisted he must go immediately. A driver volunteered.

Roosevelt's midnight ride to the presidency took nearly seven hours and required two changes of horses. But the journey had been much longer: a sickly child who had remade his body, a reform governor who had been sent to Washington to be silenced, was about to become the most important voice in the country.

At first light, a waiting train, its steam up, came into view at North Creek station. Also awaiting his arrival was a telegram from Secretary of State John Hay, which read:

THE PRESIDENT DIED AT 2:15 THIS MORNING

The Roosevelt Special reached New York's capital city of Albany by eight o'clock. Six minutes later, with a fresh locomotive coupled to the private car with its now precious passenger, the train departed for Buffalo, watched by nearly a thousand people. "The engineer opened the throttle wide," reported *The New York World* in the next morning's paper, "and the new president flew across the country at the record rate of a mile a minute."[19]

At 1:34 P.M., the train hissed to a halt in Buffalo. Wearing a top hat his secretary had borrowed in Albany, Roosevelt climbed into a carriage. After paying his respects to Ida McKinley, the dead president's widow, he took the oath of office as president of the United States, making him the youngest president in American history.

Leon Czolgosz would stand trial for murder a mere nine days later. The proceeding lasted only three days, jury deliberations twenty-five minutes. Found guilty and sentenced to death, Czolgosz claimed, "I killed the president because he was the enemy of the good people—the working people." After his electrocution at Auburn State Prison—the electric chair was a recent invention of a Buffalo dentist—Czolgosz's remains were doused with sulfuric acid to speed disintegration. His clothes and other possessions were incinerated.

As for the late president, his body would lie in state in Buffalo City Hall before being transported to Washington, D.C., for a state funeral and on to Canton, Ohio, for interment. Six years later President Roosevelt, by then in his second term, would dedicate an imposing, domed McKinley National Memorial at the grave site.

# CHAPTER SEVENTEEN

# GUESS WHO'S COMING TO DINNER

When I asked Booker T. Washington to dinner I did not devote very much thought to the matter. . . . I did not think of its bearing one way or the other, either on my future or on anything else.

THEODORE ROOSEVELT, NOVEMBER 8, 1901

Overnight, vast new responsibilities had fallen into Roosevelt's lap. While he recognized he now possessed the power to engineer change, he also felt a new obligation to be prudent: With the eyes of the world suddenly on him, he had to proceed with care as he took the country's reins, balancing his instinct to bull forward with a mindfulness of potential risks. For one thing, that meant he needed to rethink his proposed trip to the Tuskegee Institute, which was no longer feasible given his new duties.

Even so, Roosevelt, anticipating a future presidential campaign, wanted more than ever to develop stronger ties in the South. He was still in

Buffalo when, on the afternoon of September 14, 1901, he composed the one letter that he sent on the day he took office. The addressee was *Booker T. Washington, Esq., Tuskegee, Alabama.*

Typed on a single sheet of White House stationery, Roosevelt's letter read:

> *My dear Mr. Washington:*
>
> *I write you at once to say that to my deep regret my visit south must now be given up.*
>
> *When are you coming north? I must see you as soon as possible. I want to talk over the question of possible appointments in the south exactly on the lines of our last conversation together.*
>
> *I hope that my visit to Tuskegee is merely deferred for a short season.*
>
> *Faithfully yours,*
> *Theodore Roosevelt*[1]

The note, written in a tone both warm and businesslike, was uncomplicated. In a matter of weeks, it led to supper at 1600 Pennsylvania Avenue. Yet, to the amazement of both Washington and Roosevelt, that meal detonated a virtual explosion, provoking a wave of racist anger in the South that led to a national controversy. The fallout would threaten the careers and popularity of both men, as well as their shared goal of advancing the cause of Black Americans.

# PRESIDENT ROOSEVELT

Roosevelt's lazy days of summer had come to an official end earlier that afternoon, at 3:35 P.M., when he was sworn in by a U.S. district judge as

EXECUTIVE MANSION,
WASHINGTON.

Buffalo, N. Y., September 14, 1901

My dear Mr. Washington:

I write you at once to say that to my deep regret
my visit south must now be given up.

When are you coming north?  I must see you as
soon as possible.  I want to talk over the question of
possible future appointments in the south exactly on the
lines of our last conversation together.

I hope that my visit to Tuskegee is merely defer-
red for a short season.

Faithfully yours,

*Theodore Roosevelt*

Booker T. Washington, Esq.,
Tuskegee, Alabama.

*A summons to a friend: the invitation Roosevelt dispatched*
*to Booker Washington the very day of his swearing-in*
*as president of the United States.*

president of the United States. He had been handed his dream job several years earlier than he had hoped.

Some vice presidents harbor no great desire to become the nation's chief executive. A few years later, after Woodrow Wilson suffered a stroke, his vice president, a now-forgotten Indiana politician named Thomas Marshall, refused to take over for the largely incapacitated Wilson. But that was not Roosevelt.

McKinley's second-in-command had decided long before that he was better equipped to lead the nation than "Wobbly Willie," who, to Colonel Roosevelt's irritation, had hesitated for months in the lead up to the Spanish–American War. Though young, Roosevelt was widely read. He had traveled the world. In Albany, he had gained legislative and executive experience. In Washington, he had held federal administrative offices. He possessed wide knowledge of his fellow citizens as the child of a New Yorker father and a Southern mother and was a man at home in the American West. He felt ready to lead the nation.

Since the people had elected McKinley, President Roosevelt quickly announced he would keep McKinley's cabinet and stay true to his predecessor's policies. Yet not being elected to the presidency also brought certain advantages. He had made no deals with power brokers in order to gain their support, which meant no one would be knocking on his door knowing they were owed something. Rare in the blood sport that was party politics, Roosevelt was his own man.

*The new president in a 1901 photograph.*

He also brought a range of personal qualities to the first office in the land. One was his intense curiosity, another his abundant, driving energy. People admired the raw physical courage he had displayed in the Cuba fight. His focused and organized mind had served him well before and would again as he went about learning the levers of presidential power, aided by a profound self-confidence.

One of his great strengths was on the gentler, kinder side. His was an empathic personality, and as president, he pledged to himself to act "for the public welfare, . . . for the common well-being of all our people."[2]

A final and essential trait Roosevelt brought to his new office was the desire to win the 1904 election. The new president believed that one man who might help him do that was Booker T. Washington.

## THE PRESIDENT'S HOUSE

Roosevelt's first week at his White House desk was a blur. Everybody wanted a piece of him: cabinet officers, senators, and congressmen; loyal Republicans who expected something and opposition Democrats who wanted a sense of how firm an antagonist he would be. His callers the last full week of September 1901 included not just politicians but ordinary citizens, since anyone could present his calling card and ask for an appointment. Conscious as always of the usefulness of the press, Roosevelt made himself available to editors and reporters, too.

He reveled in the attention. "Washington, the whole country, was in mourning," wrote legendary journalist Lincoln Steffens, "and no doubt the president felt he should hold himself down; he didn't; he tried to, but his joy showed in every word and movement. I think he thought he was suppressing his feelings . . . [but] he laughed with glee at the power and place that had come to him."[3]

He was still working on the Saturday night when, following up on the invitation issued from Buffalo two weeks before, Booker Washington arrived for a 9:00 P.M. appointment. The place was quiet—most of the household had gone to bed, the staff gone home. But Roosevelt was always ready to talk, and they settled into chairs in the president's library.

As a civil service commissioner a decade before, Roosevelt had waged war on patronage. He had dedicated himself to seeing to it that jobs were filled with the best and most qualified men, disregarding favoritism, nepotism, and political payback. As president he wanted to do the same, especially in the South, and he told Senator Lodge that on his watch there would be no more "scalawags . . . whose venality make them a menace."[4] He also saw a chance to address the volatile subject of race.

Roosevelt had decided there was no one better to consult than Booker T. Washington. Booker was uniquely positioned to help identify the best men in the South, Republican or Democrat, Black and White. He was a man whose entire adult life had been consciously, intentionally, rigorously apolitical.

Seated across from Washington, Roosevelt laid out his ground rules. According to Washington's recollections, "he said that wherever he appointed a white man to office in the South he wished him to be the very highest type of native Southern white man . . . regardless of political influences or political consequences." But Roosevelt was also candid about how far he could go in appointing Black men:

> He stated to me, quite frankly, that he did not propose to appoint a large number of coloured people to office . . . but that he did propose to do two things which had not been done before that time. . . . Whenever he did appoint a coloured man to office in the south, he said that he wanted him to be not only a man of ability, but of character—a man who had the confidence of his white and colored neighbours. He did not propose to appoint a coloured man to office simply for the purpose of temporary political expediency.[5]

Finally, the new president proposed putting good men of color into offices in the North, a nearly unprecedented promise.

Booker left the meeting with Theodore buoyed with hope. With Washington's guidance, jobs could be filled with men who genuinely believed in the rights of Black people. They were out there, White men who had publicly taken strong public positions in favor of fair elections and Black education, and against lynching—and, more than anyone else, the well-traveled Washington knew the talent pool. He had much direct experience with all sorts of Southern men. He was a solid judge of character and could separate the hypocrites from the men of their word. The "Washington Machine," his informal network of Black and White journalists, educators, and philanthropists, further extended his reach.

Booker's optimism was tempered by Roosevelt's practicality. But this direct access to presidential power was extraordinary—and any improvements in racial fairness, even if slow and incremental, would be welcome. And also something different: Though Washington had supported McKinley, the late president's chief counselor Mark Hanna had consistently drawn his appointments from the bloc of Southern Republicans known as Lily Whites, men who wanted to exclude all Black Americans from government.

Signs that Roosevelt was serious were almost immediate. Following their Saturday meeting, the president appointed a new judge in Alabama—but only after Washington reported back that "he is head and shoulders above any of the other persons," a man who favored fair election laws and education for Black Americans.[6] In the days that followed, Washington wrote a series of letters of reference for other candidates for federal appointments, Black and White. He understood that putting good men into the right slots could help reverse the tide of racially discriminatory laws and policies. This was a real chance to change things: For years, the federal government had consistently taken a hands-off approach in Southern states, but this could signify a shift in momentum. Plus, Roosevelt made it clear to members of his administration that Washington's was a voice to be listened to, and after Washington wrote to the U.S. attorney general recommending a judge—he called him a "Gold Standard Democrat"—for U.S. attorney in Alabama, the man got the job.[7] The postmaster general, too, reached out directly to Washington.

Washington's secretary functioned as a messenger, calling upon Roosevelt and reporting back that he found the president "brimming with good will for you."[8] Washington and Roosevelt's quiet, behind-the-scenes collaboration was working well. But their next meeting would change everything.

# THE INVITATION

When Roosevelt heard that Washington was due back in town, he beckoned to a secretary. "It seemed to me that it was natural to ask him to dinner," Roosevelt later recalled. Without devoting much thought to the matter—he regularly mixed business with dining pleasure—Theodore dictated a short note, inviting the out-of-towner to come to the Executive Mansion at 7:30 P.M. that evening, October 16, 1901.

Then he hesitated, feeling what he later described as "a moment's qualm . . . because of his color." Roosevelt's better instincts quickly suppressed his uncertainty—the thought "made me ashamed of myself"— and the note was dispatched to 1918 Eleventh Street, the home of a prominent Black businessman named Whitefield McKinlay, which Washington sometimes used as his headquarters on visits to the nation's capital.[9]

On his arrival at McKinlay's, Booker saw nothing improper about the envelope marked "Executive Mansion." He supposed that the president wanted to meet again to talk; given their ongoing correspondence, that made good sense.

When he read the note inside, he, like Roosevelt, felt uneasy.

This would not be a quiet, late-night meeting when most of the city was asleep. This was *dinner*; the piece of paper in his hand was an invitation to sup at the president's table. He would not be the only Black person there—but the others would be servants, the butlers and waiters among the largely Black staff at the Executive Mansion.

On the other hand, Booker had often dined in the homes of White families across the North. He had slept in their guest bedrooms. White men and White women had been his dinner partners at banquets. Still, this seemed quite different, in part because Washington was still a Southern city, one where slavery had been the law until 1862. Senators, congressmen, and uncounted other political operatives from the South called the capital city home. Washington understood in a heartbeat that to say yes to Roosevelt could provoke outrage. If this became public knowledge, White people across in the South would make much of it.

Yet this was a direct invitation from a man he knew and liked, and who held the nation's highest office. Setting aside his misgivings, he penned a polite reply.

*My dear Mr. President,*

*I shall be very glad to accept your invitation for dinner this evening at seven-thirty.*

*Yours very truly,*
*Booker T. Washington*[10]

That evening, dressed in a freshly pressed black suit, Washington climbed into the carriage provided by Mr. McKinlay for the mile-and-a-half

*Always a man of good manners, Washington politely accepted*
*Roosevelt's kind invitation to dinner on October 16, 1901.*
*This innocent RSVP soon exploded into controversy.*

ride to the Executive Mansion, which, by presidential order, would that
very month officially become the White House.

# DINNER WITH THE FAMILY

With the nation still in mourning for the murdered President McKinley, this evening's dinner would not be an elaborate affair. As Booker T. awaited admittance beneath the entrance portico, the White House seemed a quiet place. But appearances can be deceiving.

As he was ushered from the entrance hall to the private quarters, the nation's first house began to feel very full of energy. The two youngest Roosevelt children, seven-year-old Archibald and Quentin, almost four, had arrived that day from Sagamore Hill. They were delighted to be reunited with their father; he was their favorite playmate and always seemed to find time for horseplay. On this Wednesday evening, Archie and Quentin were boys busily being boys, exploring the wonders of the immense mansion around them.

Although Teddy, an exact contemporary of Booker Junior, was away at school, the president's second son, Kermit, twelve, and daughter Ethel, age ten, would be at the dinner table, too. While sources differ, the eldest Roosevelt child may also have been in attendance, seventeen-year-old Alice. Like Booker's own daughter Portia, Alice was headstrong and independent, and at times tested her stepmother's patience. In any case, this would be a family affair.

He had met his gracious hostess before. Edith favored white clothes that set off her fair, freckled complexion and red hair. A woman of warm and sunny disposition, she liked people, and it showed as she greeted "Dr. Washington," as many people respectfully called Tuskegee's head.*

---

* The award of an honorary doctorate from Dartmouth College that year, which entitled him to be called "Dr. Washington," solved a problem for many in the South. As Northern journalist Ray Stannard Baker learned in his research, "No Negro is ever called Mr. or Mrs. by a white man; that would indicate social equality." Ray Stannard Baker, *Following the Color Line* (New York: Doubleday, Page & Company, 1908), 63.

*Washington and family about 1899. Left to right: sons Ernest
Davidson and Booker T. Jr. (known as "Baker"); Booker's wife
Margaret ("Maggie"); Booker; and daughter Portia.*

When they entered the dining room, no one played "Hail to the Chief";
presidential pomp and circumstance had its place, but this was an evening
for family and friends. Rambunctious Quentin and Archie were strategically seated on either side of their mother where, if necessary, she could
exercise a controlling hand with her irrepressible and mischievous younger
boys. On the opposite side of the oval table sat the president, with Washington, his honored guest, on one side, and Philip Stewart, a Colorado
mining executive on the other. Stewart, who had hunted with Roosevelt in
the West, was happy to swap tales of tracking grizzly bear and elk.

High spirits prevailed. Although many homes of the era operated
under the principle that children are best seen and not heard, the Roosevelts encouraged children to participate in the banter at the table. Theodore loved food, conversation, and best of all an audience. What better

*The First Family as photographed in 1903. Left to right: sons Quentin, Ted Jr., and Archie flank their father; daughter Alice from his first marriage; son Kermit; wife Edith; and daughter Ethel.*

than a crowd of adoring children and friends? Edith enjoyed entertaining almost as much as her husband and seemed in her element, despite the newness of both the place and the role of First Lady so recently thrust upon her.

Into this circle of family affection and friendship, however, Washington was a stranger. Despite the homey and welcoming air, Washington felt that, as always in the presence of rich and powerful White people, he needed to be dignified, if not aloof. Yet here he was, seated at the president's elbow—and Roosevelt was clearly enjoying himself, holding nothing back, laughing and eating, engaging everyone, as if everything was just as it should be.

When dinner was finished, Roosevelt and Washington retired to the Red Room to talk about the South and further appointments, a lengthy conversation that ended only when the guest thanked his host and excused himself at about ten o'clock. He had a night train to catch for New York. The work of raising money for Tuskegee never ceased.

As the train rumbled north, Booker T. Washington was acutely aware that, for the first time in the nation's history, a Black man—one who had been formerly enslaved—had broken bread at the nation's first table. The simple fact it happened underscored that he could now truly be called the most important member of his race in the country and perhaps an avatar for some brighter future. While such thoughts must have elevated Washington's spirits, his anxiety about the risks of this moment surely weighed them down.

# CHAPTER EIGHTEEN

# THE MORNING AFTER

There came a cry from Dixie
And a fire was set ablaze.
"You insult us, you outrage us!
You commit an awful sin!
When you welcome to your table
That—er—man with a dark skin!"

*Mobile Weekly Press*, DECEMBER 14, 1901

E ven before Booker stepped off the train early Friday morning
in New York, news of the previous night's dinner was spread-
ing. After a routine check of the president's guest list for the
previous day, an Associated Press reporter had issued a seemingly in-
nocuous dispatch at 2:00 A.M.:

BOOKER T. WASHINGTON, OF TUSKEGEE, ALABAMA,
DINED WITH THE PRESIDENT LAST EVENING.[1]

Reactions soon appeared in papers across the country. A few were fair but most of them foul.

In North Carolina, one disapproving writer managed to take the high road. "A man's home is his castle," observed the *Raleigh News*, "whether it be a home in the White House or in an humble cabin. He has the right to choose his guests, and to sit down at his own table with whomsoever he pleases to invite to break bread with him."[2]

The *Nashville American* got tougher, calling the White House dinner an "error of judgement and a breach of good taste."[3]

The editor of *Confederate Veteran* blamed Roosevelt's impulsive nature for breaking the racial code. "The President's life as a Rough Rider and hunter, whereby customs are naturally ignored, and his impulsive disposition should induce lenience of popular judgment. The insult to all the best people of America, whether Southern or Northern, was evidently not intended to be as severe as it is in fact, and it should be forgotten as soon as possible . . . in the hope that the President may do great good in restoring real sectional peace."[4]

From there, however, the anger escalated. When the president "invited a n—— to dine with him at the White House," insisted the *Memphis News-Scimitar*, it was the "greatest outrage which has ever been perpetrated by any citizen of the United States."[5]

"A leak in the dam is dangerous to the dam's safety," the *Nashville American* elaborated. "There is danger that the leak may grow larger until the dam is destroyed and hopeless havoc and ruin are wrought. To accord social equality to negroes of Booker Washington's stamp would be a leak in the dam. It would cause other negroes to seek and demand the same recognition. It would be an example which would encourage the lower classes of negroes and whites to mingle together socially; miscegenation would follow and a mongrel race would be the result. Save the South from that!"[6]

A U.S. senator from South Carolina lent his voice to the shrieking chorus of indignant denunciations. Benjamin Tillman—known as "Pitchfork Ben" because of the barnyard vulgarity of his language—insisted that Roosevelt's decision to entertain Washington "will necessitate our killing a thousand n———s in the South before they will learn their place again."[7]

Some of the racist fearmongering got specific. Not only was the very idea of interracial dining wrong, but the presence of Edith, and perhaps, young Alice, at the same table as Booker Washington was seen as an insult to all White women. The suggestion that a virginal teenage girl had dined at table with a Black man—whether it happened or not—invited hysterical visions of rape in the bigoted mind.

The story assumed a power all its own, inspiring the journalistic imagination. Kentucky's *Courier-Journal* supplied a fictitious menu—"Teddy and Booker hobnob[ed] over their possum and potatoes"—and the *Richmond Times* saw the social intermingling of Black and White people as an invitation to interracial marriage.[8]

Northern papers responded; a mini-lecture in *The New York Times* was typical.

> The Southern papers are not well advised in their severe criticism of the President for inviting Dr. Booker Washington to dinner at the White House. They sat down together on that occasion two gentlemen, one white and the other colored, who are two of the truest Americans born on our soil, and two of the best and most intelligent and influential friends of the South now living.[9]

A simple supper had become a reminder of how deeply divided the nation remained almost four decades after emancipation.

# BEWILDERED AND BAFFLED

Roosevelt was as puzzled as he was shocked. "The outburst of feeling in the South . . . is to me literally inexplicable," he told a New York congressman he had known since their Harvard days. "It does not anger me," he added, "but I am very melancholy that such feeling should exist in such bitterly aggravated form in any part of our country."[10]

In public, the president kept resolutely silent, refusing to answer questions about the dinner. He understood very well that the publicity had cost him. He had gained political respect in the South by calling himself "half a Southerner"; that seemed fair enough, thanks to Georgia roots on his mother's side. He was also known to speak admiringly of the soldiers who "wore the gray" and of General Robert E. Lee, the all-but-anointed patron saint of the Civil War South.

Almost overnight, however, he'd become the most despised president south of the Mason–Dixon Line since Abraham Lincoln. "At one stroke, and by one act," according to the *Richmond Times*, President Roosevelt "has destroyed the kindly, warm regard and personal affection for him which were growing up fast in the South. Hereafter . . . it will be impossible to feel, as we were beginning to feel, that he is one of us."[11]

Roosevelt sent word to Washington via a private channel that he "did not care . . . what anybody said or thought about" their evening together.[12] He told another friend that despite the damage done, he would not bow to the pressure and distance himself from Washington. "The idiot or vicious Bourbon element of the South is crazy because I have had Booker T. Washington to dine. *I shall have him to dine as often as I please.*"[13] But Roosevelt couldn't quite put the episode behind him as the papers continued to debate what had happened.

One of his motives in cultivating a friendship with Washington in the first place had been to enhance his standing in the South, but now his spur-of-the-moment dinner invitation had more than erased any regional political benefit. That their connection was now national news meant that, in the eyes of some Southerners, Roosevelt had committed a double sin. As if dining with a Black man wasn't damning enough, Roosevelt was clearly taking Washington's advice concerning appointments, and, some believed, even allowing a Black man to help shape national policy.

As a Memphis newspaper reported, "[Booker Washington] seems to be very influential with the administration."[14] To the New Orleans *Daily Picayune*, that made Roosevelt "the worst enemy to his race of any white man who has ever occupied so high a place in this republic."[15]

In any case, Roosevelt's planned Southern tour, postponed by McKinley's death, would have to wait for the overheated rhetoric to cool.

# WHAT WOULD MARK TWAIN SAY?

Neither Roosevelt nor Washington wished to feed the flames of controversy, but just a week after the now infamous dinner, both men were expected in New Haven. Yale University was awarding dozens of honorary degrees to the great men of the day on the occasion of its bicentennial, and word leaked out that Washington and Roosevelt might dine together again.

A worried minister friend telegraphed Washington from Alabama with a warning: "REPORTED HERE THAT YOU ARE TO MEET ROOSEVELT AND DAUGHTER AT BANQUET THIS EVENING . . . EARNESTLY HOPE YOU WILL NOT ATTEND."[16] But good manners meant both Washington and Roosevelt, having long since accepted the college's kind invitation, made their way to Connecticut.

Whatever hope they had that their White House supper would go unmentioned was shattered when, at the commemoration ceremony on

Wednesday morning, October 23, 1901, Supreme Court Associate Justice David Brewer addressed the crowd from the podium. At the Hyperion Theater, Theodore occupied a chair onstage behind the speaker, a good distance from Booker, who sat amid of sea of colorfully gowned academics.

Justice Brewer, though no advocate for the rights of Black people, surprised his listeners by speaking to and for Roosevelt.* "I am glad there is one man in the United States who knows a true Washington," Brewer told the packed house, "whether he be a George or a Booker."[17]

The crowd erupted in an ovation. As the applause carried on—it lasted for a full three minutes—Roosevelt rose and bowed again and again. According to *The New York Times* the following day, "Booker Washington, who was in the audience, seemed greatly pleased." In the North, at least, there was nothing to forgive.

That public moment was, however, as close as they got to speaking during the Yale celebrations, as Washington acknowledged in a letter the following day. "I was unfortunate in my attempt to see you while you were in New Haven, but in any case I presume we could not have talked with any satisfaction there."[18] But Roosevelt did manage to have a quiet word with another honoree, Samuel Langhorne Clemens.

His hair white and perpetually mussed, the tails of his heavy mustache crooked around the corners of his mouth, Clemens was welcomed with cheers second only to Roosevelt's when he collected his doctor of letters. When they crossed paths at the Yale celebration, Roosevelt wanted the famous author's opinion. "He asked me," Clemens later wrote, "if I thought he was right in inviting Booker Washington to lunch at the White House."

---

* Brewer served on the court that ruled in favor of the "equal, but separate" doctrine in the *Plessy v. Ferguson* case; though absent on the day of the vote, his voting record suggests clearly which side he would have taken.

*Samuel Clemens (1835–1910), better known by the pen name Mark Twain, seemed to know everybody in turn-of-the-century America, including both Booker and Theodore. The writer and Washington became friends, while Clemens was often skeptical of Roosevelt's politics.*

Sam Clemens knew Washington—after meeting two years earlier in London, they had become friends—and he admired *Up from Slavery.* His feelings about Roosevelt, however, were more complicated, having gone on record concerning the colonel's imperialist views—Clemens was disgusted by the whole Cuban adventure and called the colonel "the little imitation cowboy." In his opinion, "Booker T. Washington [was] a man worth a hundred Roosevelts, a man whose shoe-latchets Mr. Roosevelt is not worthy to untie." But as they faced one another in New Haven, a respectful Twain noted that the president seemed worried, perhaps regretful, and in need of "a little word of comfort and approval" concerning the Washington dinner.

The great author gave Roosevelt an indirect answer. "I said it was a private citizen's privilege to invite whom he pleased to his table, but that perhaps a president's liberties were more limited."[19] Roosevelt was in no position to argue.

# BUSINESS AS USUAL?

Like Roosevelt, Washington said little in public concerning the evening of October 16. "For days and weeks I was pursued by reporters in quest of interviews. I was deluged with telegrams and letters . . . but during the whole of this period of agitation and excitement I did not give out a single interview and did not discuss the matter in any way."[20]

In private, Washington worried and wondered. Roosevelt had said he remained solidly determined, but was he? Would he give in? Would political prudence lead him to walk away from his promises? Washington, a believer at heart, hoped and thought not, but he could not be sure.

Much of the correspondence Washington received in those days came from curious journalists looking to follow up on the story, but not all: A drawer in his secretary's desk soon overflowed with letters full of violent and murderous threats.

When he had accepted Roosevelt's invitation, Washington knew he risked getting caught in a political cross fire; thus, the furor that followed stunned him less than it did his host. Yet hadn't he taken tea with the queen of England? And dined with McKinley at a Chicago banquet? When he was condemned for not knowing his place—*How dare a Negro dine with the President at the nation's house!*—that seemed absurd, too. He had been *invited*. Could one even decline a presidential invitation?

The fallout extended beyond the racist press. While some Black Americans praised him—one prominent AME bishop called him a "hero of the negro race"—others accused him of betraying them and himself.[21] As one young Boston journalist wrote privately, Washington had allowed himself to be used "as a tool or catspaw" when he was actually despised as "the most ragged loafer."[22]

In the South, however, people saw Roosevelt as the villain of the piece. This was brought home to Washington when a train on which he rode stopped just north of Gainesville, Florida. Word had spread that Dr. Washington was aboard, and a small crowd gathered to get a glimpse of the famous educator.

A White man, a farmer to judge by his working clothes and sunburned neck, entered Booker's rail car. He extended his hand and shook Booker's cordially.

"Say, you are a great man," he told Washington. "You are the greatest man in the country."

A surprised Booker replied after a moment that he thought Roosevelt was the nation's finest man.

"No, suh!" the man disagreed heatedly. "Not by a jugful; I used to think that so, but since he invited you to dinner I think he is a black scoundrel."[23]

Years later, Washington broke his long silence concerning the White House dinner in his memoir *My Larger Education*. A decade had passed, and he waxed philosophical about "the curious nature of this thing we call prejudice." Always the realist, Washington knew he could not change the thinking of those who thought as the Floridian did, illogical though it might be. From harsh experience, Washington wrote, "I have come to the conclusion that these prejudices are something that it does not pay to disturb. It is best to let 'sleeping dogs lie.'"[24]

The fallout from the dinner, at least as Roosevelt had interpreted events, set new limits on the interactions he might have with the man from Tuskegee. If he wanted to win the presidency in his own right in 1904, Roosevelt realized, he could never again invite Washington or any other Black man to dine at table. ("What I did was a mistake," he acknowledged years later.)[25] The political risks were too great; Mark Twain and countless others had told him that. Thus, Booker T. Washington made his first and last appearance at the White House dinner table on October 16, 1901. Only time would tell what the larger impact of the White House supper would be on the hopes of Black Americans.

*Images representing "The Dinner" proliferated in the days and weeks after the event. Some were racist, others admiring. This portrayal was marketed as a suitable-for-framing print in Black newspapers.*

Yet the dinner remained an important landmark for Black Americans: Roosevelt had elevated Washington's status. But the story was not a memory that Roosevelt would cherish. When he took his turn at writing an autobiography, he omitted all mention of the meal and of Booker T. Washington.

# CHAPTER NINETEEN

# "THE NEGRO QUESTION"

Few problems so severely tested the presidential leadership of
Theodore Roosevelt throughout his term of office as the so-
called Negro Question.

WILLIAM B. GATEWOOD

Roosevelt refused to permit the backlash over the Washington dinner to distract him. The office of the president was
now his, and he spent much of autumn 1901 shaping a personal vision for the nation's future. Always a confident writer, he put his
thoughts on paper for what would become his first Annual Message to
Congress.* In its finished form, the detailed document, bound in leather,
amounted to eighty typeset pages.

The twin volumes—one for the House of Representatives, the other

---

* Four decades later, during Franklin Roosevelt's administration, the Annual Message, a presidential report mandated by the Constitution, came to be known by its
more familiar name, the State of the Union Address.

for the Senate—were delivered to the Capitol by a presidential secretary at midday on December 3, 1901. Roosevelt did not accompany his text down Pennsylvania Avenue because, by tradition, the speech would be read to the separate houses by congressional clerks, the members listening in their respective chambers.

Roosevelt's message opened with a eulogy to McKinley; his murder, his successor said, was a "great calamity" for the country. Roosevelt followed with a condemnation of anarchists seeking to tear the nation apart before moving on to various policy issues.[1] As one clerk succeeded another at the podium, turning from one page to the next as they read through the twenty-thousand-word document, some of the senators drifted out of the chamber—in all, the reading would take two and a half hours.

By the time the readers finished, the young president had laid out a blueprint. Buried in the drawn-out details and rhetoric were his essential priorities, two of which, the Square Deal and the Big Stick, would be keynote issues of his administration. The former summarized his domestic concerns, in particular to control corporations and conserve natural resources for the welfare of the many, because Roosevelt believed government must not favor those with "predatory wealth" but offer every man, rich or poor, big or small, a fair shake. On the international scene, he thought the United States should be a world power, that it should "Speak softly, and carry a big stick." Over the course of his seven-and-a-half-year presidency, he would expand the role of his office as he put those principles into place to serve the American people.

Just two months later, he made good on one of those promises. The brainchild of banker J. P. Morgan and financier John D. Rockefeller, Northern Securities was a holding company that had recently consolidated control over a vast network of western railroads. In February 1902, at Roosevelt's order, the Justice Department set about breaking up the trust on the grounds of restraint of trade, under the terms of the Sherman Anti-Trust Act. "Of all the forms of tyranny," as Roosevelt saw it, "the least attractive and most vulgar is the tyranny of mere wealth."[2]

The process took time—in 1904, the Supreme Court would finally rule 5–4 in favor of dissolving the Northern Securities Company—but Roosevelt's assault on the railroad monopoly and, later, on Standard Oil, would earn him a well-deserved reputation as the trust-busting president. He would get to build a canal, too, as he had promised in that first Annual Message. The Panama Canal would be a truly long-term project (begun in 1904, it would be completed two administrations later, in 1914).

Roosevelt believed that government needed to mediate between economic forces, favoring neither side while looking to guarantee justice to both owners and workers. In an unprecedented intervention by a president, he would end a strike in the coalfields with a fair solution acceptable to both capital and labor. But he hadn't forgotten his promises to Booker Washington to appoint Black men and sympathetic White men to federal offices. Following through on that task, uncomplicated as it sounds, would be as rocky a road as any the Roosevelt administration traveled.

# DR. CRUM'S SQUARE DEAL

As far as Roosevelt could see, William Crum checked all the boxes. He was a well-respected local physician and businessman. A loyal Republican, he had for almost twenty years been the party chair in Charleston County, South Carolina, and had attended every Republican National Convention since 1884. By naming Dr. Crum to fill the vacant post of

collector of customs at the Port of Charleston, which he did in early November 1902, he was fulfilling a promise made to Booker T. Washington, who had also given Crum a full-throated recommendation.

In the eyes of many Charlestonians, however, there was a problem
with William Demosthenes Crum. As the editor of the *Charleston News
and Courier* quickly reminded Roosevelt, "First, he is a colored man,
and that of itself ought to bar him from the office."[3]

Roosevelt was in a quandary. On the one hand, he was hearing from
powerful forces in the South who were adamantly opposed to Crum's
appointment. On the other, as an influential New York journalist pointed
out, if he were to abandon his principled fight for the best candidates,
regardless of their color, "he would make himself the laughing stock of
the Country."[4]

Roosevelt reached out to Washington as he usually did regarding such
matters, asking him to dig a little deeper.

A friend of fifteen years, Crum was well-known to Washington. A
man of means and education, Crum had grown up on a plantation established by his German immigrant grandfather who had married a Black
woman; though Crum was born a freeman, the fields around him had

*For much of his time in office,
Roosevelt sparred with the Senate,
which refused for years to approve his
appointment of William D. Crum
(1859–1912) to the office of Collector
at the Port of Charleston. During the
Taft administration, Crum would
represent the United States in the
African nation of Liberia, where he
contracted blackwater fever and died
at just fifty-three.*

been tended by forty-three enslaved people. After earning his medical degree at Howard University, in 1881, he established a successful medical practice in Charleston and became head of the city's Black hospital. His wife, Ellen Craft Crum, was born in London. She was the child of formerly enslaved parents made famous by their escape from bondage in Georgia; with the help of Boston abolitionists, they had sailed to England after the passage of the Fugitive Slave Act.

William and Ellen Crum were well traveled, educated, and engaged in a mix of charities in Charleston's Black society. Furthermore, like Washington, Crum was no radical: "Social equality," he observed, "is something the white man need not fear. All we ask is the God-given right to earn an honest living, and the privilege of enjoying the fruits thereof, unmolested by the lyncher with his shotgun and rope."[5]

In response to his inquiry, Washington wrote back to Roosevelt from Boston. He reported that after asking around amongst Charlestonians, he had uncovered nothing that should disqualify Crum. In fact, he reported, "Whenever a position of responsibility is to be filled both races usually turn to him in that city."[6]

Roosevelt consulted other advisers but then decided. Even in the face of threats—the *New Orleans States* warned that his "negro appointees will be killed"—the president held firm, and on December 31, 1902, Crum's appointment was formally submitted to the United States Senate.[7] Roosevelt could hardly have known the fight would turn into a five-act drama that would last as long as his presidency.

Aside from the color his skin, William Crum had another significant liability. In 1894, he had been the Republican candidate for the U.S. Senate. The outcome of the race had never been in doubt, but his Democratic opponent, "Pitchfork Ben" Tillman, became an implacable enemy. Blocking Crum's confirmation would be a small matter for Tillman, who had merely to invoke senatorial courtesy and the Crum nomination would never reach the floor.

As for Crum, he saw the fight in plain terms, as he wrote to his and Washington's mutual friend, Whitefield McKinlay, in Washington:

> President Roosevelt . . . has been equal to the occasion, and now it remains to be seen whether the Republican Senate will support a Republican president, or allow sectional feeling against a component part of the American body politic to dominate the policy of the Republican administration.[8]

The battle lines hardened when the Senate Committee on Commerce opened its hearings in January 1903. Tillman led the attack on Crum's nomination. Crum was educated and honest, Tillman conceded. "If he were a white man he would be alright." But he wasn't.

"We still have guns and ropes in the South," Tillman reminded his fellow senators, "and if the policy of appointing the Negro to office is insisted upon, we know how to use them."[9] Crum's supporters defended his appointment, pointing out that since the state was 60 percent Black, the opposition argument that most of the people were opposed to Crum made no sense. Although the committee rejected the nomination, the publicity by then was such that newspapers in the North were describing it as a test case, one that would determine how steadfast Roosevelt was in standing up to his Southern opponents.

Roosevelt chose not to walk away from his nominee: When the senate adjourned without acting, the president used his constitutionally granted power and made a recess appointment. On March 30, 1903, Crum took office as Collector at the Port of Charleston. But that was far from the end of the matter.

Congressional inaction in ensuing sessions meant Roosevelt was forced to make recess appointments in the summer and fall of 1903 and again in April 1904; throughout, Washington's firm support helped Roosevelt keep his resolve even when the press in the North began to grumble. Only with Roosevelt's election to the presidency in his own right in the fall of 1904, and with strong support from Black voters, would Senator Tillman stop fighting. Meanwhile Crum served ably and honorably, more than doubling customs receipts. He improved the facilities, too, earning the grudging admiration of the White business community in Charleston.

As for Roosevelt, he would complain privately to a lifelong friend from his Harvard days. "The Charleston aristocrats," he wrote, "offer as melancholy an example as I know of a people whose life has been warped by their own willful perversity. . . . [A]ll I have been doing is to ask . . . that these occasional good, well educated, intelligent and honest colored men be given the pitiful chance to a little reward [and] a little respect."[10]

# POSTMISTRESS MINNIE COX

By almost any standard, Wayne and Minnie Cox were pillars of their rural Mississippi community. Both had college degrees, Minnie from Fisk University and Wayne from Alcorn Agricultural and Mechanical College. Their farming and business interests made them among the most prosperous citizens of Indianola, population 630, a flourishing town with two banks, an electric light plant, up-to-date waterworks, and a cottonseed mill.[11]

Minnie Cox worked for the United States Post Office as the town's postmaster. Because Indianola was the seat of Sunflower County, her branch served more than three thousand patrons, the majority of whom were the descendants of formerly enslaved people, who worked the rich delta soil along the Yazoo River. When appointed by President Benjamin Harrison, in 1891, Cox had been the first Black woman postmistress in the country.

*Mrs. Minnie Cox (1869–1933) was postmistress of Indianola, Mississippi— until she was driven from office for being Black. Roosevelt retaliated by closing the town's post office.*

The region's postal inspector reported Cox's office was efficiently run, tidy, and delivered good service. The locals appreciated the telephone she installed, at her own expense, for the convenience of her customers. She routinely paid delinquent box fees herself, reported the inspector, "in order to avoid any friction with the white patrons."[12] Postmistress Cox was well liked and apolitical, and Harrison's successors, Democrat Grover Cleveland and Republican William McKinley, had reappointed her at the expiration of her four-year terms.

After Roosevelt took office, however, discontented Democrats began to agitate for her ouster. No one questioned her abilities, but by virtue of her skin color she embodied what many White people now called the "Negro menace." A sometime politician and newspaper editor, James K. Vardaman, was the loudest among her critics after he announced, in the fall of 1902, he was a candidate for governor.

He had already lost twice, in 1895 and 1899, but the self-described white supremacist had a more recent and highly visible target for his diatribes. In the pages of his paper, the *Greenwood Commonwealth*, published just thirty miles from Indianola, he had excoriated Roosevelt for having Booker Washington to dinner.[13] He didn't blame Washington for the affair—"he is all right if only he keeps in his place," wrote Vardaman—but he dismissed the Black man in general as "a lazy, lying lustful animal which no conceivable amount of training can transform into a tolerable citizen." Key to his campaign platform was a plan to abolish education for Black citizens.[14]

In the autumn of 1902, Vardaman came to Indianola to deliver a campaign speech. The demagogue rebuked listeners for "tolerating a negro wench as postmaster."[15] His message was amplified by others, more than one of whom coveted the postmistress's generous salary of $1,100 a year. Vardaman excited growing racist anger in the town, and public meetings were convened. At one, Minnie Cox was ordered to leave town, and at a second, a successful Black doctor was issued a deadline for departure by January 1, 1903. In the pages of the *Commonwealth*, Vardaman congratulated the townspeople for serving notice on the powers in Washington that they were "not going to let n——s hold office."[16]

Minnie Cox submitted her resignation:

> It is my opinion that if I don't resign there will be trouble. . . . This is my home, and I feel a deep interest in the town and its people.[17]

She then left Indianola to let matters cool down. The mayor remarked after her departure she was wise to leave. If she came back too soon, he added, "she would get her neck broken inside of two hours."[18]

Booker Washington, in his role as liaison to the White House, reported in regularly to Roosevelt, as did the postmaster general. When he heard what was happening in Indianola, Roosevelt couldn't believe his ears—but his response to Cox's resignation was speedy and firm. He issued a statement that he would not "tolerate wrong and outrage of such flagrant character." Mrs. Cox, he continued, would remain on the payroll and collect her full federal salary. "The postmaster's resignation has been received, but not accepted."[19] He rejected a suggestion to send in federal troops, but effective January 2, 1903, he suspended the Indianola post office. Until Minnie Cox could resume her job, the mail would be rerouted around the town.

The result was a stalemate. Roosevelt made his point, closing the post office. But the townspeople refused to step back. Instead, they piled on bizarre and imagined arguments, including that "the very presence of negroes in the post office was a constant incitant to the less responsible negro men to rape" and that "crap-shooting darkies" congregated in the post office lobby "where white women and children had to pass and repass."[20]

The display of ignorance and hypocrisy in demonizing Minnie Cox struck Roosevelt as absurd. Indianolans did get their mail, eventually, after a roundabout route that took it to another district post office miles away. "And what do you think?" Roosevelt asked a friend. "They are having it distributed by a *Negro carrier*. How is that for consistency!"[21]

The dispute became national news, and an Ohio newspaper headline proclaimed, "Mrs. Minnie Cox, Postmistress of Indianola—A Faithful and Efficient Official Driven From Office by Southern White Brutes.[22] In the spring of 1903, Congress debated the issue at length, with one Southern senator calling the closure "a tyrannical and unconstitutional act."[23] But the post office remained closed.

Nearly a year had passed when, in late 1903, Minnie Cox notified Roosevelt that under no circumstances would she accept reappointment as postmaster. In the face of intimidation, no Black applicants dared to apply, and a White postmaster was appointed in January 1904. Postal service in Indianola was restored.

Vardaman had won his race for governor and, later in the decade, would get to spew his racist venom on the floor of Congress, together with "Pitchfork" Tillman, as a member of the U.S. Senate; he would be remembered in his home state as the "Great White Chief."*

As for Minnie Cox, she returned home in early 1904, settling back into her predominately White Indianola neighborhood without incident. Deprived of her post office job and salary, Minnie Cox, together with her husband, decided to organize a new bank. The Delta Penny Savings Bank prospered, and two years later, Booker Washington reported to Roosevelt, "The bank has the confidence of both races." Both Roosevelt and Washington noted with grim irony that the citizens of the

*Father and sons on horseback. Left to right: Booker T. Jr.,
Ernest Washington, and Booker T. Sr.*

---

* An imposing brick building on Dormitory Row at the University of Mississippi was dedicated to the late senator in 1929. More recently, despite calls to remove his name—and an announcement in 2017 by the university that it planned to do so—the building retains the name Vardaman Hall.

Mississippi town would entrust their money to Mrs. Cox but refused to let her touch their mail.[24]

# BATTERING THE RACIAL BARRIER

Roosevelt soon elevated other good men of color. One was William H. Lewis who, like Washington, embodied hope for Black Americans. His father had been born enslaved in Virginia but Lewis had graduated from Amherst College, where he was an all-American football player, and then gained a Harvard Law degree. When Roosevelt appointed him assistant U.S. attorney for Boston, Lewis assumed the highest position a Black man had ever held in the federal government.

Booker did everything he could to make the best of his insider status, even in the face of controversy and unceasing pushback across the South. When Roosevelt consulted him about a judgeship in the District of Columbia, Washington's candidate was appointed over one endorsed by the bar association. Washington got a U.S. attorney in Alabama fired, and Roosevelt laid down the law with the White replacement, whom Washington suggested, instructing that hiring decisions in his department were to be made only after consulting with Dr. Washington.[25] But after 1903, the number of Black appointments dwindled.

Roosevelt's program had been met with extraordinary anger in the South. The battles over Crum and Cox were just two of many. The idea that Roosevelt was the friend of the Black man became a cudgel that many Democrats used in their election campaigns—local, state, and national—a wedge issue that motivated voters. Typical was a candidate running for congress in Alabama who repeatedly invoked Washington's name, calling him the "Negro Patronage Boss."[26] That half-truth reinforced the prejudices of White people paranoid about racial equality.

Still, Roosevelt wanted to get it right with Black voters, to convey he was a man worth voting for, a man concerned with their interests. During the election season of 1904, Washington did everything he could to help. The president's dogged support for Crum would help him at the polls, as did Washington's quiet lobbying efforts. But Booker's work had to be behind the scenes. He could not, for example, attend the Republican convention. That would invite a new tidal wave of racist condemnation.

When Roosevelt requested it, Washington was quick to offer strategic advice. Asked what he should say about "the Southern question" while campaigning, Washington counseled Roosevelt, in a letter labeled "Personal and Confidential," that "it will be wise for you to make no reference to that subject." But he offered reassurance, too. "You have said and done so many brave things as bearing upon the race question that the colored vote is with you almost as unanimously as it could possibly be."[27]

Aided by the Black vote, Theodore won a big victory on November 8, 1904, sweeping the North, Midwest, and West, accumulating an electoral vote of 336 versus his opponent's 140. Booker hoped he would retain a hold on the president's attention, but events of the preceding four years had severely tested how much Roosevelt could do on behalf of the Black man. Still, Roosevelt remained clear about the racial divide: For him it was as a matter of conscience. When the Senate pushed back on his nomination of Dr. Crum, he hadn't given in, he recalled:

> I cannot consent by my action to take the position that the door of hope—the door of opportunity—is to be shut upon all men, no matter how worthy, purely on the grounds of color. Such an attitude would according to my convictions be fundamentally wrong.[28]

# CHAPTER TWENTY

# SOUTHERN DISCOMFORTS

When I first went South I expected to find people talking about the Negro, but I was not at all prepared to find the subject occupied such an overshadowing place in Southern affairs. . . . In the North we are mildly concerned in many things; the South is over-whelmingly concerned in this one thing.

RAY STANNARD BAKER, *Following the Color Line,* 1908

A full five years after promising Booker T. Washington that he would come to Alabama to visit the Tuskegee Normal and Industrial Institute, Theodore Roosevelt finally arrived.

His train steamed to a stop early on October 24, 1905, pausing first in the town of Tuskegee. The day was chilly for October, but many of the two thousand inhabitants, along with others from the surrounding villages of Tallassee and Cheaha, clogged the streets with wagons and carriages pulled by horses and mules. Black and White residents of Tuskegee lined the byways and town square, hoping for a glimpse of the president.

After being greeted by the mayor, Roosevelt gave a short speech. It was warmly received—this was a rare honor, having the chief magistrate of the United States stop in their little Alabama town—but folks were wary, too. Two Pinkerton detectives had arrived two days earlier to identify "suspicious characters" who might have "evil designs upon Dr. Washington."[1] Since McKinley's assassination, Roosevelt himself routinely carried a revolver when in public, but danger seemed always in the air for Washington, even close to home. Just a year earlier, the district's own congressman, Tom Heflin, had stood on the steps of Tuskegee's courthouse and threatened Washington with lynching. In response, the partisan crowd had risen to its feet in a standing ovation. But the day of Roosevelt's visit would be a peaceable one.[2]

After reboarding the presidential train, the party traveled the last mile along the private spur that connected the school to the main rail line. There Booker greeted his friend Theodore, and they took seats in a fine carriage built by students at the school, pulled by horses bred in Tuskegee's pastures, and driven by a young man dressed in his brass-buttoned blue school uniform. They went directly to an elaborately decorated reviewing stand.

Roosevelt had to see Washington's campus to truly believe it—and the president was amazed. In just under twenty-five years, enrollment at Tuskegee Normal had risen from thirty original students to fifteen hundred, a number that exceeded that of Roosevelt's own alma mater, the ancient and revered Harvard University. The physical plant, once just a single, leaky-roofed shanty, now consisted of thirty-three buildings, most of them multistory and built of brick made on site, many named for such philanthropic captains of industry as Carnegie, Rockefeller, and Huntington. Booker Taliaferro Washington had created all this and even accumulated an endowment of more than a million dollars.

A parade began with students marching past the reviewing stand, the men in their blue uniforms, white gloves, and cadet caps, the women in

*The school that Booker built: In a mere twenty years, a few tumbledown buildings became a dense college community, as pictured in this 1901 bird's-eye view.*

blue dresses trimmed with red braid and blue straw hats. A total of sixty-one floats followed, each representing a branch of activity at Tuskegee, from broom making to blacksmithing, millinery to machining, architecture to agriculture. Students on every float enacted some aspect of a discipline. Girls made butter on the creamery float, a history class examined reference books found in Roosevelt's *Winning of the West*, and men rigged wires on poles on the electrical division float.

After a tour of the grounds, which consisted of two thousand acres in tillage that produced foodstuffs, cotton, and livestock, the presidential party was serenaded in the chapel by the 150-voice Tuskegee choir. Then Washington briefly bade his guest welcome, expressing "the gratitude felt by the people of the Tuskegee Institute, and by the people of both races in this section of Alabama, for the honor" of his visit.[3] Then Roosevelt went to the podium.

First, he spoke off the cuff and from the heart. "You can't be as much inspired by any thing I may say," he told the students and teachers arrayed before him, "as I have been inspired by what I have seen here. Mr. Washington, it is a liberal education just to come here and see this great focus of civilization."[4]

When he turned to the notes of his prepared remarks, he read a speech that Washington had critiqued and shaped, one that made the familiar case for Black education. Roosevelt spoke to White citizens: "In the interest of humanity, of justice, and of self-protection, every white man in America, no matter where he lives, should try to help the Negro to help himself." He addressed "lawlessness, in all its forms," citing lynching in particular. He warned the students that their "race cannot expect to get everything at once." He pled for harmony, cooperation, and the common destiny they shared "as law-abiding American citizens."[5]

If Roosevelt's address surprised no one, his presence alone was a reward for the man standing beside him as the applause swelled. Much as he would have liked to, however, Dr. Washington could not invite his guest for lunch, though it was high noon. Both men knew the dangers, immediate and political, were too great. Thus, Washington escorted the

*Roosevelt and Washington, together at last in Tuskegee, Alabama, standing at the podium in this 1905 photograph.*

president back to his train, which soon pulled out of the Tuskegee station. Booker was left to savor Theodore's renewed promise: "While I have always stood for this institution, now that I have seen it," he had said for all to hear, "I will stand for it more than ever."[6]

# THE SOULS OF BLACK FOLK

Bigoted White Southerners posed the greatest physical danger to Booker T. Washington, the men who twisted his words, envied his ties to power, and who would have rejoiced in his death, preferably by violent means. Yet as the decade passed, Washington faced a very different threat to his leadership. This one consisted of highly educated Black men, mostly in or from the North, who dreamed of a more ambitious path than his for the advancement for Black Americans.

Among the harshest Washington critics was Bostonian William Monroe Trotter. After founding his weekly paper, *The Guardian*, in 1901, Trotter regularly targeted Washington in its pages. A recent graduate of Harvard, the Black editor accused the Alabaman of subservience to White people; of advocating second-class education; and of discouraging Black political participation. His dislike of Tuskegee's head and seemingly everything he stood for led the classically educated Trotter to add a Latin tagline to his pieces: "*Washington est delenda*," translated as "Washington must be destroyed."[7]

Trotter's hatred for Washington came to a climax when he interrupted a speech Washington was giving, in July 1903, in Boston. Standing on a chair, Trotter created pandemonium as he challenged the speaker, screaming questions and insults. A riot resulted, with one person stabbed and Trotter arrested for disturbing the peace. Washington called upon the many contacts of the Tuskegee machine—influential friends, newspaper reporters, his rich donors and supporters—to call out Trotter. In the end, the event permanently damaged Trotter's credibility, but Washington's manipulation of the press also left Trotter's friend W. E. B. Du Bois fully and finally alienated from Booker. Du Bois had concluded that Washington wielded too much power, enabling him to suppress the ideas of other Black thinkers.

Through subtler means than Trotter's, Du Bois established himself as an equally persistent Washington critic. A provocative writer, he published a book titled *The Souls of Black Folk* the same year. He and Washington had, on several occasions, nearly become close collaborators, but the fifteen essays collected in Du Bois's 1903 book, which today remains an essential work, made clear why that could never happen. While Washington had difficulty—in part because of where he lived and worked— seeing a new horizon for the Black man, Du Bois imagined a larger future.

He famously wrote of the African American, "One ever feels his twoness,—an American, a Negro; two souls, two thoughts, two unreconciled strivings; two warring ideals in one dark body, whose dogged strength alone keeps it from being torn asunder."[8] He saw a uniqueness in being Black: "We black men seem the sole oasis of simple faith and reverence in a dusty desert of dollars and smartness."[9] He also believed strongly that the best Black men—the "Talented Tenth," he called them—should be educated not as Tuskegee tradesmen but as White students were, with the same varied curriculum and at the best and most demanding universities:

> The Negro race, like all races, is going to be saved by its exceptional men. The problem of education, then, among Negroes must first of all deal with the Talented Tenth; it is the problem of developing the Best of this race that they may guide the Mass away from the contamination and death of the Worst.[10]

*The Souls of Black Folk* singled out Washington directly for stinging criticism. In the essay "Of Mr. Washington and Others," he damned Booker as a Black leader chosen by White men. He relabeled Washington's influential 1895 speech "The Atlanta Compromise," a direct dismissal; to Du Bois, Washington's fingers-and-hand metaphor now sounded like surrender. More disturbing to Washington, Du Bois called him "the most distinguished Southerner since Jefferson Davis," the president of the Confederacy.[11] It was almost an indictment:

> Mr. Washington apologizes for injustice, North or South, does not rightly value the privilege and duty of voting, belittles the emasculating effects of caste distinctions, and opposes the higher training and ambition of our brighter minds.[12]

Du Bois's prophecy that "the problem of the Twentieth Century is the problem of the color line" would prove painfully true.

Since his emergence as a national voice in 1895, Washington had captained the ship: He was accustomed to being the undisputed leader and spokesperson for Black Americans. Thanks to Roosevelt, he had gained real political power, too, and with his tight network of Northern donors, the lion's share of the philanthropic monies available for Black progress was his to disperse. Suddenly, however, with the emergence of the upstart Du Bois, there was a mutiny in the ranks.

# HARPER'S FERRY

The long line of men and women walked barefoot on the dewy grass. With the sun still rising, on August 17, 1906, the congregation marched single file to the hallowed ground where John Brown's fort once stood.

Half a century before, the abolitionist had come to launch a slave rebellion, believing that if he and his armed band of eighteen foot soldiers captured the arsenal at Harper's Ferry, Virginia, that "the bees will begin to swarm."[13] The effort had failed—but the shots fired by Captain Brown and his men did lead in the years that followed to the Civil War and to emancipation.

This was the first public meeting of the so-called Niagara Movement. A year before, W. E. B. Du Bois had summoned other highly educated writers and activists to Niagara, New York; because of the color of their skin, the organizers had been forced to find accommodations on the Canadian side of the great falls. This time the group occupied dormitories at Storer College, a mission school established by Free Baptists in Harper's Ferry to educate formerly enslaved children. The movement, its tenets agreed upon at Niagara, was now going public.

In a sense, Booker Washington had instigated the organization's formation. Recognizing that his hold on Black politics was slipping, he had held a January 1904 gathering in New York at meeting rooms in Carnegie Hall lent by Andrew Carnegie himself. He wanted the twenty-eight handpicked Black leaders in attendance to agree upon a national agenda and, after three days of talks, a consensus emerged—but one that had been carefully choreographed by Booker Washington. In the months that followed, a disgruntled Du Bois and others had distanced themselves. Washington's policy hadn't changed, they believed: The Black man, in his view, still had to accommodate White people. But channeling Frederick Douglass, Du Bois demanded true equality, as expressed in an essay published in April 1904. "The way for Black men today to make these rights the heritage of their children," he wrote, "is to struggle for them unceasingly, and if they fail, die trying."[14] With such goals, the site of John Brown's attack on the system of slaveholding seemed just the place to convene.

"The Great Accommodator"—Du Bois's unflattering nickname for Washington—was conspicuously absent: He had not been invited. Instead, these delegates and sympathizers, most of them of the Talented Tenth, with Du Bois himself at their head, cupped their hands around votive candles, paying silent homage to John Brown. Breaking the quiet of the morning, they sang "John Brown's Body" and "The Battle Hymn of the Republic."

Meetings and meals followed that weekend, including a talk delivered by Sergeant Lewis Douglass, Frederick's son, who had fought for the Union Army at Fort Wagner. But the closing session was reserved for Du Bois's "Address to the Country."

In that carefully crafted document, he set out to define new terms in the fight for equality:

> The battle we wage is not for ourselves alone but for all true Americans. It is a fight for ideals, lest this, our common fatherland, false to its founding, become in truth the land of the thief and the home of the Slave—a by-word and a hissing among the nations for its sounding pretentions and pitiful accomplishments.[15]

The events in Harper's Ferry got national attention. *The New York Times* ran a story the day after Du Bois's speech headlined NEGROES WANT EQUAL RIGHTS and quoted his demands for change.[16] Although the Niagara Movement was not destined to blossom, disbanding several years later, no one could fairly call it a failure, since that same year much of its membership consolidated into a new organization, the National Association for the Advancement of Colored People. Du Bois would be among the NAACP's first officers.

Little as he might like it, Washington had to share the American stage with Dr. Du Bois.

# THE BROWNSVILLE AFFAIR

The First Battalion, Twenty-Fifth Infantry (Colored), had come to town three weeks before. Many of the soldiers were veterans of real battles, after fighting the Sioux in the West and the Spanish in Cuba. Six had won the Medal of Honor, and one among them, First Sergeant Mingo Sanders, remembered sharing hardtack and bacon back in '98 with Colonel Roosevelt following the Battle of Las Guásimas. But their time at Fort Brown would have dire consequences: They would lose their reputations and their pensions—if not their lives—in an unfair fight with Southern racism and political expedience.

At their previous posting in Nebraska, the Twenty-Fifth saw no color line. In Brownsville, Texas, a different culture awaited them. One private walking along the sidewalk found himself shoved aside with the warning, "You black son of a bitch; don't you know this is a white man's town?" In another incident, a soldier was struck by a passing pedestrian with the butt of a revolver; he collapsed, his head bloodied.[17]

On Brownsville's Elizabeth Street, the Black soldiers were turned away at two taverns, and served only by the Jim Crow bar at the rear of the Ruby Saloon. Two enterprising soldiers decided to open a beer joint across the street from Fort Brown at the edge of town. There, even on payday, there were no drunken incidents, no fights, and no calls to the police.

On August 13, 1906, the prospect of real conflict loomed. That Monday morning, a White woman claimed that, on returning to her home the night before, a man had grabbed her by the hair and thrown her to the ground; after she screamed, she said, he ran off. Shaken up but unhurt, she could supply no description of the man, only his race and attire: "The large Negro [wore] a slouch hat, blue shirt, and khaki trousers."

With the story circulating in the town, the battalion commander ordered all his men to be in their barracks by eight o'clock that night. "While I don't think it was one of my soldiers," Major Charles Penrose, a White officer, told the town's mayor, "still they will undoubtedly have the blame for it."

Then, just before midnight, shots rang out in the town. At Fort Brown, a defensive call to arms was issued as twenty more shots echoed in the near distance over the course of the next two and a half minutes.

A fusillade of what sounded like rifle shots rang out in a downtown alleyway. Voices yelled, repeatedly, "Come out, all you black sons of bitches."

The gunfire lasted ten minutes, but B and D Companies had formed up by the time the firing stopped. C Company was slower, but all the soldiers at Fort Brown were present and accounted for.

Major Penrose then ordered one company to march into town. In front of the county jail, the troops met up with an armed mob of some fifty men. The company commander ordered his men to halt. Asked who they were, the civilians replied, "Officers of the law! Officers of the law!"

The night's drama was over, but a White man, a bartender by trade, had been shot dead in his yard. A policeman was wounded; a bullet had grazed another man. A house near the alley had been shot up.

*Who had done this? Who was responsible?* Allegations made in Brownsville rapidly rose to the highest levels of government when, two days later, a telegram arrived on Roosevelt's desk. In a rush to justice, the mayor of Brownsville claimed soldiers of the Twenty-Fifth had run amuck, "leaving our women and children terrorized."[18]

The brigadier general in charge of the Southwestern Division wasn't so sure, and soon telegraphed his superiors at the War Department:

CITIZENS OF BROWNSVILLE ENTERTAIN RACE HATRED
TO AN EXTREME DEGREE . . . PROVOCATION GIVEN
THE SOLDIERS NOT TAKEN INTO ACCOUNT.

A debate raged in the days, weeks, months, and even decades that followed. Evidence surfaced. Accusations and counteraccusations were made: The soldiers were guilty; they were being framed. The president, secretary of war, and even Congress would get involved as the focus of the confused and confusing story shifted from a dusty town on the Mexico border to the White House.

# "A TRUCKLING TO REGIONAL PREJUDICE"[19]

Since Secretary of War William Howard Taft was out of town, Roosevelt took charge. He issued an order for the War Department to conduct an investigation.

The initial evidence had not been conclusive. At Major Penrose's order, every rifle on the base was inspected after the violence in the town and no indication found that any had been fired. Then the mayor had arrived at Fort Brown to hand over a cartridge clip and some empty shells made for the Army's new Springfield rifle. They had been found, he claimed, behind a hotel in Brownsville.

"Your men did this," he said flatly.

A narrative began to emerge. According to this version of events, more than a dozen Buffalo Soldiers had managed to sneak out of the fort on a murderous venture. The spent shells and a soldier's cap were proof. Penrose and his four junior offices, all White men, reluctantly concluded that, given the physical evidence, soldiers of the Twenty-Fifth must be guilty.

Advised of the open hostility toward the troops in Brownville, Roosevelt ordered the men to march to a nearby fort. After an inspector general's report confirmed the preliminary finding, the Twenty-Fifth Infantry was moved again, this time to Fort Reno in Oklahoma. A dozen soldiers identified by an investigator were separated and put under arrest in a guardhouse at San Antonio.

Yet no soldier in the First Battalion, Twenty-Fifth Infantry (Colored) would admit to any role whatsoever in the midnight melee on August 13 and 14, 1901. Their commanding office, Major Penrose, tried to get someone to confess or implicate a brother soldier, but none would name names. They were innocent, one and all, they insisted.

An impatient Roosevelt ordered his new inspector general to head west in early October. He was to interrogate the soldiers in Texas and Oklahoma—and he was to get some answers. The president prided himself on his decisiveness, and the uncertainty of this Brownsville affair unsettled him. "If the guilty parties cannot be discovered," he warned, "the whole three companies implicated in this atrocious outrage should be dismissed and the men forever debarred from reenlisting in the Army or Navy of the United States."[20]

The case was far from open and shut. No one had examined the empty shells found in Brownsville to determine how recently they had been fired. It also emerged that the men of the Twenty-Sixth Infantry, the unit that preceded the Twenty-Fifth at Fort Brown, had made pocket money peddling the ammunition on the street to locals fascinated by the new long gun. No one seemed to question that, even as the last of the shots were being fired, the headcount made at the fort found no missing men. In fact, very little seemed certain about what happened, as estimates of the number of shots fired ranged widely, from one hundred to three hundred.

Even though the Black soldiers "positively denied any knowledge" of the night's events in Brownsville, the investigator refused to believe they could be telling the truth. As a South Carolinian, he knew a good deal about Black people, he believed, having grown up with enslaved children as playmates, as was common practice in the rural South. He felt confident in asserting that "the secretive nature of the race, where crimes to members of their color are charged, is well known." Since he was certain that some soldiers just had to be guilty, their denials amounted to a "conspiracy of silence." After interviewing several dozen of the 167 men of B, C, and D Companies, he decided, consistent with the president's orders, all should be dishonorably discharged, whatever their previous honorable service.[21]

The inspector general's report settled the matter for Roosevelt, but the president felt obliged to summon his adviser on Black affairs. When Washington arrived at the White House, on October 30, 1906, Roosevelt greeted him with the announcement that, except for their White officers, every member of B, C, and D Companies would be dismissed without trial.

Washington urged him to rethink the decision; as Booker told a confidant soon after, he counseled "our friend in Washington" that it would be "a great blunder."[22] He wrote to Roosevelt, begging him to wait. "There is some information which I must put before you before you take the final action."[23]

Roosevelt's painfully direct reply must have been hard to read:

> I could not possibly refrain from acting as regards those colored soldiers. You can not have any information to give me privately to which I could pay heed, my dear Mr. Washington, because the information on which I act is that which came out in the investigation itself.[24]

In Roosevelt's mind, that was that. On the following day, November 7, 1906, Special Order No. 266 was issued. The soldiers were "discharged without honor," deprived of pensions, "forever disbarred from reenlisting . . . as well as from employment in any civil capacity under the government."[25] It would be the only documented case of mass punishment in the history of the U.S. Army.

# SUMMARY JUDGMENT

The South celebrated, with the *Nashville American* calling the soldiers' dismissal "the most praiseworthy thing the President has done." The Black press, on the other hand, universally condemned Roosevelt's action.[26]

Some in the North thought the timing cynical, since Roosevelt's decree was released the day after the midterm elections, in which some five hundred thousand Northern Blacks cast ballots. In one Ohio congressional district, Nicholas Longworth III, the president's new son-in-law—he and Alice married nine months before—had been locked in a tight electoral race. He won a victory so narrow that if half of his three-thousand-odd black constituents had voted against him, he would have lost.* And Longworth's was just one of the several contests in the North in which a shift in the Black vote might have altered the outcome for Roosevelt's allies.

When he got wind of Roosevelt's decision, Samuel Clemens was livid. Although he did not say it aloud at the time—his words would be published only after both the author and Roosevelt were dead—Twain put his anger on paper. "The government and its agents acted in a shabby and dishonest and dishonorable way from the beginning to the end," he thundered, "[because] . . . Mr. Roosevelt was anxious to . . . get back into Southern favor."[27] He regarded Roosevelt's Brownsville decision a gesture of apology to the South for the Washington dinner half a dozen years before.

---

* Credit biographer Edmund Morris for doing the math. Edmund Morris, *Theodore Rex* (New York: Random House, 2001), p. 467. Longworth would go on to become Speaker of the House.

*The New York World* spoke for the angriest of Northern newspapers when it accused Roosevelt of deploying an "executive lynch law" by dismissing the Black soldiers without a court martial proceeding.[28]

Publicly, Roosevelt responded to the criticism by doubling down, claiming he would have made the same decision even if the soldiers had been White men. Privately, though, he told a journalist friend, "I have been really deprest over this Brownsville (Texas) business." What upset him most, he explained, was the reaction of Black Americans. "I had never really believed there was much justification for the claim of the Southern whites that the decent Negroes would actively or passively shield their own wrongdoers."[29] He was not doubting his own judgment—he was questioning the integrity of the accused and those who doubted him.

Washington did what he could, asking Roosevelt to reconsider, warning that "there is a deep feeling that some wholly innocent men are being punished [and] the fact that the order appeared on the night, after the election, created the impression that it was held up to secure the Negro vote."[30] Roosevelt was unmoved.

Understanding full well he was caught in the middle, Washington issued no statements. Even when some of his closest allies demanded he condemn Roosevelt's action, he refused. But that only added to the anger of many in the Black community, who then insisted Washington must be partly responsible for the injustice.

Washington could have reckoned Roosevelt's handling of the episode as a betrayal; at the very least, Roosevelt's total rejection of his counsel had been a slap in the face. Washington might have ended their relationship, but he wasn't a bridge burner; that simply wasn't in his nature after a lifetime spent mastering the art of overlooking slurs and dismissals, minimizing slights and insults. He plodded on, taking a philosophical view. As he explained to one friend, "the Colored people of this country cannot afford to place themselves in continued opposition to the President of the United States, no matter who he is."[31]

When Roosevelt summoned him, he obediently went to the White House a few days later. Theodore wanted Booker's thoughts on the president's Annual Message to Congress. They spent an hour reviewing the speech, and the president seemed somewhat receptive to Washington's suggested modifications. "He did not take all the medicine . . . [I] prescribed for him," Washington wrote after the meeting, "but he did take a portion of it."[32] When the speech was delivered, however, Roosevelt had clearly disregarded virtually all of Washington's advice. He condemned lynching, only to undercut his own words by repeating the falsehood that "the greatest existing cause of lynching is the perpetration, especially by black men, of the hideous crime of rape—the most abominable in all the category of crimes, even worse than murder." His words played into the racist stereotypes of the oversexed Black male. Echoing his irritation at the stonewalling Brownsville soldiers, he lectured, "The respectable colored people must learn not to harbor their criminals."[33]

Senator Joseph Foraker of Ohio was the man who pushed back. A former big-business lawyer and dedicated opponent of Roosevelt's trust-busting, he took up the soldiers' cause on the floor of Congress. To a man considering a run for president in 1908, the Brownsville case looked like a tool he could use to make Roosevelt and his heir apparent, Secretary of War William Howard Taft, look bad. He did exactly that with drawn-out congressional hearings in early 1907. He portrayed the army's so-called investigations as what they were, haphazard and incomplete, without due process and with a predetermined outcome.

The Brownsville episode would be remembered as a black mark on Roosevelt's reputation, and as for Washington, his impossible mission to get Roosevelt to reverse his position left Du Bois and the others in the

Niagara Movement wondering how far Washington's clout had diminished.* For better or for worse, the White House dinner and the Brownsville episode were defining moments in the narrative of Booker's and Theodore's brave—but ultimately imperfect—relationship. Once and for all, the Texas controversy signaled an end to their valiant joint effort to effect change in the country for the Black man. Both Roosevelt and Washington had again been caught in a political cross fire.

---

* Full exoneration would not come for sixty-six years, when, in September 1972, the secretary of the army acknowledged the soldiers' treatment had been a "gross injustice" and ordered the men's records be cleared and their discharges changed in the national record to honorable. "Army Clears 167 Black Soldiers Disciplined in a Shooting in 1906," *New York Times*, September 29, 1972.

CHAPTER TWENTY-ONE

# WINDING DOWN

The fact is that a large part of our racial troubles in the United
States grow out of some attempt to pass and execute a law that
will make and keep one man superior to another.

BOOKER T. WASHINGTON, *Century Magazine*, 1915

Booker and Theodore's meetings became fewer and their correspondence less frequent after Brownsville, but before Roosevelt left office, he said thanks to his friend in early 1908. "I wish to thank you now, not so much on my own account as on behalf of the people of this country, and especially the colored people, for the high character of the men whom you have suggested."[1] It wasn't quite a farewell, but Roosevelt had already decided not to seek a second full term in addition to the three and a half years he served after McKinley's murder. Instead, he would pass the torch to another friend, Secretary of War Taft.

Washington hoped his role as adviser to the president could continue, and in the months leading up the 1908 election, he offered advice to candidate Taft concerning the Black vote. He had his wish list, too; in particular that Taft and Roosevelt see to it that the party platform supported equal accommodations on railroads, which numerous Southern states had restricted, as well as Black voting rights. When November rolled around, Taft, aided by the full-throated support of the popular outgoing president, beat Democrat William Jennings Bryan handily, carrying most states outside the South. Washington promptly wrote to Taft, offering the services he had provided Roosevelt. "If I can in any degree serve you in the same manner," he wrote on December 1, 1908, "I shall be most happy."[2]

During the four years of his presidency, Taft would indeed confer with Booker Washington—but he was clear about rolling back on Roosevelt's wavering commitment. "I am not going to put in places of such prominence in the South . . . Negroes whose appointment will only tend to increase . . . race feeling." He had no wish for the sort of prolonged battle that Roosevelt had fought for Dr. Crum; in fact, at Roosevelt's request, Washington had asked for and gotten Crum's resignation, effective the day Taft was inaugurated. The new president made only a soft

*A middle-aged Booker T. Washington in 1908: the teacher still, pencil in hand.*

*At a school where so many students arrived with little more than their dreams, the support and generosity of outsiders were essential. Pictured here at Tuskegee's twenty-fifth anniversary celebration in 1906 are businessman Robert Ogden, Secretary of War William Howard Taft, Booker, and the industrialist and philanthropist Andrew Carnegie.*

promise to "look about and make appointment in the North and recognize the negro as often as I can."[3]

The gains of the early Roosevelt years had petered out, and more radical Black thinkers like Du Bois put much of the blame on Washington, accusing him of a "policy of non-resistance, giving up of agitation, and acquiescence in semi-serfdom."[4] But Booker doggedly defended himself and Theodore. "There is no man who has been in the Presidency since Lincoln," he wrote of Roosevelt, "who has been so deeply interested in the permanent and sensible elevation of our race."[5] The two publicly cemented their continuing relations when, a week after moving out of the White House, Roosevelt received a typewritten invitation from Washington, asking him to join the board at the Tuskegee Institute. The former president accepted.

## ON THE ROAD AGAIN

The turn of the decade amounted to a turn of the page for both men. Booker continued to hit the road regularly, but now he traveled more often to the South. There the murderous lynching spirit seemed to have cooled, though Jim Crow attitudes about Black inferiority and near complete disenfranchisement remained pervasive.

Washington visited seven Southern states in 1910 alone in travels extending from Oklahoma to Georgia. On one weeklong swing through North Carolina, practically the entire Black population came out to see him at every stop. "He was their friend and champion."[6]

*The proud head of school, posed with Tuskegee's class of 1910.*

Booker was just back from a European tour, where he had been fêted by many (including the king and queen of Denmark, with whom he dined), when he boldly returned to Wilmington and the site of the massacre a dozen years earlier. Concerns for his safety were quickly dispelled by the excited crowd of three thousand who jammed the rail station to greet the famous Dr. Washington. A police escort took him to the grand Academy of Music: White-owned and usually Whites only, it was the nicest theater in town. He was met by a standing-room crowd, with the White audience seated on one side of the theater, the Black audience on the other. On the stage, leading citizens of both races were eager to shake Booker's hand.

After a prayer, the singing of a few spirituals, and the mayor's introduction, Washington gave the audience what it came for, a ninety-minute talk about the status of Black Americans. At times he directed his talk to White people, at others to Black. He mentioned the tortured history of the town. He acknowledged, too, that no Black men were permitted to vote in Wilmington, but he leavened his message with his humorous stories.

One favorite he told concerned an aging Black man at a river ferry:

> A white man came along and said to him, "Uncle, lend me three cents to get across the river." The colored man looked at him and said: "Look here, boss, you look like a white man and I suppose you is, but I ain't going to lend you no three cents today. Let me tell you another thing, boss: the man that ain't got no money is just as well off on one side of the river as on the other."[7]

No one, Black or White, could argue with the very American notion of seeking prosperity.

A reporter traveling with Washington used the speaker's own words to sum up a long story on Booker's North Carolina tour that he wrote for *The Boston Transcript.* "If we learn to be frank with each other," Washington said, "to trust each other and cultivate love and toleration instead of hatred we will teach the world a lesson, how two races different in color can live together in peace and harmony and in friendship." As he saw his role in the South, Booker needed not only to promote Black progress in education and in fair treatment by the law but to do it by appealing to both Black and White. That message hadn't changed.

At a celebration of good things to come—the site would soon be Tuskegee's own
teaching hospital—Washington spoke to the crowd in September 1911. Seated
to his left is surgeon John A. Kenney, the new facility's medical director.

# FROM NAIROBI TO MILWAUKEE

Theodore traveled, too, departing for an African safari in March 1909. He
had been the conservation president—during his time in office, some 230
million acres of public land were set aside for national forests, monuments,
and game and bird reserves—but he had dreamed since his boyhood
cruise on the Nile of hunting the great beasts of East Africa. Accompanied
by son Kermit, he found what he wanted, shooting hundreds of animals,
including lions, elephants, rhinoceroses, hippos, zebra, giraffe, and birds of
many sorts. The trip lasted a year, during which he wrote a stream of articles for *Scribner's Magazine*, in part to defray expenses.

On his way home, he stopped in England to attend the funeral of

King Edward VII as President Taft's special emissary. But that didn't alter Roosevelt's sense on his return that Taft was not governing as he would have. Taft was sidelining Roosevelt's progressive ideas and allies. He just wasn't a fighter, which Roosevelt simply could not comprehend.

Admitting to himself, at last, how deeply he regretted not seeking another term in office, Roosevelt listened willingly to enthusiastic talk among his partisans that he ought to come out of retirement to run for president in 1912. A war might be coming—on the eve of a possible conflict, was Taft doing all that he could to be ready? In the end, he couldn't resist running against Taft, who never quite understood why Roosevelt turned on him.

The decision nearly cost Theodore his life. On October 14, 1912, Roosevelt's private Pullman car, dubbed the *Mayflower*, arrived in Milwaukee. After a catnap in a rocking chair at the Hotel Gilpatrick, he headed for the auditorium where he was to give yet another campaign speech. A crowd waiting on the sidewalk cheered as he clambered into an open automobile. In the press of the crowd, however, a stranger got close to the candidate, pulled a gun, and fired at close range. Roosevelt toppled into his seat without a word.

A tavern keeper from New York named John Schrank had been stalking Roosevelt for weeks. An aide drove the gunman to ground, disarming the would-be assassin. Meanwhile, Roosevelt rose up, calling "I'm all right, I'm all right" to the horrified crowd.

He ordered that the shooter be bought to him; holding the man's face between his hands and looking deeply into his eyes, the hunted asked the hunter, "What did you do it for?" His eyes cold and expressionless, Schrank said nothing. Roosevelt ordered his attacker be taken into police custody and that no violence be done to him.

Feeling inside his heavy overcoat, Roosevelt found and fingered a bullet hole the size of a dime in his right breast. No stranger to gunshot wounds, Roosevelt reasoned that since he tasted no blood, his lung must not have been perforated and the wound was unlikely to be fatal. Despite the stabbing pain, he insisted the speech must go on, overruling the appeals of those around him.

Once at the podium, he unbuttoned his vest, exposing his blood-stained shirt as he pulled his speech from the breast pocket of his jacket. To his surprise, as he unfolded the fifty-page sheaf of pages, he found it had been perforated by the bullet. The speech and his steel eyeglass case had saved his life. He told the ten-thousand-person crowd in and around Milwaukee Auditorium that, yes, he had been shot, "but it takes more than that to kill a bull moose."

After more than an hour at the podium, a tottering and white-as-a-sheet Roosevelt finally gave himself over to the care of doctors. With an X-ray machine at their command, the physicians at Milwaukee's hospital spied the bullet, lodged in Roosevelt's chest muscles. He would carry the slug in his chest the rest of his life.

Despite the performance—here was the hero of San Juan Hill, once more exhibiting his bravery under fire—he still lost the election three weeks later. He collected more votes than Taft, but Woodrow Wilson won 435 of the 531 electoral votes. This time Roosevelt's retirement from politics would be permanent.

# NOTHING PERSONAL

The election season of 1912 had posed a problem for Washington. Roosevelt was his friend, but the "Big Man," as he called the rotund Taft, who weighed well over three hundred pounds, was still the president. Must he choose?

Neither option had been a good one. In his several years as president, Taft had made only token Black appointments in the North. Still, Washington had promised to be Taft's private adviser, a role he had fulfilled from time to time. Plus, Roosevelt's new Progressive Party had become all White in the South after refusing to seat Black delegates at its convention. That robbed Washington of an incentive to shift his allegiance back to Roosevelt.

In the end, the Tuskegee board provided Booker with an answer to the riddle, recommending strongly he take no active part in the campaign. A trusted friend seconded the idea, too: "[I] suggest . . . you consider well before expressing a preference for either. Loyalty is a trait admired by all. No one condemns a man for being loyal to his friends. . . . It is my personal belief that neither [Taft nor Roosevelt] would seek to put you on the record. Go ahead just as you have been doing."[8]

After the election, Roosevelt held no grudge. In mid-January 1913, when he and Washington met in New York, Booker felt the need to explain in plain terms why he had withheld his endorsement. "Before I had time to give my reasons," Washington wrote to their mutual friend, Assistant Attorney General William Lewis, "he explained with the greatest emphasis that he considered my course the wisest one." Washington left the conversation with renewed respect for Roosevelt as "a bigger man than I thought he was before."[9]

In a different world, Washington might have expected an explanation from Roosevelt for his decision to run. It had backfired spectacularly—for practical purposes, he had handed the Democrats the presidency. The winner, Woodrow Wilson, had gotten roughly 6.3 million votes; between them, Roosevelt and Taft collected 7.5 million. Roosevelt's impetuous candidacy had thus put into office the former president of Princeton, a child of the South with an undeniable history of Black exclusion. During his tenure, Princeton had been the only Ivy League college to enroll no Black students, and Booker himself had had firsthand experience with Princeton's racism: When Wilson had been inducted as Princeton's president, Washington had been the only honored guest not given accommodations in a faculty house. Roosevelt's and Taft's defeats were a loss for Washington—and for the cause he championed.

When Wilson moved into the White House, William Lewis's tenure in federal office abruptly ended. Washington's access fell to zero. Despite Wilson's campaign rhetoric—"I will be president of the nation"—segregation became the rule within cabinet departments. Bathrooms shared by the races for half a century became "White" or "Colored." The number of appointed Black men in the executive fell by 85 percent, as the Wilson administration systematically removed virtually all of them from management positions, offering menial jobs or firing them altogether.

The same month Wilson became president-elect, an article bearing the byline "Booker T. Washington" had appeared in the magazine *The Century*. Its title asked a fair question: IS THE NEGRO HAVING A FAIR CHANCE? But coming from the usually cautious Washington, the directness of the language was surprising. Although he would never acknowledge the change, Washington, unhappy at Wilson's victory, took a new, aggressive tone.

The criminal justice system, the article pointed out, was not fair to Black people. Black lawyers reported that almost invariably "they do not have a fair chance before a white jury when a white lawyer is on the other side of the case." The ultimate intimidation, lynching, had not ceased altogether. Washington highlighted in *The Century* the discrimination Black Americans faced in education, hotel accommodations, and the workplace. When a new building was constructed at Howard University in Washington, D.C., he pointed out, the brick masons were all White, the hod carriers Black.

One cause of these inequalities, Booker explained, was the political structure, at the national, state, and local levels. He counted 1,300 counties in the South, each of which "is a law unto itself. The result is there are almost as many race problems as there are counties."[10]

In particular, he wrote, "what embitters the colored people" were the conditions of rail travel:

[It] is not the separation but the inadequacy of the accommodations. The colored people are given half of a baggage-car or half of a smoking-car. In most cases, the Negro portion of the car is poorly ventilated, poorly lighted, and, above all, rarely kept clean; and then to add to the colored man's discomfort, . . . White men are constantly coming into the car and almost invariably light cigars."[11]

Even his constant critic Du Bois voiced his approval of Washington's *Century* piece, noting in *The Crisis*, the official magazine of the National Association for the Advancement of Colored People (NAACP), that "Mr. Booker T. Washington has joined the ranks."[12]

*In adulthood, Booker T. Washington Jr., center, favored his father in looks; that's his younger brother, Ernest Davidson Washington, on the right.*

# THE ULRICH AFFAIR

A personal experience in Washington's own life was undoubtedly a factor in his willingness to issue an explicit critique of racial discrimination. The Ulrich case, from the previous year, had dealt his reputation a blow from which it would never fully recover.

On one of his periodic trips to New York, Booker checked into the Hotel Manhattan, an elegant accommodation once billed as the world's tallest hotel. After speaking at two churches on Sunday, March 19, 1911—one congregation was Black, the other White—he dined as was his habit at the hotel, then headed across town. His secretary had arranged a meeting with Tuskegee's auditor on West Sixty-Third Street, where the accountant was staying with friends.

On reaching the address, no one answered the bell. Booker walked up and down the block, then tried again. Still no answer. On his third attempt, a stranger confronted him. "What are you doing here? Are you breaking into my house? You have been hanging around here for four or five weeks."[13]

Before Booker could disagree, the man struck him with his fist.

Washington managed to escape the building's vestibule, his attacker in pursuit, but as he fled down the street, the man clubbed him with a heavy walking stick. Booker tripped and fell, but quickly got to his feet. When he reached the corner of Central Park West, his attacker not far behind, he encountered two passing policemen.

As the police tried to make sense of what had happened, an angry crowd gathered. Booker was bleeding from gashes on his head and a torn ear. The assailant, a big-boned German immigrant named Henry Albert Ulrich, accused Booker of loitering, trying to peer into his apartment windows, and sexually assaulting his wife. Someone in the crowd yelled that Booker had been after a pair of White women on the street.

Booker protested his innocence, but the police arrested him as a peeping Tom and took both accuser and accused to the Sixty-Eighth Street police station.

Still bleeding profusely, Booker produced identification and finally persuaded the police he was the noted Dr. Washington. He then pressed charges against Ulrich, accusing him of felonious assault. Released from custody, Booker got treatment at a nearby hospital, where sixteen stitches were required to close his wounds. He went back to the Hotel Manhattan, his head swathed in gauze, but a prolonged drama had just begun, one that would provide fodder for the newspapers, both respectable and not, for months to come.

Separating truth from fiction would only grow harder. The morning-after papers reported Ulrich's allegations that Washington had been intoxicated, leered at Mrs. Ulrich, and greeted her with "Hello, sweetheart." After calling the accountant's home, a reporter disputed Washington's version of the story, saying the auditor was actually at Tuskegee.

Later accusations would suggest Washington had been in the neighborhood to visit a prostitute. There would be a trial at which Washington testified before a jammed courtroom. Friends rallied, among them President Taft, who weighed in with a widely published letter insisting upon Washington's integrity and morality. Roosevelt wrote to express his indignation at the "utterly wanton" assault.[14]

Facts about the Ulriches emerged. The woman Washington had allegedly been pursuing wasn't Ulrich's wife at all; he had a wife in New Jersey and was leading a double life. Ulrich also had a criminal record, but he would be acquitted in the November trial for assault, based on the finding that his "vicious motive" had not been proven beyond a reasonable doubt.

The experience was one long trauma for Booker, a man whose life had never before been touched by scandal. The saga had made the front pages not only in New York but across the country. In the end, many people were left pondering, as one Indiana newspaper did, that "The real mystery is found in the fact that a man of Booker Washington's wisdom, knowing the prejudice against his race, would have sought a friend in strange quarters at a late hour of night."[15]

*Three generations of Washingtons.*

## LIFE STUDIES

As they approached age sixty, both men remained busy. Each looked back: Booker's updated life story, *My Larger Education*, appeared in 1911. Theodore's *An Autobiography* followed, coming off the presses in 1913.

At first, the out-of-office Roosevelt spent more time than he ever had at his Long Island, New York, home, Sagamore Hill. But his urge to travel resurfaced, and he took a trip with sons Archie and Quentin to the American Southwest, hunting and touring such sights as the Grand

Canyon. He followed with a dangerous map-making venture deep into the heart of the Brazilian wilderness. He fell gravely ill on that trip, barely making it home alive, in April 1914.

The demands of Booker's years of constant travels were taking a cumulative toll on him, too. He looked older than he was and suffered from digestive complaints, which he treated with Bell's papayan tablets, a remedy made of unripe papayas. For a time, he drank radium water, but none of the medicaments resolved his stomach pains, headaches, or other complaints.

For both men, what was even harder to accept than time's toll was the fact that neither remained at the center of the national conversation. The NAACP, with Du Bois's finely crafted essays in the pages of *The Crisis*, was driving the conversation regarding race. Roosevelt had become a former president, a role with little relevance to current events, and his failed 1912 campaign had alienated many old Republican allies.

In 1915, race hatred surfaced in a new way when *The Birth of a Nation* opened. Directed by D. W. Griffith, the silent film was a landmark, a twelve-reel epic filled with technical innovations and accompanied by an elaborate score for full orchestra. Based on a novel, *The Clansman*, the movie was, in effect, a white supremacist tract, recounting the history of the Civil War and Reconstruction era through the story of two families, one from the North, the other Southern. The movie made villains of unintelligent and oversexed Black characters, who were portrayed as a danger to democracy and American womanhood. Among the film's heroes were Ku Klux Klansmen.

*The Birth of a Nation* met with protests in Boston and boycotts in other cities. Washington hoped it would be banned altogether in the South because of its potential to stir up racial violence, but that proved to be wishful thinking. In Atlanta the streets near the theater where *The Birth of a Nation* was shown filled with men on horseback wearing Klan regalia. Moved by a scene in which a lustful Black soldier chases a White girl, a crowd in Houston, Texas, jumped to its feet yelling, "Lynch him! Lynch him!" The movie's box office gross broke all records.

The attitude toward Black citizens was as bad in Washington, D.C., where *The Birth of a Nation* would be the first film ever screened in the White House, on February 18, 1915. Woodrow Wilson declared it a triumph. "It's like writing history with lightning," the president said. "My only regret is that it is all so terribly true."[16]

# CHAPTER TWENTY-TWO

# ROAD'S END

Theodore Roosevelt and Booker T. Washington were the two greatest men of their time in the white and black races.

CHARLES W. ANDERSON

I n autumn 1915, Booker fell dangerously ill. In addition to his chronic indigestion and headaches, he now had the symptoms of diabetes, including unquenchable thirst, frequent urination, cold feet, fatigue, and blurred vision. His Chicago physician proposed a trip to Minnesota to consult the Mayo brothers, famed for their diagnostic genius. But in late October, in New York, that suddenly seemed impossible.

Just back from an event at Yale, Washington was on the verge of collapse. At the insistence of New York friends, he consulted a well-regarded Manhattan physician, who returned a diagnosis. Booker's kidneys were failing—Bright's disease, the doctor called it—and he could offer no answers beyond extended bed rest. Booker sent word for Margaret to come to New York.

Although close colleagues had for years been urging him to halt his ceaseless travels, his poor health had remained a well-kept secret. Soon, however, rumors that the famous man was seriously ill leaked out, and Booker's loose-lipped physician talked to reporters about his patient's condition. "There is a noticeable hardening of the arteries," he told them, adding "racial characteristics are, I think, in part responsible for Dr. Washington's breakdown."[1] This news was soon reported in other papers, and many readers read between the lines. His symptoms, when considered in light of the racist assumption that all Black men were oversexed, led to the conclusion that the Wizard had advanced syphilis.

By the time Margaret reached New York, Booker had been admitted to the Rockefeller Hospital where, out of thoroughness, a Wasserman test had ruled out syphilis. His problem, though not well understood at the time, was malignant hypertension; had his doctors been able to lower his blood pressure, they might have saved his life. But Margaret was greeted on arrival with a hard-to-hear prognosis: Her husband had only days to live.

Booker wanted to go home. Over the years, he had told many audiences, "I was born in the South, have lived all my life in the South, and

*Booker Washington in the last year of his life.*

289

expect to die and be buried in the South." He could remain in New York and get the best care available in one of the nation's best hospitals. But he would be true to his word. Despite warnings from his doctors that he might not survive the journey, Booker, accompanied by Margaret, boarded a train as daylight faded on Friday afternoon, November 12.

The trip was a long one, involving station changes in multiple cities; for Booker, it was an effort of will to return to the place he had made, the institution he had created from next to nothing. The last leg of the train trip on late Saturday night brought the travelers to within five miles of Tuskegee. From there an ambulance carried Washington home, and just after midnight the dying man was helped into his own bed in the Oaks, the spacious redbrick, Queen Anne–style president's house at the Tuskegee Institute.

Booker Taliaferro Washington, age fifty-nine, would die at 4:45 A.M. on November 14, 1915.

The *New York Times* obituary—it ran dead center on Monday's front page—quoted an old ally of the deceased. On being informed of Washington's death, Theodore had told the *Times*:

> I am deeply shocked and grieved at the death of Dr. Washington. He was one of the distinguished citizens of the United States, a man who rendered greater service to his race than had ever been rendered by any one else, and who, in so doing, also rendered great service to the whole country. I mourn his loss, and feel that one of the most useful citizens of our land has gone.[2]

## "A GREAT MAN HAS FALLEN"

John D. Rockefeller Sr., the richest man in the world, sent Margaret Washington a condolence note saying that her late husband had "rendered invaluable services to his race in a life devoted to their uplift, and he was most highly appreciated by multitudes of the best people in the land." Boston Mayor James Curley intoned, "[Washington] served his race with ability and fidelity unsurpassed in present American history."

Churchmen, scholars, and writers, Black and White, praised him. In a telegram, former president Taft called Washington "one of the most powerful forces for the proper settlement of the race question that has appeared in his generation." He was the "greatest member of his race since the Egyptian Kings," one friend said; another warned "the human race will feel the loss." According to Harvard's pioneering psychologist William James, Washington's death was "a National Calamity." Alabama's governor declared that "[no] man since the Civil War did more to create harmonious relations between the races."[3]

Washington's open casket lay in state in the Tuskegee chapel on Tuesday, and nearly twenty thousand mourners filed by to pay their respects. At his funeral the next day, his six-sided casket sat amid a sea of flowers, which had more than filled two rail cars. Some four thousand people squeezed into the chapel, while several thousand others remained outside. Hymns and spirituals accompanied the simple burial service of prayers and readings from scripture. Many in the crowd cried freely. He was a man that many felt they knew despite never having shaken his hand; countless families had a framed likeness of the Wizard of Tuskegee hanging over the hearth.[4]

A day of public eulogies came a month later, on December 11, when a distinguished band of Booker's friends and admirers spoke at the chapel. Invited to be the keynote speaker, Theodore returned to Tuskegee to offer homage to his friend, observing that "a genius such as he does not arise in a generation."[5] Once again, the place was packed, this time with many mourners from the North who had traveled the great distance to rural Alabama.

As a member of the Tuskegee board, Roosevelt consulted with the other trustees to select a new president, looking to ensure the survival of the institution. When Tuskegee solicited contributions to a memorial fund in the founder's honor, more than a million dollars rolled in, including donations from more than twelve thousand Black Americans.

A biography was also in the works, its preparers Emmett Scott, Washington's trusted secretary, and Mr. Lyman Beecher Stowe, grandson of Harriet Beecher Stowe. Work on the book had begun with Washington's approval some months before, and no doubt he would have been pleased at the man the Tuskegeans invited to write its preface. Roosevelt's opening words were, "It is not hyperbole to say that Booker T. Washington was a great American."[6]

*Booker's coffin lying in state in Tuskegee. The town—and the nation—mourned the passing of the man* The New York Times *described as "the foremost leader and teacher of the negro race."*

. . .

ONE MAN WHO did not travel to Tuskegee for the memorial service was W. E. B. Du Bois. He did compose an obituary for Booker, which he published in his magazine, *The Crisis.*

He began with admiring words:

> The death of Mr. Washington marks an epoch in the history of America. He was the greatest Negro leader since Frederick Douglass, and the most distinguished man, white or black, to come out of the South since the Civil War.

But he who giveth can also taketh away. Du Bois continued:

> On the other hand, in stern justice, we must lay on the soul of this man, a heavy responsibility for the consummation of Negro disfranchisement, the decline of the Negro college and public school and the firm establishment of color caste in this land.[7]

This harsh critique was a continuation of what Du Bois and other Northern Black intellectuals had been saying for years. Men like William Trotter, editor of *The Guardian*, had called Washington "the Benedict Arnold of the Negro race" and "the Great Traitor."[8] Unknown to them, however, Washington hadn't been quite so obedient to White men as it appeared.

Even as his public life earned him fame, Washington had led a shadow existence over many years, quietly fighting limitations imposed on the civil rights of African Americans. Without the knowledge of all but his closest confidants, he raised money to pay legal fees in the late 1890s to fight the so-called grandfather clause in Louisiana, which disenfranchised many formerly enslaved people and their descendants.* A few years later he fought similar changes in Alabama law. He quietly backed court battles against the Pullman car company for their separate-and-unequal treatment of Black passengers in Tennessee, Georgia, and Virginia. These legal suits—pursued by Du Bois, among others—were often lost, but not for lack of trying on Booker's part. He went so far as to write directly to Robert Todd Lincoln, son of Abraham and president of the Pullman Company, asking that the executive intervene on behalf of Black passengers. (Lincoln's response had been to do nothing.)

In the case of an Alabama farm worker named Alonzo Bailey, Washington's intervention had mattered. Indebted to a farmer for a loan of twenty dollars, Bailey was imprisoned under the state's peonage statute. With Washington's lobbying and underwriting, the case eventually reached the Supreme Court and, in 1911, the state peonage laws had been declared unconstitutional as slavery in all but name.[9]

If Du Bois's crude dismissal of Washington in *The Crisis* seems incomplete, the contrast between the two men is important. Du Bois, the young international intellectual and scholar, had remade himself as an activist; he did it in reaction to Washington, defining himself, in a sense, as the "not Booker." In the face Jim Crow hostility, cruelty, and violence, Washington's preaching about education and economic success had begun to seem insufficient to Dr. Du Bois; he thought Washington's bargaining with Southern Whites a hypocritical failure. Du Bois and the NAACP decided to fight in a way that Washington would never be willing—or able—to do. And yet, as Washington's *Century* piece made clear, their approaches grew closer in Washington's last years as he became more forthright. He no longer spoke of the "Negro Problem";

---

* An 1898 revision to the Louisiana constitution exempted anyone seeking to vote from taking a required constitutional test if he, his father, or grandfather had voted prior to 1867. It was a transparent—and effective—means of disenfranchising Black voters.

instead, he used the term "the *so-called* Negro Problem." He liked to say that "freedom is not a bequest but a conquest," an idea that Du Bois embraced.[10]

Booker resented deeply the encroachment of Du Bois and company on his power as the Black man's chief spokesman. He knew their audiences differed—Du Bois was little known to White audiences—but among the Black leadership, people increasingly listened to the younger man. Booker did everything he could to blunt his influence, using the well-established Tuskegee machine to quietly underwrite opposing newspapers and influence writers.

In the end, their differences came down to Du Bois's vision of himself as a Black man first, an American second; Washington's polarities were reversed. Du Bois was a man of ideas, a dreamer—as distinct from Washington, the pragmatic realist. Washington was a practical man with reasonable goals; Du Bois had the sensibility of a poet and high aspirations that were unrealistic in parts of Jim Crow America. Washington was also anchored to an institution, one that was firmly rooted in the South, while Du Bois had no Tuskegee to defend.

W. E. B. Du Bois lived a long life, dying almost half a century after Booker Washington, in 1963, in the newly independent African nation of Ghana. His longevity meant he helped shape how the next two generations saw Booker's legacy. He also lived to see how the Supreme Court decision in *Brown v. Board of Education* changed the education landscape, ending the separate but equal doctrine. He lived to witness the emergence of a charismatic leader named Martin Luther King, a man who merged the radicalism of Du Bois and the fame of Washington. Looking back today at Black history, Booker Washington stands shoulder to shoulder with Frederick Douglass, whom he knew; with Du Bois, with whom he wrestled; and with King, who embodied the best of the three who came before.

Theodore Roosevelt and Du Bois would meet just once, on November

2, 1918, when Du Bois introduced Roosevelt at Carnegie Hall. Ironically, his speech that evening would be Roosevelt's last.

# T.R.: R.I.P.

Theodore outlived Booker by three years, during which Roosevelt struggled to adjust to his diminishing status. He would have liked to run for president in 1916—Woodrow Wilson's governance made him crazy—but there was no path for him to the nomination.

When the United States joined the sprawling European war, in 1917, Roosevelt wanted to get back in uniform and perhaps even head to the front. He managed to arrange a meeting with Wilson to pitch the idea of raising a division, but neither Wilson nor the War Department saw a place in their command for the fearlessly independent Roosevelt.

He did, however, get all four of his sons into uniform. In the end, that brought him profound sadness: His youngest son, Quentin, an airman,

*Theodore and Edith Roosevelt, 1917. He would die one year later, at just sixty years of age, but she would live on, cherishing his memory, until 1948, when she died at age eighty-seven.*

would die in aerial combat over France, in 1918. The father never got over the young man's death at just twenty years of age.

As the year 1918 wore on, Theodore faced a series of health challenges. The jungle fever from his Amazon trip returned. He needed surgery to correct a leg injury that had never properly healed. In October, after being diagnosed with inflammatory rheumatism, he told Kermit, "I am glad to be sixty for it gives me the right to be . . . as old as I feel."[11]

Barely two months later, on January 5, 1919, he spent a long day at his desk, writing and editing; to the end, he was a prolific writer and serious historian, having served a term as president of the American Historical Association. As he prepared to go to bed that night, Theodore complained to Edith of an odd feeling that his heart or perhaps his breathing might stop. "I know it is not going to happen," he assured her, "but it is such a strange feeling."[12] But happen it did, at 4:15 A.M., when a coronary embolism killed Teddy in his sleep.

Laid to rest four days later in Oyster Bay, he was mourned as a war hero for his role in the Spanish–American War; as a president who busted trusts; as a foreign policy visionary who saw a new, international role for his country. He was a Nobel Prize winner, an award he was given in 1906 for his central role in negotiating an end to the Russo-Japanese War. To his fellow citizens and the world at large, the bespectacled Roosevelt had been for a decade the man who defined American dynamism. That he was a larger-than-life character was reinforced a half dozen years later when a sculptor named Gutzon Borglum began carving his likeness onto the immense granite face of a mountain in South Dakota. He shared that space with just three other American giants, Washington, Jefferson, and Lincoln.

# POSTMORTEM

The only wise and honorable and Christian thing to do is to treat each black man and each white man strictly on his merits as a man.

THEODORE ROOSEVELT, NOVEMBER 8, 1901

This book has revisited the lives of two men. They shared a surprising number of life facts, despite upbringings at opposite ends of the economic and social spectrum. Both had lofty goals from childhood. Each man suffered the death of his first wife. They emerged as national leaders. Both worshipped Abraham Lincoln. Each, in the best way he knew how, confronted the awful face of American racism.

They became members of a two-man mutual admiration society. Booker seems never to have been critical of his friend, while Theodore repeatedly praised Washington.

Roosevelt initiated what he hoped would be a confidential relationship because he wanted Booker's advice. His motives were partly political, but Theodore was also a man preoccupied with doing the right thing. When he saw the deplorable living conditions of the poor in a New York tenement, he set out to improve their circumstances. Having watched the rich get richer in the late nineteenth century, he looked to use his power as president to turn the tide away from corporate dominance and toward income equality and fairness. A "square deal," he called it, for average people.

Roosevelt looked back upon slavery as morally indefensible and "the South's persistence in its wickedness and folly" as the cause of the terrible war in which brother had killed brother.[1] He decried the resurgence in blind racism against Black citizens, seeing it as a threat to social order and a functioning society. He recognized the fundamental unfairness with which the Black American was treated, especially in the South. Echoing the thinking of Frederick Douglass, he worried that lynching and other violence damaged the White man as well as the Black man.

For his part, Washington saw in a Roosevelt connection the pathway to change. Washington wanted to advance his cause in every way he could; Roosevelt trusted the man he came to call his friend to help him find people who would act in the best interests of the people of the entire country. That gave Washington the chance to place not only talented Black people but also fair-minded White ones into positions of authority in the South.

Booker's influence on Theodore is impossible to quantify. Equality was never a core belief for Roosevelt. He was a Darwinist who thought mankind, White and Black, was evolving. He once wrote that the English people, after removing their king in the seventeenth century, "were not yet fit to govern themselves." That ability, he went on, "comes to a race only through the slow growth of centuries."[2] Thus, he could not and did not expect unsophisticated, poorly educated Black citizens to master the skill of governance when they were "just emerging from conditions of life which our ancestors left behind them."[3] But he was open to halfway ideas like "racial equipotentiality" and "gradualism." He hoped that by proper training, the formerly enslaved and their children might "enter into the possession of true freedom."[4]

In Booker T. Washington, however, he saw an exceptional man. Dr. Washington had created the Tuskegee Institute; he had won the trust of some of the richest and most powerful men in the world. Over the decades, Washington spoke to millions, Black and White. By the force of his personality, Booker won them—and Theodore—over to his cause.

If Roosevelt brought empathy to the circumstances of America's Black citizens, Washington more than matched it with hope. Together they shaped a highly unusual collaboration that lasted beyond Roosevelt's time in office. They could not reverse generations of racism and racist policy, but they challenged the assumptions of their fellow Americans and got Black men appointed to historically unprecedented positions of power. Although their joint victories had been limited, Roosevelt's very public recognition of Washington, brief and compromised though it was, affirmed Washington's status as the most essential spokesman of their era for Black America.

# MEN OF THEIR TIME

The usually savvy Roosevelt underestimated the risks of a liaison with a Black man. He was dumbfounded when the aftermath of a quiet family dinner at the White House became a storm with winds that blew for years. Talk of the dinner surfaced again after Washington's death when some obituary writers varied the facts, soft-pedaling their meal as an informal lunch, as if to lessen what many Southerners still saw as a Roosevelt affront to all White people. On the other hand, the *Genesee* [NY] *Republican* took a braver stance, writing that Theodore's invitation to

Booker Washington was "a recognition of the position which the educator held in the advancement of a large part of the population of the nation."[5]

In the days after Booker's death, Roosevelt got a letter from a Massachusetts Republican who was writing a book about the former president. In his reply, Theodore complained about the hysterical response more than a dozen years before. "On any rational theory of public and social life my action was absolutely proper," he observed. But he went on to offer an admission: "What I did was a mistake."

> It was misinterpreted by the white men of the South and by the black men of the South; and in the North it had no effect, for good or bad. It was one of those cases where the application of a lofty and proper code of social observance to conditions which in actual fact were certain to cause the action to be misunderstood resulted badly.[6]

Like a child who touches a hot burner, he pulled back his hand—Roosevelt never again invited Washington, or any other Black man, to take a seat at his dining table on Pennsylvania Avenue. He was forced to pause, to rethink, and as one Mississippian put it late in the Roosevelt administration, to pay for the episode of the White House dinner since it "tinged for the South every subsequent act of his in which the Negro was concerned."[7] We can only guess the extent to which Roosevelt remembered the dinner backlash when he made his impatient and infamous call regarding the Brownsville Buffalo Soldiers. But the Brownsville decision is remembered by history as racist and wrong, and Sam Clemens thought it was a cynical do-over for the dinner.

Washington, too, was forced to proceed with caution after the fact as he and Roosevelt became friends. As Booker explained to his secretary at Tuskegee a few months following the White House dinner, "I want to help [the president] and the race if I can, but at the same time I must be careful not to injure our institution."[8]

In the immediate aftermath of the dinner debacle, Roosevelt continued to believe those Black men with the "capacity" should "share in the political work of the country." He defended men and women of color like Dr. Crum, Mrs. Cox, and William Lewis.[9] Yet the Roosevelt-Washington collaboration and the Booker and Theodore friendship were surely stunted by the public furor and wave of hate produced by their 1901 dinner date.

The Roosevelt-Washington connection lives in the American memory. When the nation elected Barack Obama in 2008, thereby fulfilling a prediction Booker Washington had made that a Black man would one day become president, Obama's opponent in the race, John McCain, reminded the world of the controversial dinner. In his generous concession speech, the Arizona senator and war hero recalled the evening back in 1901 that had provoked "outrage in many quarters." McCain then pointed out proudly that "America today is a world away from the cruel and prideful bigotry of that time. There is no better evidence of this than the election of an African American to the presidency of the United States. Let there be no reason now for any American to fail to cherish their citizenship in this, the greatest nation on earth."[10] As Obama prepared to take office—a Black man would be not a guest at the White House but its host—opinion makers mused that the nation was finally transitioning to a post-racial society. Remarkable progress had been made.

Today we know the picture was and remains more complicated. Yet, as I look back at where America has been and how far we have come, I see continued progress at closing racial gaps and admire the heroes who got us this far.

Roosevelt is remembered as a great president. He gave government a fresh new conscience, modeling for his younger cousin Franklin Delano

Roosevelt how the machinery of government could be wielded for the good of all. As for Washington, his many accomplishments—at Tuskegee, as a spokesman for his race, as a leader of all men—were immense, even if he felt constrained in how directly he could confront racism on the national stage because, in a very real sense, he was fighting from behind enemy lines. Perhaps, then, he is best judged by his own words. As a very young man, he defined a successful life as one "spent in the cause of truth and virtue, by the number of men made better for our having lived in the world."[11] By that standard, he was indeed a great man.

No one is perfect; nor is any friendship. Yet Booker and Theodore were men of virtue, men who worked together in good faith to do good, to live up to Lincoln's ambitions for a "more perfect union." They were the right men for their moment even if, at times, their efforts misfired— the great make mistakes, too. But Booker T. and Teddy had vision. They had drive. And their skins were tough enough that they drove forward even in the face of often vicious criticism. We are a better nation because they chose to fight; they would not settle, recognizing that progress is always a battle.

Today America is the most successful multicultural nation in the world, but that does not mean the quest for true equality is over. We cannot stop: we must always move forward. We'll never be perfect, but what makes America great is that we will always try to be.

# ACKNOWLEDGMENTS

I am thrilled to take this moment to thank the many people who made valuable contributions to the idea, execution, and promotion of this book. First off, thanks to Rupert Murdoch, executive chairman and CEO of Fox Corporation; Lachlan Murdoch, Fox CEO; Suzanne Scott, president; and Executive Editor Jay Wallace for supporting not just this book but all my history books, and for the opportunity to produce a special for Fox News and Fox Nation. This allows me to bring these words to life and give these great men the spotlight they deserve. It's more important than ever to have context regarding race in America and to salute the men who sacrificed so much to make our country the land of the free.

A salute to Fox Nation's great executives Jason Klarman, John Finley, and Jennifer Hegseth for allowing me to walk in the footsteps of these iconic figures in between covering news in this ever-changing world. I can't say enough about Carrie Flatley, Rob Monoco, Monica Mari, Salvatore Foglio, John Case, and Mary Drabich for capturing the essence of the story and producing an incredible special.

Adrian Zackheim and Bria Sandford, you are the publishing world's All-Pro executives. Adrian, let the record show that you came up with the simple but brilliant subtitle, while Bria ushered the entire project from concept to completion. I also want to thank the people fighting to keep Booker T. Washington's and Teddy Roosevelt's stories alive, and who were open and honest about these icons. First, Tweed Roosevelt, great-grandson of Teddy, gave me great encouragement and feedback on the concept of this project. Historian Douglas Brinkley: If there is anyone who knows more about T.R., I have not met them yet. On the Booker T. side: Thonnia Lee coordinated my Tuskegee on-campus access, and I can't thank her enough for believing we were worthy of telling the unparalleled story of the man and the school. Dana Chandler seems to me to be one of the most dedicated and talented archivists in the country, and the photos and documents brought Booker T. to life in a way I didn't think possible. Dr. Kwesi Daniels's passion for the university and talent for these historical topics left my entire team in awe. Dr. William Ndi's global perspective and knowledge of not only Booker T. but the role he played in the Roosevelt administration really helped us tell the story. Thanks to you all!

Thanks to the brilliant folks on the editorial, publicity, and marketing teams at Sentinel: Mary Kate Rogers and Kristin Berndt for setting up the promotion and marketing plan and Megan Wenerstrom for hunting down photos and researching and gathering permissions. Thanks to Jason Howerton for coordinating the social media pre- and post-publish push and Lexi Smilow for contributing and coordinating daily.

With me daily and supporting me constantly are the teams of *Fox and Friends*, *One Nation*, and the nationally syndicated radio show *The Brian Kilmeade Show*, all on the world's best news network, Fox News. Thanks to Lauren Petterson; her leadership and loyalty is never taken for granted. Leading the way in the mornings is VP Gavin Hadden; Executive Producer Tami Radabaugh; Senior Producers Sara Sonneck, Kelly Nish, Rachel Rae, and Anthony Rocchio; "Get it Done Guy" AJ Hall; world's best package producer Megan Macdonald; and stellar field producer Samantha Hoenig. Without their guidance and dedication, I would never have been able to launch seven bestsellers and coordinate national book tours while still appearing every morning on *Friends*. Speaking of resourceful and helpful, the renowned radio team of Alyson Mansfield, Eric Albein, and Pete Caterina are, as Tina Turner would sing, "Simply the best." Executives who keep us growing and innovating on the audio side include Rey Erney, John Sylvester, Maria Donovan, and William Sanchez. For inspiring all our affiliates about this book tour, thanks to Tamara Karcev and Dave Manning. Endless thanks to the stellar team producing Saturday night's *One Nation*, headed up by VP Megan Albano, Executive Producer Desire Dunn, Daniele Spindler, Taylor Walters, Joey Wannet, and Krystal Shull and Alyson Mansfield. On air with me and supporting me in everything are fellow anchors Ainsley Earhardt, Steve Doocy, Janice Dean, Pete Hegseth, Will Cain, Lawrence Jones, Carly Schimkus, Todd Pirro, Ashley Strohmier, and the fiery yet friendly Rachel Campos Duffy. They all have one thing in common—every member of every show loves this country, lives a patriotic life, and wants to make sure our story is told the right way. I am fortunate that they all believe this book furthers our nation's collective cause. Thanks to you all!

New in the quest to keep America's history alive are stage shows. Thus far, we've produced eight remarkable American stories in front of live audiences thanks to my talented cohort and lifetime friends Rick Fatscher and Patrick O'Rourke. Rick and Pat succeed in making every show wildly entertaining and educational. Can't wait to add Teddy and Booker T. to the roster!

For coordinating the book and all of these entities, and for sacrificing countless family time for me, eternal thanks to the irreplaceable Alyson Mansfield. She goes above and beyond her job description every day and I can't thank her enough for doing so.

Of course, no acknowledgment would be complete without expressing my love and thankfulness for my hall-of-fame nuclear family: my wife, Dawn, Bryan, Kirstyn, and Kaitlyn. Don't know how I got so lucky!

Finally, I'd like to thank UTA super-agents Adam Leibner, Jerry Silbowitz, and Byrd Leavell for making all of the moving parts work in sync on a daily basis, and Jay Sures for forming the best agency in the country and putting me on the roster.

# FOR FURTHER READING

Adeleke, Tunde, ed. *Booker T. Washington: Interpretive Essays.* Lewiston, NY: E. Mellen Press, 1998.

Allen, Thomas. "Intelligence in the Civil War." Central Intelligence Agency, Office of Public Affairs. Undated. https://irp.fas.org/cia/product/civilwar.pdf.

Andrews, Avery Delano. "Theodore Roosevelt as Police Commissioner." *The New-York Historical Society Quarterly* 42, no. 2 (April 1958), pp. 117–41.

Baker, Ray Stannard. *American Chronicle.* New York: Charles Scribner's Sons, 1945.

_____. *Following the Color Line: An Account of Negro Citizenship in the American Democracy.* Williamstown, MA: Corner House, 1973.

Bieze, Michael Scott, and Marybeth Gasman, eds. *Booker T. Washington Rediscovered.* Baltimore, MD: Johns Hopkins University Press, 2012.

Brands, H. W. *Theodore Roosevelt: The Last Romantic.* New York: Basic Books, 1997.

Brundage, W. Fitzhugh. *Booker T. Washington and Black Progress: Up from Slavery 100 Years Later.* Gainesville: University Press of Florida, 2003.

Cecelski, David S., and Timothy B. Tyson, eds., *Democracy Betrayed: The Wilmington Race Riot of 1898 and Its Legacy.* Chapel Hill: University of North Carolina Press, 1998.

Davis, Deborah. *Guest of Honor: Booker T. Washington, Theodore Roosevelt, and the White House Dinner That Shocked a Nation.* New York: Atria Books, 2012.

Delaney, Norman C. "The End of the *Alabama.*" *American Heritage* 23, no. 3 (April 1972), pp. 58–69, 197.

Du Bois, W[illiam]. E[dward]. B[urghardt]. *The Oxford W. E. B. Du Bois Reader.* New York: Oxford University Press, 1996.

Dyer, Thomas G. *Theodore Roosevelt and the Idea of Race.* Baton Rouge: LSU Press, 1980.

Gatewood, Willard B., Jr. "Booker T. Washington and the Ulrich Affair." *Journal of Negro History* 55, no. 1 (January 1970), pp. 286–302.

———. "Negro Troops in Florida, 1898." *Florida Historical Quarterly* 49, no. 1 (July 1970), pp. 1–15.

———. *"Smoked Yankees" and the Struggle for Empire: Letters from Negro Soldiers, 1898–1902.* Urbana: University of Illinois Press, 1971.

———. *Theodore Roosevelt and the Art of Controversy: Episodes of the White House Years.* Baton Rouge: Louisiana State University Press, 1970.

———. "Theodore Roosevelt and the Indianola Affair." *Journal of Negro History* 53, no. 1 (January 1968), pp. 48–69.

———. "William D. Crum: A Negro in Politics." *Journal of Negro History* 52, no. 4 (October 1968), pp. 301–20.

Gompers, Samuel. *Seventy Years of Life and Labour: An Autobiography.* London: Hurst & Blackett, 1925.

Goodwin, Doris Kearns. *The Bully Pulpit: Theodore Roosevelt, William Howard Taft, and the Golden Age of Journalism.* New York: Simon & Schuster, 2013.

Gosnell, Harold F. *Boss Platt and His New York Machine.* Chicago, IL: University of Chicago Press, 1924.

Grantham, Dewey W., Jr. "Dinner at the White House: Theodore Roosevelt, Booker T. Washington, and the South." *Tennessee Historical Quarterly* 17, no. 2 (June 1958), pp. 112–30.

Grondahl, Paul. *I Rose Like a Rocket: The Political Education of Theodore Roosevelt.* New York: Free Press, 2004.

Hagedorn, Hermann. *Roosevelt in the Bad Lands.* Boston, MA: Houghton Mifflin Co., 1921.

Halloran, Matthew F. *The Romance of the Merit System: Forty-Five Years' Reminiscences of the Civil Service.* Washington, D.C.: Judd & Detweiler, 1929.

Hamilton, Kenneth M. *Booker T. Washington in American Memory.* Urbana, Il: University of Illinois Press, 2017.

Harlan, Louis R. *Booker T. Washington: The Making of a Black Leader.* New York: Oxford University Press, 1972.

———. *Booker T. Washington: The Wizard of Tuskegee.* New York: Oxford University Press, 1983.

———. "The Secret Life of Booker T. Washington." *Journal of Southern History* 37, no. 3 (August 1971), pp. 393–416.

Harlan, Louis R., and Pete Daniel. "A Dark and Stormy Night in the Life of Booker T. Washington." *Negro History Bulletin* 33, no. 7 (November 1970), pp. 159–61.

Hoffer, William James Hull. *Plessy v. Ferguson: Race and Inequality in Jim Crow America.* Lawrence: University Press of Kansas, 2012.

Johnson, Edward A. *History of Negro Soldiers in the Spanish–American War.* Raleigh, NC: Capital Publishing Co., 1899.

Karsten, Peter. "The Nature of 'Influence': Roosevelt, Mahan and the Concept of Sea Power." *American Quarterly* 23, no. 4 (October 1971), pp. 585–600.

Kinzer, Stephen. *The True Flag: Theodore Roosevelt, Mark Twain, and the Birth of American Empire.* New York: Holt, 2017.

Long, John Davis. *America of Yesterday.* Boston, MA: Atlantic Monthly Press, 1923.

Lord, Nathalie. "Booker Washington's Schools Days at Hampton." *Southern Workman* 31 (May 1902), pp. 255–59.

Mahan, Alfred Thayer. *The Influence of Sea Power Upon History, 1660–1783.* Boston: Little, Brown, 1890.

Malin, James C. "Roosevelt and the Elections of 1884 and 1888." *Mississippi Valley Historical Review* 14, no. 1 (June 1927), pp. 25–38.

Manning, Marable. *W. E. B. Du Bois: Black Radical Democrat.* New York: Routledge, 2005.

Marshall, Edward. *The Story of the Rough Riders, 1st U.S. Volunteer Cavalry.* New York: G. W. Dillingham, 1899.

McCullough, David. *Mornings on Horseback.* New York: Simon & Schuster, 1981.

McFarland, Philip. *Mark Twain and the Colonel: Samuel L. Clemens, Theodore Roosevelt, and the Arrival of a New Century.* Lanham, MD: Rowman & Littlefield, 2012.

Miller, Nathan. *Theodore Roosevelt: A Life.* New York: William Morrow, 1992.

Morison, Elting E., ed. *The Letters of Theodore Roosevelt.* 8 vols. Cambridge, MA: Harvard University Press, 1951–1954.

Morris, Edmund. *Colonel Roosevelt.* New York: Random House, 2010.

———. *The Rise of Theodore Roosevelt.* New York: Coward, McCann, and Geoghegan, 1979.

———. *Theodore Rex.* New York: Random House, 2001.

Norrell, Robert J. "Booker T. Washington: Understanding the Sage of Tuskegee." *Journal of Blacks in Higher Education* no. 42 (Winter 2003–2004), pp. 96–109.

———. *Up from History: The Life of Booker T. Washington.* Cambridge, MA: Harvard University Press, 2009.

Pringle, Henry F. "Roosevelt and the South." *Virginia Quarterly Review* 9, no. 1 (January 1933), pp. 14–25.

———. *Theodore Roosevelt.* New York: Harcourt, Brace, 1931.

Putnam, Carleton. *Theodore Roosevelt: The Formative Years, 1858–1886.* New York: Scribner's, 1958.

Rauchway, Eric. *Murdering McKinley: The Making of Theodore Roosevelt's America.* New York: Hill and Wang, 2003.

Riis, Jacob A. *Theodore Roosevelt, The Citizen.* New York: Macmillan, 1912.

Risen, Clay. *The Crowded Hour: Theodore Roosevelt, the Rough Riders, and the Dawn of the American Century.* New York: Scribner, 2019.

Robinson, Corinne Roosevelt. *My Brother Theodore Roosevelt.* New York: Scribner's, 1921.

Rogers, William Warren, Sr., and Robert David Ward. *August Reckoning: Jack Turner and Racism in Post–Civil War Alabama.* Tuscaloosa: University of Alabama Press, 2004.

Roosevelt, Theodore. *An Autobiography.* New York: Da Capo Press, 1913.

————. *The Naval War of 1812.* New York: G. P. Putnam's Sons, 1882.

————. *The Rough Riders.* New York: Scribner's, 1899.

————. *Theodore Roosevelt's Diaries of Boyhood and Youth.* New York: Charles Scribner's Sons, 1928.

Samuels, Peggy, and Harold Samuels. *Remembering the* Maine. Washington, D.C.: Smithsonian Institution Press, 1995.

Scott, Emmett J. "Twenty Years After: An Appraisal of Booker T. Washington." *Negro Journal of Education* 5, no. 4 (October 1936), pp. 543–54.

Scott, Emmett J., and Lyman B. Stowe. *Booker T. Washington: Builder of a Civilization.* Garden City, NY: Doubleday, 1916.

Seale, William. *The President's House: A History.* 2nd ed. 2 vols. Baltimore, MD: Johns Hopkins University Press, 1986.

Sigsbee, Charles D. *The "Maine": An Account of Her Destruction in Havana Harbor.* London: T. Fisher Unwin, 1899.

Thomas, Evan. *The War Lovers: Roosevelt, Lodge, Hearst, and the Rush to Empire.* New York: Little, Brown, 2010.

Turk, Richard W. *The Ambiguous Relationship: Theodore Roosevelt and Alfred Thayer Mahan.* New York: Greenwood Press, 1987.

Twain, Mark. *Mark Twain in Eruption.* New York: Harper & Brothers, 1922.

Washington, Booker T[aliaferro]. *The Booker T. Washington Papers.* Edited by Louis R. Harlan and Raymond Smock. 14 vols. Urbana: University of Illinois Press, 1972–1989.

————. *My Larger Education, Being Chapters from My Experience.* Toronto, Ontario: McClelland and Goodchild, 1919.

————. *The Story of My Life and Work: An Autobiography.* Toronto, Ontario: J. L. Nichols, 1901.

————. *The Story of the Negro.* 2 vols. New York: Negro Universities Press, 1909.

————. *Up from Slavery.* Boston, MA: Houghton Mifflin, 1901.

Weaver, John D. *The Brownsville Raid.* College Station, TX: University of Texas Press, 1970.

White, Richard D., Jr. "Theodore Roosevelt as Civil Service Commissioner: Linking the Influence and Development of a Modern Administrative President." *Administrative Theory & Practice* no. 4 (December 2000), pp. 696–713.

White, William Allen. *The Autobiography of William Allen White.* New York: Macmillan, 1946.

Willette, Gilson. "Slave Boy and the Leader of His Race." *New Voice*, June 27, 1899, pp. 3, 16.

Wilson, Walter E., and Gary L. McKay. *James D. Bulloch: Secret Agent and Mastermind of the Confederate Navy*. Jefferson, NC: McFarland & Co. Inc., 2012.

Wister, Owen. *Roosevelt—The Story of a Friendship*. New York: Macmillan, 1930.

Woodward, C. Vann. *Origins of the New South*. Baton Rouge: Louisiana State University Press, 1971.

————. "*Plessy v. Ferguson*: The Birth of Jim Crow." *American Heritage* 15, no. 3 (April 1964).

Wright, Stephen J. "The Development of the Hampton-Tuskegee Pattern of Higher Education." *Phylon* 10, no. 4 (4th Quarter, 1949), pp. 334–42.

# IMAGE CREDITS

p. ii Booker Washington and Theodore Roosevelt at Tuskegee Institute. Yale Collection of American Literature, Beinecke Rare Book and Manuscript Library.

p. 3 Washington, B. T. (1901). *An Autobiography: The Story of My Life and Work*. Toronto, ON: J. L. Nichols & Co., p. 26.

p. 6 Washington, B. T. (1901). *An Autobiography: The Story of My Life and Work*. Toronto, ON: J. L. Nichols & Co., p. 50.

p. 16 The procession approaching Union Square. Library of Congress Prints and Photographs Division. [LC-DIG-stereo-1s04309].

p. 19 *Theodore Roosevelt*. Theodore Roosevelt Birthplace National Historic Site.

p. 28 Hampton Normal and Agricultural Institute, from the *1876 Catalogue of the Hampton Normal Agricultural Institute, Hampton, Virginia*. University of Illinois Urbana-Champaign.

p. 32 Samuel Chapman Armstrong. Courtesy of the Hampton History Museum, Hampton, VA. Cheyne Collection, 2009.15.1859.

p. 50 Early Site of Tuskegee Institute. Bettmann Collection, Getty Images.

p. 51 "B.T. Washington." From "Men of Mark: Eminent, Progressive and Rising Collection." Schomburg Center for Research in Black Culture, Jean Blackwell Hutson Research and Reference Division, The New York Public Library. New York Public Library Digital Collections.

p. 59 Fanny Washington. The Tuskegee University Archives, Tuskegee University.

p. 61 Washington, B. T. (1901). *An Autobiography: The Story of My Life and Work*. Toronto, ON: J. L. Nichols & Co., p. 220.

p. 74 Teddy Roosevelt ranching in Dakota, 1883–1886. Theodore Roosevelt Collection, Houghton Library, Harvard University, W437051.1.

p. 76 Edith Kermit Carow Roosevelt, full-length portrait, seated on bench, facing right, holding umbrella. Library of Congress Prints and Photographs Division. [LC-USZ62-103988]

p. 78 Across the field, Sagamore Hill. Library of Congress Prints and Photographs Division. [LC-DIG-ppmsca-23796]

p. 85 Olivia Davidson Washington. University of Texas Libraries Collections. Washington, B. T. (1901). *An Autobiography: The Story of My Life and Work.* Toronto, ON: J. L. Nichols & Co.

p. 86 Booker T. Washington, three-quarter length portrait, seated, facing front. Library of Congress Prints and Photographs Division. [LC-USZ62-119924]

p. 89 Mrs. Booker Washington, portrait. Library of Congress Prints and Photographs Division. [LC-DIG-ggbain-03395]

p. 91 Classroom at Tuskegee, Frances Benjamin Johnston. From Washington, B. T. (1901). *An Autobiography: The Story of My Life and Work.* Toronto, ON: J. L. Nichols & Co., p. 222.

p. 92 Upholstery Class at Tuskegee, Frances Benjamin Johnston. From Washington, B. T. (1901). *An Autobiography: The Story of My Life and Work.* Toronto, ON: J. L. Nichols & Co., p. 225.

p. 101 Cartoon of NY Governor Theodore Roosevelt grinding policemen with mortar and pestle. It refers to the investigations into the corruption of Tammany Hall–controlled New York City. Everett Collection Inc./Alamy Stock Photo.

p. 104 Audience listening to Washington speech. The Tuskegee University Archives, Tuskegee University.

p. 105 Washington on stage. The Tuskegee University Archives, Tuskegee University.

p. 122 Henry Cabot Lodge, 1850–1924. Library of Congress Prints and Photographs Division. [LC-USZ62-78266]

p. 127 U.S.S. *Maine.* Library of Congress Prints and Photographs Division. [LC-DIG-ppmsca-40732]

p. 129 A view of our battleship MAINE as she appears today, May 10, 1900, Havana Harbor. Library of Congress Prints and Photographs Division. [LC-USZ62-65547]

p. 136 Washington with pupil. The Tuskegee University Archives, Tuskegee University.

p. 138 John Marshall Harlan, 1833–1911. Library of Congress Prints and Photographs Division. [LC-USZ62-40292]

p. 140 Hon. Fred. Douglass on platform in [the] Pavilion. Library of Congress Prints and Photographs Division. [LC-USZ62-120533]

p. 141 Washington fishing. The Tuskegee University Archives, Tuskegee University.

p. 147 [The Day Before San Juan Hill]. Library of Congress Prints and Photographs Division. [LC-DIG-ppmsca-35737]

p. 158 The Battle of Guásimas near Santiago June 24th, 1898. The 9th and 10th colored cavalry in support of rough riders. Library of Congress Prints and Photographs Division. [LC-USZ62-134]

p. 168 [Charge of the Rough Riders at San Juan Hill]. Reproduction of painting by Frederic Remington. Library of Congress Prints and Photographs Division. [LC-DIG-ppmsca-37596]

p. 170 *Charge of the 24th and 25th Colored Infantry and Rescue of Rough Riders at San Juan Hill, July 2nd, 1898.* Library of Congress Prints and Photographs Division. [LC-DIG ppmsca 69093]

p. 179 Washington, B. T. (1901). *An Autobiography: The Story of My Life and Work.* Toronto, ON: J. L. Nichols & Co., p. 174.

p. 183 [Wilmington, N.C. race riot, 1898: The wrecked "Record" building and group of vigilantes] Library of Congress Prints and Photographs Division. [LC-USZ62-51942]

p. 185 Wilmington Light Infantry, Wikimedia Commons.

p. 187 Washington, B. T. (1901). *An Autobiography: The Story of My Life and Work.* Toronto, ON: J. L. Nichols & Co., p. 280.

p. 202 W. E. B. Du Bois Papers, Robert S. Cox Special Collections and University Archives Research Center, UMass Amherst Libraries.

p. 204 Washington sitting outside. The Tuskegee University Archives, Tuskegee University.

p. 219 Letter from Roosevelt to Washington. Theodore Roosevelt Papers, Manuscript Division, Library of Congress.

p. 220 Theodore Roosevelt. Library of Congress Prints and Photographs Division. [LC-DIG-ppmsca-36063]

p. 226 Washington RSVP to White House dinner. Booker T. Washington Papers, Manuscript Division, Library of Congress.

p. 228 Washington, B. T. (1901). *An Autobiography: The Story of My Life and Work.* Toronto, ON: J. L. Nichols & Co., p. 10.

p. 229 [Pres. and Mrs. Theodore Roosevelt seated on lawn, surrounded by their family]. Library of Congress Prints and Photographs Division. [LC-DIG-ppmsca-35741]

p. 237 [Portrait of Samuel Clemens, "Mark Twain" seated in chair holding a pipe] Library of Congress Prints and Photographs Division. [LC-USZ62-28790]

p. 240 BOOKER T. WASHINGTON (1856–1915) Afro-American politician at left in a 1901 montage with President Theodore Roosevelt. Pictorial Press Ltd / Alamy Stock Photo.

p. 244 William Demosthenes Crum, 1901. C. M. Bell Collection, Library of Congress. [LC-DIG-bellcm-14837]

p. 248 Minnie Cox, Wikimedia Commons.

p. 251 Washington and sons on horses. The Tuskegee University Archives, Tuskegee University.

p. 256 Tuskegee Institute. From Washington, B. T. (1901). *An Autobiography: The Story of My Life and Work.* Toronto, ON: J. L. Nichols & Co., p. 469.

p. 257 [Theodore Roosevelt and Booker T. Washington at Tuskegee Normal and Industrial Institute, Tuskegee, Alabama]. Library of Congress Prints and Photographs Division. [LC-DIG-ds-14858]

p. 273 [Booker T. Washington, three-quarter length portrait, seated, facing slightly right with right hand in lap]. Library of Congress Prints and Photographs Division. [LC-USZ62-128954]

p. 274 [(Left to right) Robert C. Ogden, U.S. Secretary of War William Howard Taft, Booker T. Washington, and Andrew Carnegie, standing on the steps of a building, at the Tuskegee Institute's 25th anniversary celebration]. Library of Congress Prints and Photographs Division. [LC-J694-353A]

p. 275 Washington with class of 1910. The Tuskegee University Archives, Tuskegee University.

p. 277 Washington with Kenney on stage. The Tuskegee University Archives, Tuskegee University.

p. 282 Washington with sons. The Tuskegee University Archives, Tuskegee University.

p. 285 Washington with granddaughter. The Tuskegee University Archives, Tuskegee University.

p. 289 Booker T. Washington, 1915. Library of Congress Prints and Photographs Division. [LC-USZ62-25635]

p. 292 [Booker T. Washington, lying in state]. Library of Congress Prints and Photographs Division. [LC-USZ62-111867]

p. 296 Edith Kermit Carow and Theodore Roosevelt, 1918. Theodore Roosevelt Collection, Houghton Library, Harvard University. 541.9

# NOTES

## CHAPTER I: BORN "BOOKER"

1. B.T.W., *The Story of My Life and Work* (1901), p. 15.
2. Ibid., p. 15.
3. Ibid., pp. 17–18.
4. Harlan, *Booker T. Washington* (1972), p. 8.
5. Ibid., p. 7.
6. B.T.W., *Up from Slavery* (1901) in Booker T. Washington, *The Booker T. Washington Papers*. Harlan, Louis R, and Raymond Smock, eds. 14 vols. (Urbana-Champaign: University of Illinois Press, 1972–1989), vol. 1, p. 219. (Hereafter referred to as *BTW Papers*.)
7. Ibid.
8. B.T.W., *The Story of the Negro* (1909), vol. 1., no. 8., p. 116.
9. B.T.W., *Up from Slavery* (1901) in *BTW Papers*, vol. 1, p. 219.
10. John Washington, quoted in Harlan, *Booker T. Washington* (1972), p. 23.
11. B.T.W., *Up from Slavery* (1901) in *BTW Papers*, vol. 1, p. 225.
12. Ibid., p. 227.
13. Ibid., p. 228.
14. Ibid.
15. Ibid., p. 237.
16. Harlan, *Booker T. Washington* (1972), pp. 43–44.
17. B.T.W., *Up from Slavery* (1901) in *BTW Papers*, vol. 1, p. 237.

18. Harlan, *Booker T. Washington* (1972), p. 45.
19. B.T.W., *Up from Slavery* (1901) in *BTW Papers*, vol. 1, p. 236.
20. Harlan, *Booker T. Washington* (1972), p. 46.
21. B.T.W., *Up from Slavery* (1901) in *BTW Papers*, vol. 1, pp. 254–55.
22. *West Virginia Journal*, March 30, 1870.

CHAPTER 2: "TEEDIE" GROWS UP

1. Michael Beschloss, "When TR Saw Lincoln," *New York Times*, May 14, 2014.
2. Mittie Roosevelt, quoted in Putnam, *Theodore Roosevelt* (1958), p. 25.
3. Ibid.
4. Ibid.
5. T.R., *An Autobiography* (1913), p. 20.
6. T.R., Diary, December 12, 1872, quoted in Putnam, *Theodore Roosevelt* (1958), p. 148.
7. T.R., *An Autobiography* (1913), p. 4.
8. Anna Roosevelt Cowles reminiscences, quoted in McCullough, *Mornings on Horseback* (1981), p. 48.
9. T.R., *An Autobiography* (1913), p. 12.
10. *Atlanta Journal*, June 10, 1923.
11. Anna Roosevelt Cowles reminiscences, quoted in McCullough, *Mornings on Horseback* (1981), p. 60.
12. Robinson, *My Brother Theodore Roosevelt* (1921), p. 17.
13. T.R., *An Autobiography* (1913), p. 12.
14. Robinson, *My Brother Theodore Roosevelt* (1921), p. 17.
15. T.R. to T.R. Sr., October 22, 1876.
16. T.R. to Anna Roosevelt, December 16, 1877.
17. T.R., Diary, December 25, 1877.
18. Elliott Roosevelt, account of his father's death, February 9, 1878, quoted in McCullough, *Mornings on Horseback* (1981), pp. 187–88.
19. T.R., Diary, February 12, 1878.

CHAPTER 3: FROM STUDENT TO TEACHER

1. B.T.W., *Up from Slavery* (1901) in *BTW Papers*, vol. 1, p. 239.
2. Willette, "Slave Boy and the Leader of His Race" (1899), p. 3.
3. B.T.W., *Up from Slavery* (1901) in *BTW Papers*, vol. 1, p. 238.
4. Ibid., p. 239.
5. Ibid., p. 238.
6. Ibid., p. 240.
7. Ibid., pp. 240–41.
8. Ibid.

9. Mission statement, April 1, 1868, quoted at hamptonu.edu/about/history.cfm.
10. B.T.W., *Up from Slavery* (1901) in *BTW Papers*, vol. 1, p. 242.
11. Samuel C. Armstrong, "Lessons from the Hawaiian Islands," *Journal of Christian Philosophy* (January 1884), p. 213.
12. B.T.W., *Up from Slavery* (1901) in *BTW Papers*, vol. 1, pp. 242–43.
13. The several quotes in this passage from Miss Lord came from her article "Booker Washington's School Days at Hampton" (1902), pp. 255–59.
14. B.T.W., *My Larger Education* (1919), pp. 103–4.
15. B.T.W., *Up from Slavery* (1901) in *BTW Papers*, vol. 1, p. 249.
16. Italics added; quoted in *Commercial Tribune* [Cincinnati], February 26, 1899.
17. B.T.W., *Up from Slavery* (1901) in *BTW Papers*, vol. 1, p. 253.
18. Ibid.
19. William T. McKinney to B.T.W., September 11, 1911.
20. B.T.W., Commencement Speech, quoted in Lord, "Booker Washington's School Days at Hampton" (1902), p. 258.

### CHAPTER 4: THEODORE, HUSBAND AND WRITER

1. Richard Saltonstall, quoted in Putnam, *Theodore Roosevelt* (1958), p. 138.
2. T.R. to Martha Bulloch Roosevelt, October 8, 1878.
3. T.R. to Henry Minot, July 5, 1880.
4. T.R., Diary, January 25, 1880.
5. T.R. to Corrine Roosevelt, March 8, 1881.
6. Putnam, *Theodore Roosevelt* (1958), p. 167.
7. T.R, *An Autobiography* (1913), p. 28.
8. T.R., Diary, August 18, 1879; T.R., *An Autobiography* (1913), p. 28.
9. Quoted in Morris, *The Rise of Theodore Roosevelt* (1979), p. 565.
10. T.R., *An Autobiography* (1913), p. 24.
11. Wister, *Roosevelt—The Story of a Friendship* (1930), p. 24.
12. T.R., *The Naval War of 1812* (1882), pp. 4–5.

### CHAPTER 5: "MY LIFE-WORK"

1. B.T.W., *Up from Slavery* (1901) in *BTW Papers*, vol. 1, p. 271.
2. Ibid.
3. Harlan, *Booker T. Washington* (1972), p. 110.
4. B.T.W., *Up from Slavery* (1901) in *BTW Papers*, vol. 1, p. 271.
5. Acts of the General Assembly of Alabama, Passed at the Session of 1880–1881. Montgomery, AL, 1881, pp. 395–96.
6. B.T.W., *Up from Slavery* (1901) in *BTW Papers*, vol. 1, p. 272.
7. B.T.W. to J. F. B. Marshall, June 25, 1881.
8. B.T.W., *Up from Slavery* (1901) in *BTW Papers*, vol. 1, p. 280.

9. B.T.W. to Frank Briggs, June 28, 1881.

10. B.T.W., *Up from Slavery* (1901) in *BTW Papers*, vol. 1, p. 273.

11. B.T.W., *The Story of My Life and Work* (1901), p. 69.

12. Ibid., p. 75.

13. Scott and Stowe, *Booker T. Washington* (1916), p. 6.

14. B. T. Washington and O. A. Davidson, "The Tuskegee, Alabama, Normal School," *Southern Workman* 11 (May 1882), p. 56.

15. Bill Arp, *Atlanta Constitution*, March 19, 1882.

16. Rogers and Ward, *August Reckoning* (2004), p. 10.

17. Ibid., pp. 91–92.

18. *Meridian Mercury*, August 23, 1882.

19. *New Orleans Daily Picayune*, August 24, 1882.

20. *Meridian Mercury*, August 23, 1882.

21. *New-York Tribune*, August 23, 1882. For a more detailed recounting of Turner's story, see Rogers and Ward, *August Reckoning* (2004).

22. B.T.W., *Up from Slavery* (1901) in *BTW Papers*, vol. 1, p. 298.

23. B.T.W., *The Story of My Life and Work* (1901), p. 65.

24. B.T.W. to the editor of the *Southern Workman*, February 19, 1883.

25. B.T.W., *Up from Slavery* (1901) in *BTW Papers*, vol. 1, p. 294.

26. B.T.W. to J.F.B. Marshall, March 26, 1883.

27. Harlan, *Booker T. Washington* (1972), p. 147.

## CHAPTER 6: LESSONS AND LOSSES

1. T.R., *An Autobiography* (1913), p. 57.

2. *New York Herald*, November 1, 1881.

3. T.R. to C. Washburn, November 10, 1881.

4. Gompers, *Seventy Years of Life and Labour* (1925), p. 192.

5. Ibid., p. 188.

6. Ibid., p. 527.

7. Roosevelt, "Machine Politics in New York City," *Century Magazine* 33, no. 1 (November 1886).

8. T.R., *An Autobiography* (1913), p. 82.

9. George Spinney, quoted in Brands, *Theodore Roosevelt* (1997), p. 141.

10. Hermann Hagedorn, *The Roosevelts of Sagamore Hill* (New York: Macmillan, 1954), p. 7.

11. T.R. to Alice Lee Roosevelt, January 22, 1884.

12. Alice Lee Roosevelt to T.R., February 11, 1884.

13. *New York Times*, February 13, 1884.

14. Corinne Roosevelt Robinson interview, September 18, 1930.

15. Ibid.

16. Arthur Cutler, quoted in Morris, *The Rise of Theodore Roosevelt* (1979), p. 243.

17. T.R. to Carl Schurz, February 21, 1884.
18. T.R., *An Autobiography* (1913), p. 328.
19. T.R. to Simon Newton Dexter North, April 30, 1884.
20. T.R. to Martha Bulloch Roosevelt, March 16, 1879.
21. T.R., *An Autobiography* (1913), pp. 94, 97.
22. Ibid., p. 94.
23. Putnam, *Theodore Roosevelt* (1958), p. 452.
24. T.R., *An Autobiography* (1913), p. 98.
25. Ibid., p. 99.
26. Theodore Roosevelt, *Hunting Trips of a Ranchman*, in *Works of Theodore Roosevelt*, vol. 1 (New York: Scribner's, 1926), pp. 27–28.
27. Putnam, *Theodore Roosevelt* (1958), p. 525.
28. T.R. to Anna Roosevelt, September 20, 1884.
29. T.R., Memorial to Alice, 1884, quoted in Putnam, *Theodore Roosevelt* (1958), p. 391.
30. T.R. to Henry Cabot Lodge, April 20, 1887.
31. T.R., *An Autobiography* (1913), p. 122.

## CHAPTER 7: "LIKE CLOCK WORK"

1. Quoted in Norrell, *Up from History* (2009), p. 67.
2. *Catalogue of the Tuskegee State Normal School, 1883–84*, quoted in Harlan, *Booker T. Washington* (1972), p. 140.
3. B.T.W., *The Story of My Life and Work* (1901), pp. 85–86.
4. Samuel Armstrong to B.T.W., May 5, 1887.
5. William Jenkins to B.T.W., March 31, 1889.
6. B.T.W. to Samuel Armstrong, April 4, 1889.
7. B.T.W. to Warren Logan, April 17, 1889.
8. B.T.W. to Samuel Armstrong, April 21, 1889.
9. B.T.W. to Warren Logan, May 2, 1889.
10. B.T.W. to Samuel Armstrong, May 18, 1889.
11. B.T.W., *Up from Slavery* (1901) in *BTW Papers*, vol. 1, p. 292.
12. B.T.W. to Warren Logan, April 15, 1893.
13. B.T.W., *The Awakening of the Negro* (1896), quoted in Norrell, *Up from History* (2009), p. 98.
14. Ida B. Wells, "Lynch Law in All Its Phases," *New York Age*, June 25, 1892.
15. *Tuskegee Reporter*, November 13, 1896.

## CHAPTER 8: ROOSEVELT THE REFORMER

1. T.R., *Letters*, vol. 1, p. 149.
2. T.R. to Henry Cabot Lodge, March 28, 1889.

3. James G. Blaine, quoted in Goodwin, *The Bully Pulpit*, p. 130.
4. Halloran, *The Romance of the Merit System* (1929), p. 59.
5. Ibid., p. 56.
6. Riis, *Theodore Roosevelt* (1912), p. 106.
7. Civil Service Commission, 1893–1894, quoted in White, "Theodore Roosevelt as Civil Service Commissioner" (2000), p. 703.
8. Quoted in White, "Theodore Roosevelt as Civil Service Commissioner" (2000), p. 705.
9. Goodwin, *The Bully Pulpit* (2013), p. 141.
10. T.R., *An Autobiography* (1913), pp. 162–63.
11. Morris, *The Rise of Theodore Roosevelt* (1979), p. 473.
12. T.R. to Anna Roosevelt, October 13, 1894.
13. T.R. to Anna Roosevelt, April 14, 1895.
14. T.R., *An Autobiography* (1913), p. 174.
15. Andrews, "Theodore Roosevelt as Police Commissioner" (1958), p. 120.
16. Grondahl, *I Rose Like a Rocket* (2004), p. 219.
17. T.R., *An Autobiography* (1913), p. 175.
18. Ibid., p 28.

## CHAPTER 9: THE SPEECH THAT ECHOED

1. Henry McNeal Turner, *Atlanta Constitution*, July 23, 1893.
2. "A Circular Announcing the Tuskegee Negro Conference, January 1892," quoted in Norrell, *Up from History* (2009), p. 106.
3. B.T.W. to Samuel Armstrong, February 26, 1892.
4. B.T.W. to William Torrey Harris, May 4, 1892.
5. Wylie Harris's name is also spelled "Wyley" and "Wiley" in various accounts of events.
6. *Montgomery Advertiser*, April 30, 1890.
7. *Tuskegee News*, May 8, 1890, June 13, 1895.
8. *Tuskegee News*, June 13, 1895.
9. B.T.W. to F. J. Grimké, November 27, 1895.
10. *Tuskegee News*, June 13, 1895.
11. *Washington Bee*, October 26, 1895.
12. B.T.W. to F. J. Grimké, November 7, 1895.
13. Thomas Harris to B.T.W., October 7, 1895, December 22, 1895.
14. B.T.W., *Up from Slavery* (1901), p. 100.
15. An Account of Testimony before the House Committee on Appropriations, May [15], 1894.
16. Irving Penn to B.T.W., August 23, 1895.
17. *Atlanta Constitution*, August 23, 1895.
18. Bill Arp, *Atlanta Constitution*, October 14, 1891.

19. B.T.W., Speech at Old South Meeting House, Boston, December 15, 1891, in *BTW Papers*, vol. 3, p. 201.
20. Harlan, *Booker T. Washington* (1972), pp. 198–99.
21. B.T.W. to Charles Collier, September 3, 1895.
22. B.T.W., *Up from Slavery* (1901), p. 213.
23. Ibid., p. 215.
24. W. J. McKee, quoted in Harlan, *Booker T. Washington* (1972), p. 216.
25. James Creelman, *New York World*, September 19, 1895.
26. Here and after, Address of Booker T. Washington, September 18, 1895, in *Up from Slavery* (1901) in *BTW Papers*, vol. 1, pp. 330–34.
27. *New York World*, September 19, 1895.
28. Grover Cleveland to B.T.W., October 6, 1895.
29. Clark Howell, letter to the editor of *The New York World*, reprinted in B.T.W., *The Story of My Life and Work* (1901), p. 79.
30. W. E. B Du Bois, *What the Negro Wants*, Rayford W. Logan, ed. (Chapel Hill: University of North Carolina Press, 1944).
31. Ibid.
32. Ibid.
33. W. E. B. Du Bois to B.T.W., September 24, 1895.

### CHAPTER 10: AMERICA THE UNREADY

1. Mrs. Bellamy [Maria Longworth] Storer, "How Theodore Roosevelt Was Appointed Assistant Secretary of the Navy: A Hitherto Unrelated Chapter of History," *Harper's Weekly*, June 1, 1912.
2. Grondahl, *I Rose Like a Rocket* (2004), p. 241.
3. T.R. to Alfred Thayer Mahan, May 12, 1890.
4. T.R., *The Naval War of 1812* (1882), p. 21.
5. T.R to William McKinley, April 26, 1897.
6. T.R. to Anna Roosevelt, January 2, 1897.
7. T.R. address to Naval College, June 2, 1897.
8. T.R. to John Long, September 17, 1897; T.R. to Henry Cabot Lodge, September 24, 1897.
9. T.R. to Henry Cabot Lodge, September 11, 1897.
10. T.R. to Bellamy Storer, August 19, 1897.
11. Pringle, *Theodore Roosevelt* (1931), p. 175.
12. John Long, Diary, January 13, 1898.
13. Ibid.
14. Sigsbee, *The "Maine"* (1899), pp. 62–64.
15. Facsimile reproduced in ibid., facing p. 76.
16. *New York Evening Journal*, February 16, 1898.
17. Ibid.

18. Quoted in Thomas, *The War Lovers* (2010), pp. 210–11.
19. Long, Diary, February 16, 1898.
20. T.R. to Benjamin Diblee, February 16, 1898.
21. T.R. to George Dewey, April 25, 1898.
22. Henry Cabot Lodge, Senate speech, April 13, 1898.
23. Long, *America of Yesterday* (1923), p. 170.
24. Ibid., p. 186.
25. Ibid., pp. 186–87.

### CHAPTER 11: THE MOSES OF HIS PEOPLE

1. Portia Washington to B.T.W., November 19, 1893.
2. Taylor himself left the most detailed report of the encounter. See Robert Taylor to William Baldwin Jr., September 23, 1895.
3. Woodward, "*Plessy v. Ferguson*: The Birth of Jim Crow" (1964).
4. The Separate Car Act, enacted on July 10, 1890.
5. *The Times-Democrat*, June 8, 1892.
6. Justice Henry Billings Brown, majority opinion, *Plessy v. Ferguson*, May 18, 1896.
7. *Dred Scott v. John F. A. Sandford*, March 6, 1857.
8. Hoffer, *Plessy v. Ferguson* (2012), 146.
9. Timothy Fortune to B.T.W., September 26, 1895.
10. Norrell, *Up from History* (2009), p. 132.
11. B.T.W., "Who Is Permanently Hurt," in *Our Day*, June 16, 1896.
12. Harlan, ed., *The Booker T. Washington Papers* (1975), vol. 4, p. 185, n1.
13. B.T.W., "An Address at the Harvard University Alumni Dinner," June 2, 1896, in *BTW Papers*, vol. 4, pp. 183–85.
14. B.T.W., "A Speech at the Unveiling of the Robert Gould Shaw Monument," May 31, 1897.

### CHAPTER 12: A SPLENDID LITTLE WAR

1. T.R., *An Autobiography* (1913), p. 223.
2. Ibid., p. 222.
3. T.R., *The Rough Riders* (1899), p. 46.
4. Morris, *The Rise of Theodore Roosevelt* (1979), p. 620.
5. T.R., *The Rough Riders* (1899), pp. 15–16.
6. Ibid., p. 37.
7. Marshall, *The Story of the Rough Riders* (1899), p. 47.
8. T.R., *The Rough Riders* (1899), p. 53.
9. Ibid.
10. Quoted in Thomas, *The War Lovers* (2010), p. 279.
11. Edith Roosevelt to Emily Carow, June 3, 1898.

12. Norrell, *Up from History* (2009), p. 164.
13. *Cleveland Gazette*, May 13, 1898.
14. Gatewood, "Negro Troops in Florida, 1898" (1970), pp. 8–9.
15. Morris, *The Rise of Theodore Roosevelt* (1979), p. 626.
16. T.R. to Corrine Roosevelt Robinson, June 15, 1898.
17. *Manchester Guardian*, May 9, 1898.
18. Marshall, *The Story of the Rough Riders* (1899), p. 81.
19. Ibid., p. 91.
20. T.R., *The Rough Riders* (1899), pp. 86–87.
21. Marshall, *The Story of the Rough Riders* (1899), pp. 99–100.
22. T.R., *The Rough Riders* (1899), p. 89.
23. Marshall, *The Story of the Rough Riders* (1899), p. 119.
24. George Washington to John Augustine Washington, May 31, 1754.
25. Marshall, *The Story of the Rough Riders* (1899), p. 104.
26. T.R., *The Rough Riders* (1899), p. 91.
27. T.R. to Henry Cabot Lodge, June 27, 1898.

## CHAPTER 13: THE CROWDED HOUR

1. T.R., *The Rough Riders* (1899), p. 109.
2. *San Francisco Call*, July 3, 1898.
3. *Washington Bee*, July 9, 1898.
4. T.R., *An Autobiography* (1913), p. 245.
5. T.R., Interview with Hermann Hagedorn, August 18, 1918, quoted in Brands, *Theodore Roosevelt* (1997), p. 347.
6. T.R., *An Autobiography* (1913), p. 122.
7. Ibid., pp. 123–24.
8. T.R., *The Rough Riders* (1899), p. 126.
9. Ibid.
10. Ibid., p. 127.
11. T.R., *An Autobiography* (1913), pp. 247–48.
12. Marshall, *The Story of the Rough Riders* (1899), p. 191.
13. Richard Harding Davis, quoted in Risen, *The Crowded Hour* (2019), p. 206.
14. T.R., *The Rough Riders* (1899), p. 134.
15. Thomas, *The War Lovers* (2010), p. 327.
16. T.R., *The Rough Riders* (1899), p. 138.
17. Morris, *The Rise of Theodore Roosevelt* (1979), p. 564.
18. Gatewood, *"Smoked Yankees" and the Struggle for Empire* (1971), p. 42; Richard Harding Davis, *The Cuban and Puerto Rican Campaigns* (New York: Scribner's, 1904), p. 244.
19. Gatewood, *"Smoked Yankees" and the Struggle for Empire* (1971), p. 44.
20. *Chicago Tribune*, September 14, 1898.

21. Marshall, *The Story of Rough Riders* (1899), p. 240.
22. *New York Times*, August 16, 1898.
23. Morris, *The Rise of Theodore Roosevelt* (1979), p. 664.
24. T.R., "The Strenuous Life," April 10, 1899.
25. T.R. to Cecil Rice, November 25, 1898.

### CHAPTER 14: MAN IN THE MIDDLE

1. Collis Huntington to B.T.W., October 28, 1898.
2. Here and after, B.T.W., "An Address at the National Peace Jubilee," October 16, 1898, in *BTW Papers*, vol. 4, pp. 490–93.
3. Washington himself told the story of his Chicago speech in *The Story of My Life and Work* (1901), pp. 224–36.
4. B.T.W., "An Address at the National Peace Jubilee," October 16, 1898.
5. B.T.W., *The Story of My Life and Work* (1901), p. 232.
6. *Atlanta Constitution*, October 18, 1898.
7. Here and after, the story of the events at Wilmington in 1898 is drawn from Prather, "We Have Taken the City," in Cecelski and Tyson, eds., *Democracy Betrayed* (1998); and Wilmington Race Riot Report, state publication.
8. Wilmington *Weekly Star*, August 26, 1898.
9. Mike Ogle, "Manly McCauley, 1880–1898, at http://www.occrcoalition.org/wp -content/uploads/2019/11/MANLY-McCAULEY-PAPER-OCCRC-2.pdf.
10. John V.B. Metts to "Dear Elizabeth," November 12, 1898.
11. B.T.W., *Up from Slavery* (1901), p. 304.
12. Ibid., p. 307.
13. B.T.W., Welcoming Address, December 16, 1898, in *BTW Papers*, vol. 4, pp. 531–32.
14. Ibid., p. 308.
15. B.T.W., "Impressions of Holland and France," *Southern Workman* 30 (November 1901), p. 613.
16. B.T.W., "Letter to the Editor," *Colored American*, July 22, 1899, p. 2.
17. Quoted in Rachel M. Arauz, "Identity and Anonymity in Henry Ossawa Tanner's *Portrait of the Artist's Mother*." *Rutgers Art Review* 19 (2001), p. 41.
18. B.T.W., *Up from Slavery* (1901) in *BTW Papers*, vol. 1, pp. 365–67.
19. B.T.W., *The Future of the American Negro* (1899), in *BTW Papers*, vol. 5, pp. 374–75.
20. Ibid., p. 372.

### CHAPTER 15: THE NEW CENTURY DAWNS

1. T.R., *An Autobiography* (1913), p. 294; Gosnell, *Boss Platt and His New York Machine* (1924), p. 319.
2. T.R., *An Autobiography* (1913), p. 294.
3. Ibid.

4. Ibid., p. 308.
5. *New York Times,* January 15, 1899.
6. Thomas Fortune to B.T.W., October 1, 1898.
7. B.T.W., *My Larger Education* (1919), p. 167.
8. Ibid., p. 168.
9. Norrell, *Up from History* (2009), p. 240.
10. White, *The Autobiography of William Allen White* (1946), p. 297.
11. *Emporia Gazette,* June 26, 1899.
12. T.R. to Henry Cabot Lodge, July 1, 1899.
13. T.R. to Anna Roosevelt Cowles, December 17, 1899.
14. T.R. to Henry Cabot Lodge, January 22, 1900.
15. Ibid.
16. Quoted in Morris, *The Rise of Theodore Roosevelt* (1979), p. 719.
17. *New-York Tribune,* June 21, 1900.
18. Lyman Abbott to B.T.W., December 9, 1899; Lyman Abbott, "Booker T. on Our Racial Problem," *Outlook,* January 6, 1900, pp. 14–17.
19. Walter Hines Pages to B.T.W., October 14, 1896.
20. J. D. McCall to B.T.W., February 19, 1900.
21. *The Nation,* April 4, 1901.
22. Lyman Abbott to B.T.W., October 1, 1900.
23. Ibid.
24. William T. Harris to B.T.W., January 8, 1901.
25. W. E. B. Du Bois, *The Suppression of the African Slave-Trade to the United States of America, 1638–1870* (Cambridge, MA: Harvard Historical Studies Series, 1895).
26. W. E. B. Du Bois to B.T.W., February 16, 1900.
27. W. E. B. Du Bois, "Great Barrington Notes," *New York Globe,* September 29, 1883.
28. W. E. B. Du Bois, "The Conservation of Races," 1897, quoted in Marable, *W. E. B. Du Bois* (2005), p. 36.
29. W. E. B. Du Bois, *The Dial,* July 1, 1901, pp. 53–55, in *BTW Papers,* vol. 6, pp. 175–78.
30. B.T.W., *My Larger Education* (1919), p. 168.

CHAPTER 16: DEATH OF A PRESIDENT

1. T.R. to B.T.W., November 10, 1900.
2. T.R. to B.T.W., March 21, 1901.
3. Davis, *Guest of Honor* (2012), p. 120.
4. T.R. to B.T.W., July 9, 1901.
5. Ibid.
6. Miller, *Theodore Roosevelt* (1992), p. 348.
7. Eyewitness Louis Babcock, quoted in Grondahl, *I Rose Like a Rocket* (2004), p. 364.

8. *Atlanta Constitution*, September 8, 1901.
9. T.R. to Leonard Wood, April 17, 1901.
10. *New York Times*, September 8, 1901.
11. Rauchway, *Murdering McKinley* (2003), p. 11.
12. T.R. to Henry Cabot Lodge, September 9, 1901.
13. Ibid.
14. T.R. to B.T.W., September 7, 1901.
15. Edith Roosevelt, quoted in Grondahl, *I Rose Like a Rocket* (2004), p. 373.
16. T.R., *An Autobiography* (1913), p. 364.
17. The compelling story of Roosevelt's journey from Mount Marcy to Buffalo is recounted in detail by Paul Grondahl in his *I Rose Like a Rocket* (2004), pp. 374ff.
18. L. Vernon Biggs, *The Manner of Man That Kills* (Boston, MA: Richard G. Badger, 1921), p. 241n3.
19. *New York World*, September 15, 1901.

CHAPTER 17: GUESS WHO'S COMING TO DINNER

1. T.R. to B.T.W., September 14, 1901.
2. T.R., *An Autobiography* (1913), p. 372.
3. Lincoln Steffens, *The Autobiography of Lincoln Steffens* (New York: Harcourt, Brace, 1931), p. 503.
4. T.R. to Henry Cabot Lodge, October 11, 1901.
5. B.T.W., *My Larger Education* (1919), pp. 170–71.
6. B.T.W. to T.R., October 2, 1901.
7. B.T.W. to Philader Chase Knox, October 4, 1901.
8. Emmett Scott to B.T.W., October 4, 1901.
9. T.R. to Albion Tourgee, November 8, 1901.
10. B.T.W. to T.R., October 16, 1901.

CHAPTER 18: THE MORNING AFTER

1. Morris, *Theodore Rex* (2001), p. 54.
2. Quoted in Grantham, "Dinner at the White House" (1958), p. 118.
3. *Nashville American*, October 19, 1901.
4. *Confederate Veteran*, October 19, 1901.
5. Quoted in Grantham, "Dinner at the White House" (1958), p. 116.
6. *Nashville American*, October 23, 1901.
7. Quoted in Grantham, "Dinner at the White House" (1958), p. 118.
8. Quoted in Davis, *Guest of Honor* (2012), pp. 207, 213.
9. *New York Times*, October 20, 1901.
10. T.R. to Lucious Littauer, October 24, 1901.
11. *Richmond News*, October 18, 1901.

12. Quoted in Morris, *Theodore Rex* (2001), p. 55.
13. Italics added. T.R. to Curtis Guild, October 28, 1901.
14. *Memphis Commercial Appeal*, October 17, 1901.
15. Quoted in Grantham, "Dinner at the White House" (1958), p. 117.
16. Edgar Gardner Murphy to B.T.W., October 23, 1901.
17. *New York Times*, October 24, 1901.
18. B.T.W. to T.R., October 24, 1901.
19. Twain, *Mark Twain in Eruption* (1922), pp. 30–31.
20. B.T.W., *My Larger Education* (1919), p. 176.
21. Henry M. Turner to B.T.W., November 5, 1901.
22. William Ferris to B.T.W., [January 1902].
23. Harlan, *Booker T. Washington* (1972), pp. 318–19; B.T.W., *My Larger Education* (1919), pp. 177–78.
24. B.T.W., *My Larger Education* (1919), pp. 177–78.
25. T.R. to Charles Washburn, November 20, 1915.

CHAPTER 19: "THE NEGRO QUESTION"

1. Here and after, T.R., First Annual Message to Congress, December 3, 1901.
2. T.R., *An Autobiography* (1913), p. 439.
3. Quoted in T.R. to James Smyth, November 26, 1902.
4. Francis Leupp, quoted in Whitefield McKinlay to B.T.W., November 30, 1902.
5. Gatewood, "William D. Crum: A Negro in Politics" (1968), p. 309.
6. B.T.W. to T.R., December 1, 1902.
7. *New Orleans States*, quoted in Gatewood, *Theodore Roosevelt and the Art of Controversy* (1970), p. 106.
8. William Crum to Whitefield McKinlay, January 10, 1903.
9. *Charleston News and Courier*, January 24, 1903.
10. T.R. to Owen Wister, April 27, 1906.
11. Here and after, Gatewood, "Theodore Roosevelt and the Indianola Affair" (1968), pp. 49ff; Gatewood, *Theodore Roosevelt and the Art of Controversy* (1970), pp. 62ff.
12. Charles Fitzgerald, quoted in Gatewood, *Theodore Roosevelt and the Art of Controversy* (1970), p. 65.
13. *Greenwood Commonwealth*, January 31, 1903.
14. Gatewood, *Theodore Roosevelt and the Art of Controversy* (1970), p. 69.
15. Ibid., p. 71.
16. *Greenwood Commonwealth*, November 28, 1902.
17. Minnie Cos to Charles Fitzgerald, December 4, 1902.
18. Morris, *Theodore Rex* (2001), p. 199.
19. Ibid.
20. Gatewood, "Theodore Roosevelt and the Indianola Affair" (1968), pp. 58, 64.

21. Baker, *American Chronicle* (1945), p. 225.
22. *Cleveland Gazette*, February 7, 1903.
23. Gatewood, *Theodore Roosevelt and the Art of Controversy* (1970), p. 80.
24. B.T.W. to T.R., June 19, 1906.
25. Norrell, *Up from History* (2009), pp. 254–55.
26. Ibid., p. 308.
27. B.T.W. to T.R., July 29, 1904; August 24, 1904.
28. Quoted in Gatewood, *Theodore Roosevelt and the Art of Controversy* (1970), p. 90.

### CHAPTER 20: SOUTHERN DISCOMFORTS

1. Report of Pinker Detective #58, October 22, 1905, in *BTW Papers*, vol. 8, p. 418.
2. *Nashville American*, October 19, 1904.
3. "A Press Release: Visit of the President of the United States to Tuskegee Institute," October 24, 1905, in *BTW Papers*, vol. 8, pp. 426–27.
4. T.R. address, preliminary remarks, October 24, 1905, in *BTW Papers*, vol. 8, p. 431n1.
5. Ibid.
6. Ibid.
7. Harlan, *Booker T. Washington* (1983), p. 36.
8. W. E. B. Du Bois, *The Souls of Black Folk* (1903), reprinted in *The Oxford W. E. B. Du Bois Reader* (1996), p. 102.
9. Ibid., p. 106.
10. W. E. B. Du Bois, "The Talented Tenth," in *The Negro Problem* (New York: James Pott, 1903), p. 33.
11. Du Bois, *The Souls of Black Folk* (1903), p. 123.
12. Ibid., p. 131.
13. Frederick Douglass, *Life and Times of Frederick Douglass* (Hartford, CT: Park Publishing, 1881), p. 325.
14. W. E. B. Du Bois, "The Parting of the Ways," *World Today*, no. 6 (April 1904), p. 523.
15. W. E. B. Du Bois, "Address to the Country," August 19, 1906.
16. *New York Times*, August 20, 1906.
17. Here and after, unless otherwise cited, the facts and quotations concerning the Brownsville affair are from Weaver, *The Brownsville Raid* (1970).
18. Frederick J. Combe to T.R., August 16, 1906.
19. *New York Times*, November 19, 1906.
20. T.R. to Inspector General Ernest A. Garlington, October 4, 1906.
21. General Earnest Garlington, quoted in Weaver, *The Brownsville Raid* (1970), p. 94.
22. B.T.W. to Charles Anderson, November 7, 1906.
23. B.T.W. to T.R., November 2, 1906.

24. T.R. to B.T.W., November 5, 1906.
25. Special Order 266, November 7, 1906, cited in Morris, *Theodore Rex* (2001), p. 467.
26. *Nashville American*, November 10, 1906.
27. Twain, *Mark Twain in Eruption* (1922), p. 32.
28. Quoted in Harlan, *Booker T. Washington* (1983), p. 311.
29. T.R. to Ray Stannard Baker, March 30, 1907.
30. B.T.W. to T.R., November 26, 1906.
31. B.T.W. to Samuel Bacote, May 5, 1908.
32. B.T.W. to Whitefield McKinlay, November 8, 1906.
33. T.R., Sixth Annual Message to Congress, December 3, 1906.

#### CHAPTER 21: WINDING DOWN

1. T.R. to B.T.W., April 2, 1908.
2. B.T.W. to William Howard Taft, December 1, 1908.
3. William Howard Taft to Henry F. Pringle, February 23, 1909.
4. W. E. B. Du Bois, *New York Post*, April 1, 1910.
5. B.T.W. to Robert J. Reyburn, February 22, 1908.
6. Here and after, this account of Booker's visit is based upon a report published in the *Boston Evening Transcript*, November 12, 1910. It's cited in *BTW Papers* as the *Boston Transcript*.
7. B.T.W. in *BTW Papers*, vol. 10, p. 465.
8. George Myers to B.T.W., February 26, 1912.
9. BTW to William Lewis, January 12, 1913.
10. Booker T. Washington, "Is the Negro Having a Fair Chance?" *Century Magazine*, November 1912.
11. Ibid.
12. W. E. B. Du Bois, *Crisis*, December 1912.
13. Here and after, Gatewood, "Booker T. Washington and the Ulrich Affair" (1970), pp. 286–302.
14. T.R. to B.T.W., March 27, 1911.
15. *Lafayette Indiana Journal*, March 22, 1911.
16. Norrell, *Up from History* (2009), p. 413. There is some dispute among Wilson biographers concerning the accuracy of the quote. However, when asked to condemn the film's racist theme, Wilson refused.

#### CHAPTER 22: ROAD'S END

1. *New-York Tribune*, November 10, 1915.
2. *New York Times*, November 15, 1915.
3. For these and other comments on Washington's life and legacy, see chapter 1, Hamilton, *Booker T. Washington in American Memory* (2017), pp. 14–37.

4. Baker, *American Chronicle* (1945), p. 222.
5. T.R. to Julius Rosenwald, December 15, 1915.
6. T.R., Preface to Scott and Stowe, *Booker T. Washington* (1916), p. ix.
7. W. E. B. Du Bois, *Crisis*, December 1915.
8. Norrell, *Up from History* (2009), p. 264.
9. Harlan, "The Secret Life of Booker T. Washington" (1971).
10. Italics added. Scott, "Twenty Years After: An Appraisal of Booker T. Washington (1936), p. 53.
11. T.R. to Kermit Roosevelt, October 27, 1918.
12. Brands, *Theodore Roosevelt* (1997), p. 811.

### EPILOGUE: POSTMORTEM

1. T.R. to James Ford Rhodes, February 20, 1905.
2. Theodore Roosevelt, *Oliver Cromwell* (New York: Scribner's, 1900), p. 100.
3. T.R., Speech at Arlington, Virginia, May 30, 1903, cited in Dyer, *Theodore Roosevelt and the Idea of Race* (1980), p. 97.
4. "The Negro Problem," cited in Dyer, *Theodore Roosevelt and the Idea of Race* (1980), p. 110.
5. *Genesee Republican*, November 15, 1915.
6. T.R. to Charles Washburn, November 12, 1915.
7. Although Alfred Holt Stone was a racist ideologue, he likely spoke accurately enough for his peers. See Grantham, "Dinner at the White House" (1958), p. 130
8. B.T.W. to Emmett Scott, June 23, 1902.
9. Dyer, *Theodore Roosevelt and the Idea of Race* (1980), p. 110.
10. John McCain, concession speech, November 5, 2008.
11. B.T.W., Commencement Speech, quoted in Lord, "Booker Washington's School Days at Hampton" (1902), p. 258.

# INDEX

Note: Italicized page numbers indicate material in tables or illustrations.

Abbot, Lyman, 199–200
abolitionists, 4, 33–34
Adams, Henry, 97, 98
Adams, Lewis, 48, 50
"Address to the Country"
    (Du Bois), 262
Alabama, 55, 83, 139, 252, 294
Alabama State Teachers' Association, 88
Alger, Philip, 130
American Federation of Labor, 66
American Missionary Association, 30
American Museum of Natural
    History, 20
*The American Spelling Book* (Webster), 8
Anderson, Charles W., 288
Anthony, Susan B., 189
Apache Wars, 145
Armstrong, Samuel Chapman
    and funding for Tuskegee School, 87
    Washington's admiration for, 31–32
    and Washington's commencement
        address, 37
    and Washington's drive, 81
    and Washington's educational
        aspirations, *32*
    and Washington's graduation from
        Hampton, 34
    as Washington's mentor, 32, 38
    and Washington's recruitment to
        Tuskegee, 46–47
    and Washington's wife Olivia's
        death, 87
    Washington warned about politics
        by, 55
Arp, Bill, 113
"The Atlanta Compromise"
    (Washington), 260
*The Atlanta Constitution*, 54
*An Autobiography* (Roosevelt)
    Alice's death omitted from, 79
    publication of, 285
    on respect, 39
    on tenements of New York City, 65
    on time as governor of New York, 194

*An Autobiography* (Roosevelt) (*cont.*)
  and Tom Harris incident, 110,
  Washington omitted from, 240

Bailey, Alonzo, 294
Baker, Ray Stannard, 227*n*, 254
Baldwin, William H., Jr., 177
Battle of Lake Erie, 43
Benton, Thomas Hart, 77
*The Birth of a Nation* (film), 286–87
Black Americans
  and Black Codes, 139
  and Brownsville affair, 263–71, 271*n*
  caricatured in news media, 103–4
  and caste system, 136, 138, 184,
    260, 293
  and Civil Rights Act of 1875, 54, 54*n*
  and criminal justice system, 281
  and *Dred Scott* case, 138–39
  education of, 8, 29–30, 83, 249, 257,
    259 (*see also* Tuskegee Institute)
  elected to office, xiv, 54
  and emancipation of the enslaved,
    5–6, *6*, 54
  and interracial relationships, 55,
    181–82
  military service of, 143, 151–52, 178,
    263–71, 271*n* (*see also* Buffalo
    Soldiers)
  and "miscegenation," 107, 107*n*
  mortgaging of crops, 113
  and "Negro Problem" debate, 117,
    119, 294–95
  and Niagara Movement, 261
  oversexed stereotypes, 270, 286, 289
    (*see also* sexual accusations and
    stereotypes of Black people)
  political appointments of, 222–23,
    235, 281, 300
  and presidential election of 1904, 247
  and racial divide, 12–14, 187, 231–33
  and Reconstruction era, xiii

  rights of (*see* civil rights; equality)
  and segregation, 55, 117, 136–39
    (*see also* discrimination, racial;
    Jim Crow era)
  as sharecroppers, 104
  and Tom Harris incident, 106–10
  violence suffered by (*see* lynchings;
    violence aimed at Black
    Americans)
  voting rights of, xiii–xiv, 36, 94,
    181, 184
  and Washington on race relations, 83
  and Washington's dinner at the
    White House, 230, 240
Borglum, Gutzon, 297
Brewer, David, 236, 236*n*
brickmaking program at Tuskegee
  Normal School, 59–61, *61*
Brown, Herd, 56
Brown, John, 260–61
Brownsville affair, 263–71, 271*n*, 301
*Brown v. Board of Education*, 295
Bryan, William Jennings, 102, 273
Buffalo Soldiers, *170*
  and Battle of San Juan Hill, 172
  and Brownsville affair, 263–71,
    271*n*, 301
  as caregivers for sick soldiers, 172
  casualties among, 155
  courage of, 143
  and Kettle Hill assault, 166, 167
  in Port Tampa military camp, 151–52
  and Roosevelt's body servant, 162
  and violence in Wilmington, North
    Carolina, 185
  and Washington's speech in Chicago,
    178–79, *179*, 180
Bulloch, Irvine, 23, 41–42
Bulloch, James (father), 21
Bulloch, James (son), 22, 23, 41–42, 43,
  44, 44*n*
Bulloch family, 21, 22–23, 41–42

Burroughs, James, 2–3
Burroughs, William, 4
Burroughs family, 4
Byrnes, Thomas F., 101

"The Call" (Mordaunt), 166*n*
Campbell, George W., 46
Camp Wood, 148
Carnegie, Andrew, 255, 261
caste system, race-based, 136, 138, 184,
 260, 293
*The Century Magazine*, 65, 272,
 281–82, 294
Chase, Calvin, 188
cigar-making in tenements, 64–66
civil rights
 corrosion of, 44, 135, 180
 and *Dred Scott* case, 138–39
 and equal protection clause, 137
 and *Plessy v. Ferguson*, 136–39
 Washington's fight for, 293–94
 *See also* equality
Civil Rights Act of 1875, 54, 54*n*
Civil Rights Acts of 1964 and 1968, 54*n*
Civil Service Commission, 95–98
Civil War, American
 and *The Birth of a Nation* (film), 286
 and Bulloch family, 22–23, 41–42
 and Burroughs family, 4–5
 commencement of, 4–5
 and *Dred Scott* case, 138–39
 and education at Hampton, 29–30
 end of, xiii, 6, 15
 and Harper's Ferry, 261
 military service of Black Americans
 in, 178
 and news of emancipation, 5–6, 6
 Reconstruction following, xiii, xiv, 54
 Roosevelt, Sr.'s refusal to fight in,
 22, 23
 and Roosevelt family, 22–23, 41–42, 299
 and Shaw's sacrifice, 143

Clemens, Samuel Langhorne (Mark
 Twain), 189, 236–37, *237*, 239,
 268, 301
Cleveland, Grover, 93–94, 97, 117
Columbia Law School, 41
"committee of safety" and lynching of
 Turner, 56–57
Compromise of 1877, xiv
Coolidge, Calvin, 26
Cotton States and International
 Exposition, 111–18
Cox, Minnie, 247–52, *248*, 302
criminal justice system, 281
*The Crisis*, 282, 293, 294
Crum, Ellen Craft, 245
Crum, William D., 243–47, *244*, 252,
 253, 273, 302
CSS *Alabama*, 42
CSS *Florida*, 42
Cuba
 civil war in, 124–25, 126–27
 and explosion on USS *Maine*, *127*,
 128–31, *129*
 and independence from Spain, 171*n*
 and naval readiness of United States,
 124, 125–26
 *See also* Spanish–American War
Curley, James, 291
Czolgosz, Leon Frank, 206, 209–11, 215

Dakota Badlands, 71–76
Dancy, John Campbell, 181
Dartmouth College, 227*n*
Davis, Richard Harding, 151, 153, 159,
 168, 172
Delta Penny Savings Bank, 251
Democratic Party. *See* Southern
 conservatives/Democrats
Dewey, George, 131, 146
discrimination, racial
 and *The Birth of a Nation* (film), 286–87
 and Black Codes, 139

discrimination, racial (*cont.*)
 and Civil Rights Act of 1875, 54, 54*n*
 codified, 135, 136–39
 and *Plessy v. Ferguson*, 135, 136–39
 and progress made in U.S., 302–3
 Roosevelt's condemnation of, 299
 and "separate but equal" doctrine,
  136–39, 236*n*, 294, 295
 and Ulrich affair, 283–85
 Washington on incidence of, 281
 *See also* Jim Crow era
Douglass, Frederick
 autobiography of, 139, 201
 background of, 139–40
 death of, 139
 on degradation, 110
 equality demanded by, 261
 influence on Washington, 33–34
 intellectual approach of, 141
 and Lincoln, xv, 140
 at Tuskegee Institute, 140, *140*
 and Washington's status, 295
Douglass, Lewis, 262
*Dred Scott* case, 138–39
Du Bois, W. E. B., *202*
 "Address to the Country," 262
 and *American Negro* exhibition, *202*
 background of, 118–19
 criticisms of Washington, 120,
  259–60, 274, 293, 294
 death of, 295
 demand for equality, 261, 262
 differences between Washington and,
  203–5, 294, 295
 influence and power of, 262, 286, 295
 as intellectual, 203, 205, 295
 and NAACP, 262
 and Niagara Movement, 261, 262
 positions at Tuskegee Institute
  offered to, 202–3
 on racial divide, 260
 and Roosevelt, 295–96

*The Souls of Black Folk*, 259, 260
 on Washington's *Century* article, 282
 and Washington's death, 293
 and Washington's Exposition
  address, 120
 and Washington's influence, 270–71
 and Washington's reticence on
  race-based violence, 188

education and schools
 for Black Americans, 8, 29–30, 83,
  249, 257, 259 (*see also* Tuskegee
  Institute)
 and *Brown v. Board of Education*, 295
 segregation of, 55
Edward VII, King of Great Britain, 278
Egypt, Roosevelt family in, 18–19, 20
Elkhorn Ranch of Roosevelt, 72–73, 75
Emancipation Proclamation, 5–6
equality
 actively thwarted in the South,
  227*n*, 232
 Crum's approach to, 245
 Douglass's call for, 33–34, 261
 Du Bois's demand for, 261, 262
 Founders' promise of, xiv
 and *Mr./Mrs.* used when addressing
  Black Americans, 227*n*
 as the norm in Europe, 189
 quest for, 303
 and Reconstruction Amendments,
  54–55
 Roosevelt's perspective on, 299–300
 and "separate but equal" doctrine,
  136–39, 142, 236*n*, 294, 295
 as threat to status quo in the South, 107
 Washington's approach to, 91, 117,
  261, 273

farmers' mortgaging of crops, 113
Felton, Rebecca, 181
Ferguson, John H., 137

Ferguson, Washington ("Wash"), 2, 7–8
Fifteenth Amendment, xiii
Fifth Army Expeditionary Force, 150
First United States Volunteer Cavalry.
    *See* Rough Riders
Fisk University, 88, 119
Florida, 181
*Following the Color Line* (Baker),
    227*n*, 254
Foraker, Joseph, 270
"The Force That Wins" (Washington's
    commencement address), 37
Fort Brown, 263–71, 271*n*
Fort Reno, 265
Fortune, Timothy Thomas, 142, 196
Fourteenth Amendment, xiii, 137
Framingham Normal School in
    Massachusetts, 52–53
French and Indian War, 159
*The Future of the American Negro*
    (Washington), 190, 199

Gatewood, William B., 241
Gideon's Band, 12–14
Goldman, Emma, 210
Gompers, Samuel, 64–66
*Gone with the Wind* (Mitchell), 22
Grant, Ulysses S., xiii, 6, 23
Griffith, D. W., 286
Grimké, Francis J., 109
*The Guardian*, 258, 293

Hampton Normal and Agricultural
    Institute, 26–38
    and Armstrong, 31–32
    campus of, 27–28, *28*
    establishment of, 29–30
    first class of students at, 29–30
    Lord as instructor at, 33, 34, 36, 37
    mission of, 30
    transformative experience of, 35
    and Tuskegee Institute, 51

Washington as instructor at, 37–38
Washington's arrival at, 26–29
Washington's first knowledge of,
    11–12
Washington's graduation from, 34–35
Washington's life at, 30–31
Washington's work as janitor at, 30
Hanna, Mark, 199, 223
Harlan, John Marshall, 138–39, *138*
Harper's Ferry, Virginia, 260–61, 262
Harris, Tom, 106–10
Harris, William T., 201
Harris, Wylie, 106, 108
Harrison, Benjamin, 93–94, 97, 102,
    247, 248
Harvard College/University, 23–24,
    39–40, 142–43, 255
Hay, John, 192, 215
Hayes, Rutherford B., xiv, 55
Hearst, William Randolph, 126
Heflin, Tom, 255
HMS *Guerrière*, 43
Hobart, Garret A., 198
Hose, Sam, 187, 188, 190
House Bill No. 165, 47–48
House Committee on Appropriations,
    111–12
Howard University, 281
*How the Battleship Maine Was
    Destroyed* (Rickover), 132*n*
*How the Other Half Lives* (Riis), 99
Huntington, Collis P., 89–90, 177, 255

immigrants, 99
Indianola, Mississippi, 247–52
Indian Wars, 152
*The Influence of Sea Power upon
    History, 1660–1783* (Mahan),
    123–24
interracial relationships, 55, 181–82
"Is the Negro Having a Fair Chance?"
    (Washington), 281–82

Jackson, Andrew, 96, 178
James, William, 291
Jefferson, Thomas, 123, 297
Jim Crow era
    and Black Codes, 139
    and Brownsville affair, 263
    Du Bois's difference with Washington
        on, 203–4
    laws enforcing, 55
    and military service of Black
        Americans, 152
    pervasiveness of attitudes, 275
    and *Plessy v. Ferguson*, 136–39
    violence and intimidation associated
        with, xiv
    *See also* discrimination, racial
J. L. Nichols and Company, 200
John F. Slater Fund for the Education of
    Freedmen, 119

Kenney, John A., 277
King, Martin Luther, Jr., 295
Ku Klux Klan, xiv, 12, 13, 117, 286

Lamb, Hugh, 67
Lawrence, James, 43–45
Lee, Robert E., 4, 6, 15, 23, 234
Lewis, William H., 252, 280, 281, 302
Lincoln, Abraham
    ambitions of, 303
    assassination of, 15–16
    and Civil War, 4
    and Douglass, xv, 140
    Emancipation Proclamation, 5–6
    and Mount Rushmore, 297
    and Platt, 193
    portrait of, in Tuskegee Institute, *91*
    and Roosevelt, 16, 298
    and Washington, 33, 298
Lincoln, Robert Todd, 294
Lodge, Henry Cabot
    as friend and ally to Roosevelt, 70, *122*

on naval power, 124
and Roosevelt as assistant secretary of
    the navy, 122
and Roosevelt as vice president,
    198, 199
and Roosevelt's political ambitions, 94
and Roosevelt's political
    appointments, 222
and Spanish–American War, 131–32
Long, John D.
    and explosion on USS *Maine*, 130
    and Roosevelt's authority, 125
    and Roosevelt's hotheadedness, 132
    and Roosevelt's military service,
        126–27, 146
    on Roosevelt's political ascent, 133
    and Spanish–American War, 132
Longworth, Nicholas, III, 268, 268*n*
Lord, Nathalie, 32–33, 34, 36, 37
Lost Cause narrative, 22
Louisiana, 136, 293–94, 294*n*
lynchings
    and *The Birth of a Nation* (film), 287
    as commonplace, 180, 208, 208*n*
    death toll from, xiv
    decline in, 275
    Roosevelt's statements on, 257, 270, 299
    of Turner, 55–57
    Washington on incidence of, 281
    Washington's reticence on, 57, 90–91
    Washington threatened with, 255
    in Wilmington, North Carolina, 182
    *See also* violence aimed at Black
        Americans

Mackie, Mary F., 29, 31, 32
Madison, James, 42–43, 123
Mahan, Alfred Thayer, 123–24
Malden, South Carolina, 7, 7*n*
Manly, Alex, 181
Mann, Horace, *85*
Marcy, William Learned, 213*n*

Marshall, Edward, 147, 162
Marshall, J. F. B., 51, 59, 60
Marshall, Thomas, 220
McCain, John, 302
McKinlay, Whitefield, 224, 225, 246
McKinley, Ida, 215
McKinley, William
  assassination of, 206, 209–15, 242, 255
  cabinet and policies of, 220
  and Cuban civil war, 127
  and explosion on USS *Maine*, 130, 131
  political appointments of, 223
  and presidential election of 1896,
    102, 121
  and presidential election of 1900,
    206, 207
  and Roosevelt as assistant secretary of
    the navy, 122, 124, 126
  and Roosevelt as vice president,
    198–99
  Roosevelt's frustrations with, 220
  and Roosevelt's hawkish tendencies,
    122, 174
  and Spanish–American War, 132, 153,
    173, 220
  at Tuskegee Institute, 185–87, *187*
  and Washington's speech in Chicago,
    177–80, 238
  Washington's support for, 223
  Wood's service as physician to, 145
McKinley National Memorial, 216
Merriam brothers, 58
military service of Black Americans,
    143, 151–52, 178, 263–71, 271*n*.
    *See also* Buffalo Soldiers
Mitchell, Margaret, 22
Mordaunt, Thomas Osbert, 166*n*
Morgan, J. Pierpont, 177, 242
Morris, Edmund, 268*n*
mortgaging of crops by Black
    farmers, 113
Mount Rushmore, 297

Murray, Joe, 64
*My Larger Education* (Washington),
    239, 285

*Narrative of the Life of Frederick
    Douglass, an American Slave*
    (Douglass), 139, 201
National Association for the
    Advancement of Colored People
    (NAACP), 262, 282, 286, 294
National Educational Association, 82
National Peace Jubilee, Chicago,
    177–80, *179*
Native Americans, 38, 148
*The Naval War of 1812* (Roosevelt),
    45, 123
"Negro Problem" debate, 117, 119, 254,
    294–95
*New York Age*, 142
New York Customs House, 96
New York State
  and Boss Platt, 192–95
  Roosevelt as governor of, 173, 174,
    192–95, 205
Niagara Movement, 261, 262, 271
Northern Securities Company, 242–43

Obama, Barack, 302
"Of Mr. Washington and Others" (Du
    Bois), 260
O'Neill, William "Buckey," 165

Panama Canal, 243
Pan-American Exposition, 209–11
Parker, James B., 210–11
Pendleton Civil Service Act (1883),
    95–96
Penrose, Charles, 264, 265, 266
peonage laws, 294
Perry, Oliver Hazard, 43
*The Philadelphia Negro* (Du Bois), 202
Philippines, 126, 146

Plant, Henry, 150
Platt, Thomas C., 192–95, 193n, 198, 199
Plessy, Homer Adolph, 136–39
Plessy v. Ferguson, 135, 136–39, 142, 236n
Police Commission in New York City, 99–102
Porter, Alfred, 53
presidential elections
  election of 1876, xiv
  election of 1888, 93–94
  election of 1896, 102, 121
  election of 1900, 206, 207
  election of 1904, 221, 247
  election of 1908, 272–73
  election of 1912, 278, 279, 280, 286
  election of 1916, 296
  election of 2008, 302
Princeton University, 280–81
Pulitzer, Joseph, 126
Pullman Company, 294

railroads, 136–39, 243, 273, 282, 294
Ranch Life and the Hunting Trail (Roosevelt), 77
Ransom, Reverdy, 188
Reconstruction Amendments, 54–55
Reconstruction following Civil War, xiii, xiv, 54, 286
Remington, Frederic, 168
Republican Association in Manhattan, 63–64
The Resurrection of Lazarus (Tanner), 189
Rich, Charles Alonzo, 67
Rickover, George Hyman, 132n
Riis, Jacob, 99–100, 102, 208
Rockefeller, John D., 176–77, 242, 255, 290–91
Roosevelt, Alice Hathaway Lee (wife), 229
  death of, 68–69, 72, 78–79
  European vacation of, 44

marriage of, 40–41, 70
pregnancy and childbirth, 66, 67, 68, 72
and property in Oyster Bay, 67
Roosevelt, Alice Lee (daughter)
  Bamie's caretaking of, 69, 77, 79
  birth of, 68
  christening of, 69
  father's visits to see, 77
  marriage of, 268
  and political career of father, 98
  and stepmother, 79, 227
  and Washington's dinner at the White House, 227, 233
Roosevelt, Anna ("Bamie"; sister)
  as caregiver for Alice Lee, 69, 77, 79
  and education of siblings, 19
  health issues of, 69, 69n
  and sale of parents' home, 70
  and Theodore's property in Oyster Bay, 67
Roosevelt, Archibald (son), 98, 227, 228, 229, 285
Roosevelt, Corinne ("Conie"; sister), 19, 23, 69
Roosevelt, Edith Kermit Carow (wife), 76, 229, 296
  and Alice Lee, 79, 227
  children of, 98, 144
  as First Lady, 229
  health of, 144
  hostess duties of, 97
  marriage of, 76–77
  and Theodore's military service, 144, 151
  and Theodore's political career, 95, 97
  and Washington's dinner at the White House, 227, 233
Roosevelt, Elliott ("Ellie"; brother), 19, 68
Roosevelt, Ethel (daughter), 98, 227, 229
Roosevelt, Franklin D., 241n, 302–3
Roosevelt, Kermit (son), 98, 227, 229, 277, 297

Roosevelt, Martha "Mittie" Bulloch
(mother)
courtship and marriage of, 21–22
death of, 67, 68–69, 72, 78
Southern roots of, 21, 22
and Theodore's property in Oyster
Bay, 67
and Theodore's time at Harvard, 24
Roosevelt, Quentin (son), 126, 144, 227,
228, 229, 285, 296
Roosevelt, Ted (son), 79, 98, 227, 229
Roosevelt, Theodore, Jr.
advocacy for working class, 65–66,
96, 102, 195, 299
African safari of, 277
ambitions of, 298, 303
attempted assassination of, 278
as attorney, 41
autobiography of, 39, 65 (see also An
Autobiography)
bear encounter of, 74–75
books published by, 45, 70, 77,
94, 123
and Brownsville affair, 264, 265, 266,
267, 268, 269, 272, 301
cattle investment of, 72, 73, 79, 93
celebrity and fame of, 173–74
children of, 68, 98, 126
and Clemens, 237
conservation of public lands, 79,
194, 277
critics of, 199
in the Dakota Badlands, 71–76, 77,
78, 79, 93
death of, 296, 297
deaths of wife, Alice, and mother,
68–69, 72, 78–79, 298
and Du Bois, 295–96
education of, 23–25, 39–40, 41
in Egypt, 18–19
eyesight and glasses of, 18, 75,
146, 149

hawkish tendencies of, 122, 126, 174
health of, 17–18, 17n, 20, 24–25, 77,
173, 297
impulsiveness/hotheadedness of, 122,
132, 199, 232
and Lincoln, 16, 298
marriages of, 40–41, 70, 76–77 (see
also Roosevelt, Alice Hathaway
Lee; Roosevelt, Edith Kermit
Carow)
and military/naval history, 41–45, 123
military service of, 102, 143, 146–47,
296 (see also Rough Riders;
Spanish–American War)
and Mount Rushmore, 297
The Naval War of 1812, 45, 123
and Nobel Prize, 297
personal philosophy of, 98
and politics, 70 (see also Roosevelt's
political career)
and racial equality, 223, 299–300
reading habits of, 123
and Sagamore Hill home in Oyster
Bay, 66–67, 70, 78, 78, 285
on slavery, 299
and Taft's presidency, 278
at Tuskegee Institute, ii
on Tuskegee Institute board, 274,
291–92
Tuskegee Institute visited by, ii, 217,
254–58, 257
Washington praised by, vii, 290, 298
Washington's collaboration with, 218,
219, 235, 298–99, 300, 302
and Washington's death, 290,
291–92
Washington's early relationship with,
195–97, 208–9
Washington's influence on, 299, 300
Washington's parallels with, 70, 98,
298–99
youth of, 15–25, 16, 19

Roosevelt, Theodore, Sr. (father)
and Civil War, 22
courtship and marriage of, 21–22
death of, 25, 39
influence on Theodore, 16, 20, 96
and Lincoln's funeral cortege, 16
philanthropy of, 20, 96
Roosevelt family
and Civil War, 22–23
in Egypt, 18–19, 20
and the South, 21
wealth of, 19–20
Roosevelt's political career
after Spanish–American War, 173–75
and ambitions of Roosevelt, 94, 197,
207, 220, 298, 303
as assistant secretary of the navy,
122–33
and Boss Platt, 192–95, 198, 199
as civil service commissioner, 95–98
and Gompers, 64–66
as governor of New York, 173, 174,
192–95, 205
and Harrison's campaign, 93–94, 102
key lessons learned in, 97–98
Long on ascent of, 133
mayoral campaigns in New York,
77–78, 98–99
and McKinley's assassination, 209–15
and McKinley's campaign, 102, 121
as muckraker, 101
in New York state legislature, 64, 70
patronage/corruption fought by
Roosevelt, 95–98, 222
paying dues in, 121
as police commissioner in New York,
99–102, 151
and popularity of Roosevelt, 199
and presidential election of 1900,
206, 207
and presidential election of 1912, 278,
279, 280, 286

and presidential election of
1916, 296
and Republican Association in
Manhattan, 63–64
retirement from, 272, 279
and Southern strategy for presidential
campaign, 207, 217–18
transparency prioritized in, 195
as vice president of the United States,
195, 197–99, 206, 208, 211–13
work habits, 205–6
See also Roosevelt's presidency
Roosevelt's presidency, 229
Annual Message to Congress,
241–43, 270
assassination of McKinley, 209–15
and cabinet and policies of
McKinley, 220
and collaboration with Washington,
221–23
and Cox (postmistress), 247–52, 302
and Crum's nomination/appointment,
243–47, 252, 253, 302
and desire to collaborate with
Washington, 218, 219
domestic agenda (Square Deal),
242, 299
foreign policy agenda (Big Stick), 242
and Panama Canal, 243
and political ambitions of, 197, 220
political appointments of, 221–23,
235, 243–47, 252–53, 300
presidential election of 1904, 221,
247, 253
and respect for Washington, 224
and Southern strategy, 217–18,
234–35, 268
swearing in, 215, 218
and trust busting, 242–43
Washington's dinner at the White
House, 218, 224–30, 226, 231–36,
237, 238–40, 240, 268, 300–302

Roswell, Georgia, 21–22
Rough Riders (First United States
    Volunteer Cavalry)
  and Battle of Las Guásimas,
    157–60, *158*
  and Bloody Ford, 164–65
  boot camp of, 147–48
  casualties in, 161
  on foot in Cuban jungle, 155–56
  as infantry unit, 153
  McKinley's visit with, 173
  name of, 147
  recruitment of, 146
  Remington's portrayal of, *168*
  return home, 172–73
  reunion of, 197
  Roosevelt offered command of,
    144–45
  Roosevelt's promotion to colonel, 163
  and San Juan Hill, 165, 169–71
  in Tampa, 149–51
  transport to Cuba, 153–54
  and violence in Wilmington, North
    Carolina, 185
  Wood's command of, 144–45
Ruffner, Lewis, 9, 12–14, 32
Ruffner, Viola Knapp, 9–11, 29, 32, 34
Russo-Japanese War, 297

Saint-Gaudens, Augustus, 143
Saltonstall, Richard, 39–40
Sanders, Mingo, 263
Schrank, John, 278
Scott, Emmett, 292
Scott, Sir Walter, 166*n*
*Secret Service of the Confederate States in
    Europe* (Bulloch), 44*n*
segregation, 55, 117, 136–39
"separate but equal" doctrine, 136–39,
    142, 236*n*, 294, 295
sexual accusations and stereotypes of
    Black people
  aimed at Washington, 283–84
  and *The Birth of a Nation* (film), 286–87
  and Brownsville affair, 263–71
  lynchings following, 90, 181
  and opposition to Cox as
    postmistress, 250
  oversexed stereotype, 270, 286, 289
  and racist fearmongering, 181, 233
  and Washington's declining health, 289
sharecroppers, 104
Shaw, Robert Gould, 143
Sherman Anti-Trust Act, 243
Sigsbee, Charles, 128–29
slavery and enslaved people
  and abolitionism, 4, 33–34
  education withheld from, 4, 10
  and emancipation of the enslaved,
    xiii, 5–6, *6*, 54
  enslaved people held by
    Burroughs, 2–3
  living conditions of people in, 3–4
  Roosevelt's condemnation of, 299
  in Washington, DC, 225
  Washington on history of, 178
  *See also* Black Americans
*The Souls of Black Folk* (Du Bois),
    259, 260
the South
  and *The Birth of a Nation* (film),
    286–87
  Black people elected to office in, xiv
  and Bulloch family, 21, 22
  Cotton States and International
    Exposition in, 111–18
  demonization of Black Americans
    in, 104
  education withheld from the enslaved
    in, 10
  and Gideon's Band, 12–14
  and interracial relationships, 181–82
  lack of opportunities for Black
    Americans in, 104

the South (*cont.*)
massacre at Wilmington, North
Carolina, 180–85, 186
"Negro Problem" debate in, 117, 119,
254, 294–95
racial divide in, 12–14, 187, 231–33
and Roosevelt's condemnation of
slavery, 299
Roosevelt's connection to, 21
and Roosevelt's political
appointments, 222–23
segregation in, 55, 117, 136–39
(*see also* discrimination, racial;
Jim Crow era)
and Tom Harris incident, 106–10
unwritten laws of, 91
violence in (*see* lynchings; violence
aimed at Black Americans)
voter suppression in, xiii–xiv, 36, 94,
181, 184
Washington on race relations in, 83,
90, 115–18
and Washington's dinner at the
White House, 231–33, 234–35,
238–39, 268, 300–301, 302
Washington's travels to, 275–76
South Dakota, 297
Southern conservatives/Democrats
backlash against racial progress, xiv
and Jim Crow era, 55
and race relations, 90
and Turner, 55–56
Southern Railway, 135
Spain, 124–27, 130, 132*n*, 177
Spanish–American War, 144–60
and Battle of Las Guásimas,
157–60, *158*
and Battle of San Juan Hill, 165,
169–71, 172–73, 174
Black soldiers serving in (*see* Buffalo
Soldiers)
and Bloody Ford, 163–66
casualties in, 159, 161, 168
Clemens's disgust with, 237
and explosion on USS *Maine*,
126–32, *127*
and fight for Santiago, 171
and Kettle Hill assault, 166–70
and living conditions of soldiers, 162
long-term impact of, 174
and McKinley, 132, 153, 173, 220
military objective in, 155
news accounts of, 161
Remington's portrayal of, *168*
Roosevelt's heroism in, 297
(*see also* Rough Riders)
Spain's surrender, 171–72, 171*n*
staging for, in Tampa, 149–54
victory of, 177
and yellow fever, 172
*See also* Rough Riders
Spanish Atlantic Squadron, 153
Standard Oil, 243
Steffens, Lincoln, 221
Stewart, Philip, 228
*The Story of My Life* (Washington), *6*, 200
Stowe, Lyman Beecher, 292
Strong, William, 99
Stuart, J. E. B., 4

Taft, William Howard, 272–74, 278,
279–80, 284, 291
Tampa Bay Hotel, 150–51
Tanner, Henry Ossawa, 189
Taylor, Robert, 134–35
Tenement House Commission, 194
tenements of New York City, 65–66, 96,
100, 299
Thirteenth Amendment, xiii
Thrasher, Max Bennett, 200–201
Tilden, Samuel J., xiv
Tillman, Benjamin, 233, 245, 246,
247, 251
Trotter, William Monroe, 258–59, 293

trust busting, 242–43
Turner, Jack, 55–57
Tuskegee, Alabama
  economic impact of school in, 53–54
  Washington lying in state in, *292*
  Washington's arrival in, 47–50
Tuskegee Institute (formerly Tuskegee
    Normal School for Colored
    Teachers), *275*
  Armstrong Hall, 59
  brickmaking program at, 59–61, *61*
  building construction at, 88
  campus of, 50–51, *50*, 58–60, 61, *91*,
    255, *256*
  Douglass's address at, 140, *140*
  Du Bois offered positions at, 202–3
  Du Bois's criticisms of, 204
  early years at, 49–50, *50*
  endowment of, *255*
  enrollment at, 52, 82, 88, 176, *255*
  establishment of, 48
  first class of students at, 49–50, 53
  funding shortfalls at, 87
  fundraising for, 58–59, 89–90, 176–77,
    188, 229, 260
  graduates from, 54
  instructional programs offered at, 81
  McKinley's visit to, 185–87, *187*
  name of, 115
  night school at, 82
  Porter Hall, 53, 58–59
  recruiting students to, 49, 52
  respect and recognition of, 82, 85, 88
  Roosevelt on board of, 274, 291–92
  Roosevelt's visit to, ii, 217, 254–58, *257*
  staff/faculty members at, 82, 88, 176
  and Taft, *274*
  Teacher's Cottage, 59
  and teaching hospital, *276*
  and Tom Harris incident, 108
  and Washington's death, 292
  Washington's recruitment to, 46–47

work required of students in, 52, 59,
    *61, 92*
Tuskegee Negro Conference, 104–6
*The Tuskegee News*, 106
Twain, Mark (Samuel Langhorne
    Clemens), 189, 236–37, *237*, 239,
    268, 301
Twenty-Fifth Infantry (Colored),
    263–71, 271*n*

Ulrich, Henry Albert, 283–85
United States Post Office, 247–52
University of Mississippi, 251*n*
*Up from Slavery* (Washington), 113–14,
    200–201, 202, 205, 208, 237
U.S. Army, 263–71, 271*n*
U.S. Congress, 241–43, 245–47, 265
U.S. Department of Justice, 242–43
U.S. Department of the Navy, 122–33, 146
U.S. Department of War, 149, 264,
    265, 296
U.S. House of Representatives, 154
U.S. Navy, 43–45
  construction of ships, 124, 125, 126
  emphasis on readiness of, 124, 125, 126
  and Spanish–American War, 153,
    154–55
USS *Chesapeake*, 43
USS *Constitution* ("Old Ironsides"), 43
USS *Indiana*, 124
USS *Maine*, 127–32, *127*, *129*, 132*n*, 170
USS *Massachusetts*, 124
USS *New York*, 153
USS *Oregon*, 124, 153
U.S. Supreme Court, 135, 243

Vardaman, James K., 248–49, 250–51
Victoria, Queen of Great Britain,
    189, 238
violence aimed at Black Americans, 270
  as commonplace, 134, 135, 180,
    208, 208*n*

violence aimed at Black Americans (*cont.*)
  death toll from, xiv
  decline in, 275
  massacre at Wilmington, North
    Carolina, 180–85, 186, 275
  in Port Tampa military camp, 152
  Postmistress Cox threatened with,
    249–50
  rise in, 176, 187
  Roosevelt on broad impact of, 299
  threatened by Senator Tillman, 246
  and Tom Harris incident, 106–10
  torture and murder of Hose, 187,
    188, 190
  and Washington on race relations, 117
  Washington's reticence on, 57, 91, 188
  Washington's speech addressing,
    190–91
  Washington threatened, 238, 255
  Whites' celebration of, 187, 191
  witnessed by Portia on train,
    134, 135
  *See also* lynchings
voting rights
  enforcement of, xiii–xiv
  suppression of, xiii–xiv, 36, 94, 181,
    184, 294*n*
  and Taft, 273
  Washington on, 191

Waddell, Alfred, 183
War of 1812, 42–45, 178
War of Independence, 178
Washington, Amanda (sister), 2, 5–6, 36
Washington, Baker T. (son), 84, 84*n*,
    228, 282
Washington, Booker T., *86, 136, 289*
  accused of accommodating White
    people, 205, 261–62
  admiration and respect for, 85, 103,
    *104*, 117, 203, 227
  ambitions of, 11, 36, 188, 303
    appearance of, 203
  "The Atlanta Compromise," 260
  as attorney, 36
  autobiographies/memoirs of, 113–14,
    199–201, 202, 208, 239, 285
  birth of, 1–2, 2*n*
  book collecting of, 11
  and Brownsville affair, 267, 272
  "cancer gnawing" imagery of, 179, 180
  celebrity and fame of, 103–4, *104,*
    134, 186, 196, 208, 293
  children of, 58, 79, 84, 85–86, 87, 89,
    *251, 282, 285*
  and Clemens, 237, *237*
  critics of, 120, 188, 196, 258–60, 274,
    293 (*see also* Du Bois, W. E. B.)
  and Crum's nomination/appointment,
    245, 273
  death of, 290–93, *292*
  and deaths of wives, 61–62, 81, 84, 298
  demeanor/manner of, 177
  on dignity in work, 52
  doctorate, honorary, 227*n*
  as Douglass's heir, 141–42
  education (*see* Washington's
    education)
  and emancipation of the enslaved,
    5–6, *6*
  employment of, 9–11, 30, 32–33, 35,
    36, 37–38 (*see also* Tuskegee
    Institute)
  and equality, 91, 117, 261
  European travels of, 188–90, 275
  and fishing, *141*
  fundraising, 58–59, 176–77, 188,
    229, 260
  hand-and-fingers metaphor of, 103,
    116–17, 190, 260
  Harvard's honorary degree bestowed
    on, 142–43
  health of, 84, 188, 286, 288–90
  house fire of, 86

influence (*see* Washington's influence and power)

interventions behind-the-scenes of, 293–94

"Is the Negro Having a Fair Chance?" 281–82

and Lincoln, 298

marriages of, 58, 84, 89 (*see also* Washington, Fanny Smith; Washington, Margaret Murry; Washington, Olivia Davidson)

and military service of Black Americans, 152

name of, 1, 9, 9*n*

on "Negro Problem" debate, 117, 294–95

and Niagara Movement, 261–62

parents of, 2

and politics, 55, 57

practicality of, 111, 295

and presidential election of 1888, 94

on race relations, 83–84, 90, 190–91

and reading, 4, 8–9

respect and recognition of, 227, 227*n*

reticence on race-based violence, 57, 91, 188

and rights of Black Americans, 44

Roosevelt influenced by, 299, 300

Roosevelt praised by, vii

and Roosevelt's 1912 campaign, 279–80

Roosevelt's collaboration with, 218, 219, 235, 298–99, 300, 302

Roosevelt's dinner invitation, 218, 224–30, 226, 231–36, 237, 238–40, 240, 268, 300–302

Roosevelt's early relationship with, 195–97, 208–9

Roosevelt's parallels with, 70, 98, 298–99

and Roosevelt's political appointments, 221–23, 235, 244, 245

Roosevelt's praise for, ii, 290, 298

Roosevelt's rejection of counsel, 267, 269, 270

and Roosevelt's Southern strategy, 218, 234–35

and Roosevelt's visit to Tuskegee, 254–58, 257

on self-care and cleanliness, 35

self-discipline of, 10

as self-made man, 9

and "separate but equal" doctrine, 139, 142, 294

in the South, 275–76

speaking skills/style of, 11, 34, 36, 115, 140–41, 141*n*

speech at Cotton States and International Exposition in, 112–18

speech at National Educational Association, 82

speech at National Peace Jubilee, Chicago, 177–80, 179, 238

speech before House Committee on Appropriations, 111–12

speeches compiled and published, 190

and Taft, 272–74, 279–80

as teacher, 4, 35, 273

and threats of violence, 238, 255

and Tom Harris incident, 106–10

travels of, 58, 84, 88, 89, 188–90, 274–75, 286, 289

and Turner's lynching, 57

and Tuskegee Negro Conference, 104–6

and Ulrich affair, 283–85

*Up from Slavery*, 113–14, 200–201, 202, 205, 208, 237

as voice of moderation, 91, 139

writing skills of, 11

youth of, 2–14, 3

*See also* Tuskegee Institute

Washington, DC, 225

Washington, Ernest Davidson (son), 85–86, 228, 251, 282

Washington, Fanny Smith (wife), 47, 58, 59, 61–62, 81
Washington, George (president), 91, 125, 158–59, 297
Washington, James (brother), 36
Washington, Jane (mother), 2, 3, 5–6, 7, 8–9, 36
Washington, John Henry (brother), 2, 2n, 5, 26–27, 82
Washington, Margaret Murray (wife), 228
  and Booker's health, 288, 289, 290
  and Booker's speeches, 113
  European vacation of, 188–90
  marriage of, 89
  position sought at Normal School, 88–89
  and Tuskegee Negro Conference, 105
Washington, Olivia Davidson (wife), 52, 58, 84, 85–87, 85
Washington, Portia (daughter)
  birth of, 58
  death of mother, 61–62
  education of, 134
  in family portrait, 228
  and Olivia as stepmother to, 84
  violence on train witnessed by, 134, 135
Washington's education
  and desire to learn, 1, 4, 26, 27, 33
  funding for, 26–27
  at Hampton, 11–12, 26–38
  and reading, 8–9, 33
  Ruffner's encouragement of, 10–11
  at Wayland Baptist Theological Seminary, 36–37
Washington's influence and power
  development of, 14, 110–11
  diminishment of, 261, 270–71, 281
  Du Bois's criticisms of, 259, 260, 261
  on Roosevelt's policies, 299
  Roosevelt's public recognition of, 300
  and Tuskegee Negro Conference, 104–5
  as voice of moderation, 139

  and Washington's collaboration with Roosevelt, 235
Wayland Baptist Theological Seminary, 36–37
Webber, Edgar, 200
Webster, Noah, 8
White, William Allen, 197
white supremacists
  and Cox's postmistress appointment, 248–52
  and "miscegenation," 107n
  prevalence of, in the South, 53, 90
  Red Shirts, 185
  rise of, xiv
  and violence in Wilmington, North Carolina, 180–85
  See also lynchings; violence aimed at Black Americans
Wilberforce University, 119
wilderness conservation, 79, 194, 277
Wilmington, North Carolina, racially motivated violence in, 180–85, 186, 275
Wilmington Daily Record, destruction of, 181–83, 183
Wilson, Woodrow, 220, 279, 280–81, 287, 296
Winning of the West (Roosevelt), 256
Wood, John, 17
Wood, Leonard
  and army encampment in Tampa, 150
  background of, 145
  and Battle of Las Guásimas, 157, 158
  and boot camp, 148–49
  command of Rough Riders, 144–45
  and soldiers on foot in Cuban jungle, 155–56
work, Washington on dignity in, 52
World War I, 296
Wright, Daniel, 184

Yale University, 235